W9-BVD-096

STUDY GUIDE

Stephen C. Schaefer
Contra Costa College

Hilary Becker
Carleton University

FINANCIAL ACCOUNTING

Second Canadian Edition

Walter T. Harrison, Jr., Baylor University
Charles T. Horngen, Stanford University
W. Morley Lemon, University of Waterloo
Ray F. Carroll, Dalhousie University
Sandra Robertson Lemon, Consultant

PEARSON
Prentice Hall

Toronto

Copyright © 2007 Pearson Education Canada, a division of Pearson Canada Inc., Toronto, Ontario

Original edition published by Pearson Education, Inc., Upper Saddle River, New Jersey, USA. Copyright © 2006 by Pearson Education, Inc. This edition is authorized for sale only in Canada.

Pearson Prentice Hall. All rights reserved. This publication is protected by copyright, and permission should be obtained from the publisher prior to any prohibited reproduction, storage in a retrieval system, or transmission in any form or by any means, electronic, mechanical, photocopying, recording, or likewise. For information regarding permission, write to the Permissions Department.

0-13-187930-8

Executive Editor: Samantha Scully
Developmental Editor: Paul Donnelly
Production Editor: Mary Ann Field
Production Coordinator: Deborah Starks

1 2 3 4 5   11 10 09 08 07

Printed and bound in Canada.

PEARSON
Prentice
Hall

CONTENTS

PREFACE

This Study Guide will assist you in mastering *Financial Accounting*, Second Canadian Edition, by Walter T. Harrison, Jr., Charles T. Horngren, W. Morley Lemon, Ray F. Carroll, and Sandra Robertson Lemon. The chapters in this Study Guide correspond to the chapters in the textbook. Each chapter of this Study Guide contains four sections: Chapter Overview, Chapter Review, Test Yourself, and Demonstration Problems.

Chapter Review: The Chapter Review parallels the chapter in your textbook. It is organized by learning objective and provides a concise summary of the major elements in each objective. Emphasis is given to new terms and concepts, particularly in the earlier chapters where it is essential for you to be conversant with accounting terminology. A Chapter Overview links each chapter to previous or subsequent topics.

Test Yourself. The Test Yourself section is divided into six parts: matching, multiple choice, completion, true/false, exercises, and critical thinking. Answers are provided for each section along with explanations, when appropriate. The six sections provide a comprehensive review of the material in each chapter and should be used after you have read each chapter thoroughly to determine which topics you understand and those requiring further study.

Demonstration Problems: Two Demonstration Problems are provided for each chapter. These problems attempt to incorporate as many of the topics in the chapter as possible. For some chapters, the first demonstration problem must be completed before the second one is attempted. For those chapters, complete the first one, check your answers, make any necessary corrections, then go on to the second problem. The solutions to the demonstration problems provide explanations as well.

THIS STUDY GUIDE IS NOT A SUBSTITUTE FOR YOUR TEXTBOOK. It is designed as an additional support tool to assist you in succeeding in your accounting course.

Comments about the Study Guide are encouraged and should be sent to phcinfo.pubcanada@pearsoned.com.

Hilary M. Becker
Carleton University

CHAPTER 1—THE FINANCIAL STATEMENTS

CHAPTER OVERVIEW

Chapter 1 introduces you to accounting and its use in decision making. Some of the topics covered in this chapter are the types of business organization, the basic accounting equation, and financial statements. Like many disciplines, accounting has its own vocabulary. An understanding of accounting terminology and the other topics covered in this chapter will give you a good foundation toward mastering the topics in upcoming chapters. The specific learning objectives for this chapter are to

1. **Use** accounting vocabulary for decision making
2. **Apply** accounting concepts and principles
3. **Use** the accounting equation to describe an organization
4. **Evaluate** operating performance, financial position, and cash flows
5. **Explain** the relationships among the financial statements

CHAPTER REVIEW

Objective 1 - Use accounting vocabulary for decision making

Accounting is the information system that measures business activities, processes data into reports, and communicates results to decision makers. (Helpful hint: review Exhibit 1-1 in your text.)

There are many users of accounting information. Individuals use accounting information to make decisions about purchases and investments and to manage their bank accounts. Businesses use accounting information to set goals for their businesses and to evaluate progress toward achieving those goals. Investors use accounting information to evaluate the prospect of future returns on their investments. Lenders (creditors) use accounting information to evaluate a borrower's ability to meet scheduled repayments of money loaned. Accounting information is also used by government regulatory agencies, taxing authorities, and nonprofit organizations.

While there are many users of accounting information, they can be grouped into two broad categories—external users and internal users. **Financial accounting** provides information useful to managers and individuals outside the organization while **management accounting** provides information exclusively to internal decision makers.

Each of the three professional accounting bodies in Canada has developed a code of conduct to guide its members in the production of accurate information for decision making.

Ethical behaviour $\Rightarrow$ reliable information $\Rightarrow$ decision

The three forms of business organization are:

1. **Sole proprietorship**—a business owned by one person.
2. **Partnership**—a business owned by two or more individuals.
3. **Corporation**—a business owned by shareholders, which conducts its business in its own name. Shareholders have no liability for business debts. The amount a shareholder can lose is limited to the amount the shareholder invested in the corporation.

In Canada, proprietorships are numerically the largest form of business, whereas corporations are the dominant form in terms of total assets, income, and number of employees. (Helpful hint: review Exhibit 1-2 in the textbook for a summary of the three forms of business ownership.)

A corporation is formed under federal or provincial law and has a legal identity distinct from its owners, the shareholders. Unlike in a proprietorship or partnership, the shareholders have no personal liability for the corporation's liabilities. The shareholders elect a board of directors who appoint officers to manage the organization.

Objective 2 - Apply accounting concepts and principles

Canadian Securities Administrators, the *Canadian Business Corporations Act*, and the *Ontario Securities Act* have each designated the *CICA Handbook* as Generally Accepted Accounting Principles (GAAP). In these ways the CICA became the official promulgator of GAAP. (Helpful hint: review Exhibit 1-3 and 1-4 in the textbook.) **Generally Accepted Accounting Principles** (GAAP) are the rules governing accounting, which include five important standards: 1) the **entity concept**, 2) the **reliability principle**, 3) the **cost principle**, 4) the **going-concern concept**, and 5) the **stable-monetary-unit concept**.

The **entity concept** states that the records of a business entity should be separate from the personal records of the owner(s). For example, if a business owner borrows money to remodel her home, the loan is a personal debt, not a debt of the business.

The **reliability principle** states that accountants should attempt to provide reliable, accurate records and financial statements. All data that the accountant uses should be verifiable by an independent observer. Ideally, accounting records should be determined by objective evidence. For example, the most objective and reliable measure of the value of supplies is the price paid for the supplies. The objective evidence documenting the price is the bill from the supplier.

The **cost principle** states that the assets and services should be recorded at their actual (historical) cost. For example, if a firm pays $150,000 for land, then $150,000 is the value recorded in the books even if an independent appraiser states that the land is worth $200,000.

The **going-concern concept** holds that the entity will remain in operation for the foreseeable future. The cost principle states that the relevant measure of the entity's assets is historical cost. However, if the entity were going out of business, the relevant measure of its assets would be market value.

The **stable-monetary-unit concept** holds that the purchasing power of the dollar is relatively stable. Therefore, accountants may add and subtract dollar amounts as though each dollar had the same purchasing power.

GAAP is based on a conceptual foundation, with the **primary objective** being information that is useful for investment and credit decisions. (Helpful hint: review Exhibit 1-4 in the textbook.) The primary characteristics are **Relevance, Reliability, Comparability,** and **Understandability.**

The **limitations of GAAP** include situations when: 1) GAAP does not lead to fair presentation, 2) the financial statements are prepared in accordance with regulatory legislation, and 3) the financial statements are prepared in accordance with contractual requirements. In each case, professional judgment must be used.

Objective 3 - Use the accounting equation to describe an organization

The **accounting equation** is expressed as

$$\text{ASSETS} = \text{LIABILITIES} + \text{OWNERS' EQUITY}$$

Assets are a firm's resources that are expected to provide future benefits. **Liabilities** are claims by outsiders (creditors) to those resources. Claims by insiders (owners) are called **owners' equity** or **capital**.

Examples of assets are cash, merchandise, supplies, land, and buildings. Merchandise inventory is the items a business sells to its customers. Long-lived assets, such as equipment, land, buildings, etc., are also called **capital assets**.

Examples of liabilities are accounts payable and notes payable, which arise when the business makes purchases on credit.

Owners' equity is what is left of the assets after subtracting the liabilities:

$$\text{ASSETS} - \text{LIABILITIES} = \text{OWNERS' EQUITY}$$

The owners' equity of a proprietorship and partnership is called **capital**. The owners' equity of a corporation is called **shareholders' equity** and is divided into two categories: **contributed capital** and **retained earnings**. **Contributed capital** is the amount invested in the corporation by its owners. **Common stock** is a basic component of contributed capital. **Retained earnings** is the amount earned by the corporation to date that has not been paid out in dividends. Revenues increase retained earnings, whereas expenses decrease retained earnings. Net income results when revenues exceed expenses. A net loss results when expenses exceed revenues.

Dividends are proportional distributions of assets, usually cash, to the owners of the corporation (called shareholders). Dividends are not expenses. (Helpful hint: review Exhibit 1-6.)

Objective 4 - Evaluate operating performance, financial position, and cash flows

Accountants summarize the results of business activity in four primary financial statements: 1) the **income statement**, 2) the **statement of retained earnings**, 3) the **balance sheet**, and 4) the **cash flow statement**.

The **income statement** presents a summary of the firm's revenues and gains and expenses and losses for some period of time, such as a month, and reports net income if total revenues exceed total expenses. A net loss occurs if total expenses are greater than total revenues.

The **statement of retained earnings** presents a summary of changes in retained earnings during the same period as the income statement. Retained earnings increase with income and decrease with dividends and net losses.

The **balance sheet** (also called the statement of financial position) reports all assets, liabilities, and owners' (shareholders') equity as of a specific date. That date will be the same date as the last day of the period for which activities are summarized in the income statement and the statement of retained earnings. Assets are divided into two major categories—current and long term. Current assets are ones that will convert to cash or be consumed within one year or within the operating cycle if it is longer. Liabilities are also divided into two categories—current and long term—using the same standard (one year or the operating cycle if it is longer). Note that the term balance sheet comes from the fact that the report balances; that is, total assets equal total liabilities plus total shareholders' equity.

The **cash flow statement** shows the cash inflows and outflows, organized into three areas—operating activities, investing activities, and financing activities. The cash flow statement can be prepared using either the direct or indirect approach.

The major source of cash receipts from operating activities will be the cash received from customers, whereas the major source of cash payments will be the cash disbursed to suppliers and employees. Investing activities include the acquisition and sale of long-term assets—things such as buildings and equipment. Financing activities include short-term and long-term debt, the sale or repurchase of the company's stock, and the payment of dividends. These three sections each result in a net cash inflow or outflow, which are then summarized into a "net" cash increase or decrease for the period. This final "net" reconciles the difference between the beginning cash balance and the ending cash balance. Study carefully Exhibit 1-6 and the financial statements for Sun-Rype Products Ltd. (Exhibits 1-8, 1-9, 1-10, and 1-11) in your text.

Objective 5 - Explain the relationships among the financial statements

All financial statements begin with three-line headings as follows:

Company Name

Statement Name

Appropriate Date

The income statement is prepared first, listing the revenues and expenses for the period. The result is either net income (when revenues are greater than expenses) or net loss (when revenues are less than expenses). This result is carried forward to the next statement.

The statement of retained earnings is prepared after the income statement. It details the amounts and sources of changes in retained earnings during the period as follows:

	Beginning Retained Earnings
+	Net Income (or - Net Loss)
-	Dividends
=	Ending Retained Earnings

The result, listed as Ending Retained Earnings, is carried forward to the next financial statement.

The balance sheet is a formal listing of the accounting equation as of the last day in the financial period. The individual assets are added together to equal total assets. The liabilities are totaled and added to shareholders' equity.

The cash flow statement reports cash receipts and payments for operating, investing, and financing activities. Each section results in a net cash inflow or outflow. These three sections are then summarized in one net amount for the period. This final figure is added (if a net inflow) to the beginning cash balance or deducted (if a net outflow) from the beginning cash balance to arrive at an ending cash balance. This ending cash balance is reported on the balance sheet. Review Exhibit 1-12 in your text to become more familiar with these relationships.

Study Tip: The statement order is important to remember.
1. Income Statement
2. Retained Earnings Statement
3. Balance Sheet
4. Cash Flow Statement
Memorize the acronym IRBC to help you.

TEST YOURSELF

All the self-testing materials in this chapter focus on information and procedures that your instructor is likely to test in quizzes and examinations.

I. Matching

1. *Match each numbered term with its lettered definition.*

_____ 1. shareholders' equity
_____ 2. assets
_____ 3. corporation
_____ 4. expenses
_____ 5. GAAP
_____ 6. income statement
_____ 7. liabilities
_____ 8. common shares

_____ 9. partnership
_____ 10. proprietorship
_____ 11. revenues
_____ 12. cash flow statement
_____ 13. statement of retained earnings
_____ 14. dividends
_____ 15. contributed capital

A. a summary of revenues and expenses for a period
B. a business owned by one person
C. a financial statement summarizing changes in retained earnings
D. a legal entity owned by shareholders, which conducts its business in its own name
E. shareholders' ownership interest in the assets of a corporation
F. resources expected to provide future benefit
G. the "rules" of accounting
H. claims on assets by outsiders
I. increases in retained earnings from delivering goods and services to customers
J. a business co-owned by two or more individuals
K. decreases in retained earnings that result from operations
L. certificates representing ownership in a corporation
M. details the net change in cash from one period to the next
N. the amount invested in the corporation by the owners
O. a distribution of assets to the owners of a corporation

2. *Match each numbered term with its lettered definition.*

_____ 1. financial accounting
_____ 2. management accounting
_____ 3. entity
_____ 4. objectivity principle
_____ 5. cost principle

_____ 6. historical cost
_____ 7. going-concern concept
_____ 8. accounting equation
_____ 9. owners' equity
_____ 10. cash flow statement

A. the residual claim to assets after satisfaction of all liabilities
B. provides information to managers and external users
C. ensures that accounting records and financial statements are based on the most reliable data available
D. the cash equivalent cost of acquisition
E. presents the resources (assets) of the business and the claims against those assets
F. provides information for internal decision makers
G. a statement summarizing the business's sources and uses of cash for the period
H. an organization or section of an organization that is accounted for as a separate economic unit
I. holds that an entity will remain in operation for the foreseeable future
J. holds that acquired assets should be recorded at their historical cost

II. Multiple Choice   *Circle the best answer.*

1. An example of a liability is

    A. supplies expense
    B. equipment
    C. notes payable
    D. dividends

2. Which of the following appears on the income statement?

    A. cash receipts from customers
    B. revenues from customers
    C. cash paid to employees
    D. cash paid to suppliers

3. Which of the following does not appear on the cash flow statement?

    A. dividends paid
    B. proceeds from short-term borrowing
    C. payments for new equipment
    D. accounts payable

4. The proper order for financial statements preparation is

    A. income statement, balance sheet, cash flow statement, statement of retained earnings
    B. income statement, cash flow statement, statement of retained earnings, balance sheet
    C. income statement, statement of retained earnings, balance sheet, cash flow statement
    D. balance sheet, cash flow statement, income statement, statement of retained earnings

5. If the date on a financial statement is August 31, 2006, then the financial statement must be

    A. the income statement
    B. the statement of retained earnings
    C. the balance sheet
    D. the cash flow statement

6. If the financial statement is dated "For the Month Ended August 31, 2006," then the financial statement must be

   A. the income statement
   B. the statement of retained earnings
   C. the balance sheet
   D. either the income statement or the statement of retained earnings

7. Net income equals

   A. Assets - Liabilities
   B. Liabilities + Shareholders' Equity
   C. Revenues + Expenses
   D. Revenues - Expenses

8. If liabilities are $90,000 and shareholders' equity is $120,000, what are total assets?

   A. $30,000
   B. $210,000
   C. $120,000
   D. $90,000

9. If the beginning balance in retained earnings was $920, the ending balance is $1,035, and net income for the month was $240, how much were dividends during the period?

   A. $1,160
   B. $115
   C. $125
   D. $355

10. On January 1, 2006, Francois' Design Corporation had assets of $160,000 and shareholders' equity of $75,000. During the year, assets increased by $45,000 and shareholders' equity decreased by $22,000. What were the liabilities on December 31, 2006?

    A. $85,000
    B. $152,000
    C. $53,000
    D. $205,000

11. The purpose of the cash flow statement is to show

    A. the sources and uses of cash for the period
    B. the net income for the period
    C. the resources of the entity and the claims to those resources
    D. an explanation of the changes in retained earnings for the period

12. During the year, Vicky Corporation earned revenues of $18,000, incurred expenses of $6,000, and paid dividends to shareholders in the amount of $2,000. The amount Vicky Corporation should report as net income for the year is

    A. $18,000
    B. $10,000
    C. $16,000
    D. $12,000

13. The following information is available for Charming Limited:

Total revenues	$18,000	Beginning retained earnings	$7,000
Total assets	$40,000	Total expenses	$10,000
Total equity	$15,000	Dividends paid to shareholders	$2,000

Determine Charming's ending retained earnings.

    A. $15,000
    B. $13,000
    C. $17,000
    D. $21,000

14. The following information is available for Charming Limited:

Total revenues	$18,000	Beginning retained earnings	$7,000
Total assets	$40,000	Total expenses	$10,000
Total equity	$15,000	Dividends paid to shareholders	$2,000

Determine Charming's total liabilities.

    A. $25,000
    B. $55,000
    C. $33,000
    D. $28,000

15. The following information is available for Charming Limited:

Total revenues	$18,000	Beginning retained earnings	$7,000
Total assets	$40,000	Total expenses	$10,000
Total equity	$15,000	Dividends paid to shareholders	$2,000

Determine Charming's contributed capital.

    A. $15,000
    B. $7,000
    C. $25,000
    D. $2,000

16. The statement that identifies the profitability or earnings of the company over a period of time is the

    A. balance sheet
    B. income statement
    C. statement of retained earnings
    D. cash flow statement

III. Completion   *Complete each of the following statements.*

1. The four primary financial statements are 1) _____, 2) _____, 3)_____, and 4) _____.

2. Keeping accounting records for a business separate from the owner's personal accounting records follows from the _____ concept.

3. Revenues are _____.

4. _____ are the costs incurred in operating a business.

5. The cash flow statement can be prepared using either the _____or the _____ method.

6. Identify the accounting equation. _____

7. When assets are purchased by a firm, they are recorded at _____.

8. _____is the clerical recording of the data used in an accounting system.

9. All financial statements begin with a three-line heading as follows:

_____

_____

_____

10. Assuming the purchasing power of the dollar remains relatively stable over time underlies the _____ concept.

11. The cash flow statement details cash inflows/outflows from three activities. These are _____, _____, and _____.

12. Which item appears on both the income statement and the statement of retained earnings?

_____

13. _____ appears on both the retained earnings statement and the balance sheet.

14. The payment of dividends appears in which section of the cash flow statement?

_____

15. You would look to the _____ to determine if a company was profitable.

16. The balance sheet represents the entities assets, liabilities, and owners' equity _____ of time.

IV. True/False   *For each of the following statements, circle* T *for true or* F *for false.*

1. T F   Net income is most closely associated with operating activities.
2. T F   An example of an investing activity is repurchasing outstanding common stock.
3. T F   Net loss is subtracted from the beginning retained earnings on the statement of retained earnings.
4. T F   The corporate form of business allows owners the most flexibility in running the business.
5. T F   Shareholders in corporations have personal liability for the corporation's obligations.
6. T F   The sale of a building would be included under operating activities on the cash flow statement.
7. T F   The organization most closely associated with GAAP is the Canadian Institute of Chartered Accountants (CICA).
8. T F   The terms "capital" and "creditor" are synonymous.
9. T F   The income statement details activity for a specific period of time.
10. T F   The excess of revenues over expenses is called a net loss.
11. T F   Assets and expenses are listed on the balance sheet.
12. T F   The balance sheet is a detailed expression of the accounting equation.
13. T F   The income statement is prepared after the statement of retained earnings.
14. T F   Shareholders' equity consists of contributed capital and retained earnings.
15. T F   On the cash flow statement, financing activities refer to borrowing funds and repaying them and transactions involving the shareholders.

V. Exercises

1. Freon Corp. specializes in providing technical services to corporations in the Halifax area. At the end of its first year of operation, the company had the following cash flows:

    a. $466,000 was received from clients for services provided during the year.
    b. Employees were paid a total of $192,500.
    c. The company paid a total of $82,680 in interest charges during the year and received $1,275 in interest on a savings account.
    d. The outside consultants who provided the technical assistance were paid a total of $210,000 during the year.
    e. A total of $7,500 was paid in taxes during the year.

    In the space below, present the cash flows from operating activities for Freon Corp.

2. Presented below are the balances in the assets, liabilities, and shareholders' equity for Kerri's Juice Bar Inc. on January 31, 2006. The balance for common shares has been intentionally omitted.

Accounts Payable	$1,225
Accounts Receivable	1,480
Cash	508
Common Shares	?
Equipment	14,400
Retained Earnings	2,580
Supplies	75

Prepare a balance sheet for Kerri's Juice Bar on January 31, 2006.

Kerri's Juice Bar Inc.
Balance Sheet
January 31, 2006

Assets:
Cash
Accounts receivable _____
Supplies _____
Equipment _____

Total assets _____

Liabilities:
Accounts payable
Total liabilities _____
Shareholders' equity:
Common shares _____
Retained earnings _____
Total liabilities
and shareholders' equity _____

3. The following are the balances in the accounts of Brandy's Ltd. on August 31, 2006.

Accounts Receivable	$ 41
Accounts Payable	53
Advertising Expense	185
Common Shares	64
Dividends	42
Equipment	298
Fees Earned	756
Notes Receivable	100
Retained Earnings, July 31	92
Salary Payable	18
Salary Expense	70
Supplies	24
Supplies Expense	32
Truck Rental Expense	124
Utilities Expense	106

Prepare an income statement for Brandy's Ltd. for the month of August 2006.

Brandy's Ltd. Income Statement For the Month Ended August 31, 2006		
Revenues		$
Expenses:		
	$	
Net income (loss)		$

Prepare the statement of retained earnings for Brandy's Ltd. for the month of August 2006.

Brandy's Ltd. Statement of Retained Earnings For the Month Ended August 31, 2006		
Beginning Retained Earnings, July 31, 2006		
Add/Subtract Net Income (loss)		$
Dividends		
Ending Retained Earnings, August 31, 2006	$	

VI. Critical Thinking

1. Can a profitable business (one where revenues consistently exceed expenses) become insolvent (unable to pay its bills)? Conversely, can an unprofitable business remain solvent?

2. Explain the reasoning behind the order of preparation of the financial statements (income statement, statement of retained earnings, balance sheet, cash flow statement).

DEMONSTRATION PROBLEMS

Demonstration Problem #1

The following list summarizes the cash transactions for Ronson Refinishers, Inc. at the end of its most recent fiscal period:

1. Additional shares of common stock were sold for $275,000.
2. $20,000 was used to pay off some short-term notes payable.
3. A new building was acquired during the year—the total cost was $920,000. A cash down payment of $240,000 was made at the time the building was purchased.
4. Some old equipment was sold and replaced with newer, more sophisticated equipment. The old equipment was sold for $9,200. The new equipment cost $105,000, paid in cash.
5. At the beginning of the year, customers owed a total of $71,500. During the year, invoices totaling $1,205,400 were sent to customers. At the end of the year, the total amount owed to Ronson Refinishers was $116,770.
6. Dividends of $80,000 were paid to shareholders during the year.
7. The total amount paid to employees during the year was $362,500.
8. Ronson Refinishers borrowed $150,000 from its bank, signing a two-year promissory note.
9. The business earned $2,452 in interest during the year.
10. Suppliers were paid $184,270 during the year.
11. The company repurchased 10,000 of its outstanding common shares, paying $28.50 per share.
12. The company paid $52,290 for income taxes during the year.
13. $27,415 was paid in interest during the year.

Required

1. Classify each of the cash flows as operating, investing, or financing activities.

1. _____	8. _____
2. _____	9. _____
3. _____	10. _____
4. _____	11. _____
5. _____	12. _____
6. _____	13. _____
7. _____	

2. Using the following form, prepare a cash flow statement for Ronson Refinishers (check your answers to Requirement 1 with the solution before proceeding with the statement).

Ronson Refinishers, Inc.		
Cash Flow Statement		

Demonstration Problem #2

Sarah Smart is a media consultant living in Toronto. Her business is called Smart Advice Inc. From the following information, prepare an income statement, statement of retained earnings, and balance sheet for Smart Advice Inc. for the month of July 2006.

Accounts Payable	$ 700
Accounts Receivable	1,800
Advertising Expense	5,000
Building	55,000
Cash	65,700
Commissions Earned	72,000
Common Shares	60,000
Dividends	2,000
Equipment	6,600
Interest Expense	200
Interest Receivable	100
Notes Payable	4,000
Notes Receivable	1,000
Retained Earnings, beginning	17,325
Salaries Expense	9,750
Salaries Payable	250
Supplies	2,325
Supplies Expense	2,900
Utilities Expense	100
Vehicle	3,800

Income Statement

Statement of Retained Earnings

Balance Sheet

SOLUTIONS

A. TEST YOURSELF

I. Matching

1.

1. E	4. K	7. H	10. B	13. C
2. F	5. G	8. L	11. I	14. O
3. D	6. A	9. J	12. M	15. N

2.

1. B	4. C	7. I	10. G
2. F	5. J	8. E	
3. H	6. D	9. A	

II. Multiple Choice

1.   C   Of the choices given, only "Notes Payable" meets the definition of a liability. Insurance Expense is an expense, Equipment is an asset, and Dividends are reductions in equity.

2.   B   Cash receipts from customers, cash paid to employees, and cash paid to suppliers all appear on the cash flow statement.

3.   D   Accounts payable are a liability and are listed on the balance sheet.

4.   C

5.   C   The balance sheet lists all the assets, liabilities, and shareholders' equity as of a specific date. The income statement, statement of retained earnings, and cash flow statement cover a specific time period.

6.   D   The income statement and statement of retained earnings cover a specific period of time. The balance sheet lists all the assets, liabilities, and shareholders' equity as of a specific date.

7.   D   Revenues minus expenses equals net income. Assets minus liabilities equals shareholders' equity. Liabilities plus shareholders' equity equals assets. Revenues plus expenses has no meaning.

8.   B   The accounting equation is:
Assets = liabilities + owners' equity
Total Assets = $90,000 + $120,000
Total Assets = $210,000

Study Tip: Memorizing and understanding the basic accounting equation is important and will be helpful in future chapters.

9.   C

Beginning balance in Retained Earnings	$920
+ Net Income	240
Subtotal	1,160
- Dividends	125
Ending balance in Retained Earnings	$1,035

Study Tip: There is an important concept in this problem that you can use over and over throughout your accounting course. In general terms, the concept can be stated as: Beginning balance + Additions - Reductions = Ending balance.

10.   B   Assets   = Liabilities + Shareholders' Equity

$160,000 = $ 85,000   + $ 75,000   Jan. 1

+45,000   - 22,000

$205,000 = $152,000   + $ 53,000   Dec. 31

11.   A.   The cash flow statement identifies the sources and uses of cash by the company.

12.   D.   Revenue – expenses = net income; $18,000 - $6,000 = $12,000. Remember, dividends are not an expense.

13.   B.   Beginning retained earnings plus net income minus dividends equals ending retained earnings:

$7,000 + ($18,000 - $10,000) - $2,000 = $13,000

14.   A.   Assets equal Liabilities plus Owners' Equity:

$40,000 = Liabilities + $15,000

Liabilities = $25,000

15.   D.   Total Equity equals Contributed Capital plus (ending) Retained Earnings:

$15,000 = Contributed Capital + $13,000

Contributed Capital = $2,000

16.   B   The income statement identifies the earnings/loss of a period for a company.

III. Completion

1. income statement, statement of retained earnings, balance sheet, and cash flow statement
2. entity (the most basic concept in accounting is that each entity has sharp boundaries between it and every other entity)
3. amounts earned by delivering goods and services to customers
4. Expenses
5. direct, indirect
6. Assets = Liabilities + Owners' equity
7. cost
8. Bookkeeping

9. company name, statement name, date
10. stable-monetary-unit
11. operating, investing, financing activities
12. net income (loss)
13. Ending retained earnings
14. financing activities
15. income statement
16. at a specific date

IV. True/False

1.	T	
2.	F	Repurchasing common stock is a financing activity.
3.	T	
4.	F	The greatest flexibility for an owner is the proprietorship form of business. The owners of a corporation are the shareholders, and they have no direct involvement in "running" the business.
5.	F	Shareholders have no personal obligation for a corporation's liabilities as a corporation is a separate legal entity.
6.	F	GAAP stands for Generally Accepted Accounting Principles.
7.	T	
8.	F	The terms are similar in that both represent claims on the economic resources of the organization; however, capital represents the claims of owners, whereas creditors are non-owners who have claims on the economic resources.
9.	T	
10.	F	The excess of revenues over expenses is called net income.
11.	F	Assets are on the balance sheet, but expenses are on the income statement.
12.	T	
13.	F	The income statement is prepared first, before the statement of retained earnings, because you need net income from the income statement to complete the statement of retained earnings.
14.	T	
15.	T	

V. Exercises

1.

Cash received from clients	$466,000
Cash received from interest	1,275
Cash paid to suppliers and employees	(402,500)
Cash paid for interest	(82,680)
Cash paid for taxes	(7,500)
Cash flows from operating activities	($25,405)

2.

Kerri's Juice Bar Inc.
Balance Sheet
January 31, 2006

Assets:		Liabilities:	
Cash	508	Accounts payable	1,225
Accounts receivable	1,480	Total liabilities	1,225
Supplies	75	Shareholders' equity:	
Equipment	14,400	Common shares*	12,658
		Retained earnings	2,580
		Total liabilities and	
Total assets	16,463	shareholders' equity	16,463

* common shares = X

X = total assets – liabilities – retained earnings

X = 16,463 – 1,225 – 2,580

X = 12,658

3. a.

Brandy's Ltd.
Income Statement
For the Month Ended August 31, 2006

Revenues: Fees earned		$756
Expenses:		
Salaries	$ 70	
Truck rental	124	
Supplies	32	
Advertising	185	
Utilities	106	517
Net income (loss)		$239

Study Tip: Net income results when revenues are greater than expenses. Net loss results when revenues are less than expenses.

Study Tip: Dividends are not an expense of the business.

---

b.

Brandy's Ltd.
Statement of Retained Earnings
For the Month Ended August 31, 2006

Beginning Retained Earnings, July 31, 2996	$42
Add/Subtract Net Income (loss)	239
	281
Dividends	(42)
Ending Retained Earnings, August 31, 2006	$239

VI. Critical Thinking

1. The answer to both questions is "yes." How is this possible? Profitability is presented on the income statement and occurs when revenues exceed expenses. Solvency is analyzed by examining the balance sheet and comparing assets (specifically, cash and receivables) with liabilities. A business is solvent when there are sufficient assets on hand to pay the debt as the debt becomes due. Remember, however, there is another financial statement—the statement of retained earnings—which links the income statement to the balance sheet. A profitable business will become insolvent if, over time, the owners withdraw assets (dividends) in excess of net income. Conversely, an unprofitable business can remain solvent over time if the owner is able to contribute assets in excess of the net losses.

2. The income statement is prepared first to determine the total income for the period. This must be performed first to be able to update the statement of retained earnings, which adds net income to the beginning retained earnings less dividends to determine the ending retained earnings. This, in turn, is used to update the balance sheet with the proper retained earnings figure. Once the ending retained earnings is determined, one can explain the changes in total cash during the period.

DEMONSTRATION PROBLEMS

Demonstration Problem #1 Solved and Explained

Requirement 1

1. Financing activity
2. Financing activity
3. Investing activity
4. Investing activity
5. Operating activity
6. Financing activity
7. Operating activity
8. Financing activity
9. Operating activity
10. Operating activity
11. Financing activity
12. Operating activity
13. Operating activity

Remember, operating activities are those relating to the company's operations (i.e., why they are in business). Operating activities can be traced back to the income statement. Investing activities detail the acquisition and disposition of long-term assets. Financing activities refer to debt and shareholders' equity.

Requirement 2

Ronson Refinishers, Inc.
Cash Flow Statement

Cash flows from operating activities:		
Cash received from customers	$1,160,130 [1]	
Cash received from interest	2,452	
Cash paid to suppliers and employees	(546,770) [2]	
Cash paid for interest	(27,415)	
Cash paid for taxes	(52,290)	
Net cash flows from operating activities		$536,107
Cash flows from investing activities:		
Cash paid for new building	(240,000) [3]	
Proceeds from sale of equipment	9,200	
Cash paid for new equipment	(105,000)	
Net cash flows from investing activities		(335,800)
Cash flows from financing activities:		
Cash paid for short-term debt	(20,000)	
Proceeds from long-term borrowing	150,000	
Proceeds from sale of common stock	275,000	
Repurchase of common shares	(285,000) [4]	
Payment of dividends	(80,000)	
Net cash flows from financing activities		40,000
Net increase (decrease) in cash		$240,307

[1] Remember the Study Tip given to you earlier: Beginning balance + additions - deductions = ending balance.
[2] $184,270 (suppliers) + $362,500 (employees) = $546,770.
[3] While the building cost $920,000, only $240,000 in cash was used; therefore, only $240,000 appears on the cash flow statement.
[4] 10,000 shares × $28.50 =$285,000

Demonstration Problem #2 Solved

Smart Advice Inc.
Income Statement
For the Month Ended July 31, 2006

Commissions earned		$72,000
Less: Expenses		
Advertising	$ 5,000	
Interest	200	
Salaries	9,750	
Supplies	2,900	
Utilities	100	
Total expenses		17,950
Net income		$ 54,050

Smart Advice Inc.
Statement of Retained Earnings
For the Month Ended July 31, 2006

Retained earnings July 1, 2005		$ 17,325
Add: Net income	54,050	
Less: Dividends	2,000	52,050
Retained earnings July 31, 2005		$69,375

Smart Advice Inc.
Balance Sheet
July 31, 2006

ASSETS			LIABILITIES		
Cash	$ 65,700		Accounts payable	$ 700	
Accounts receivable	1,800		Notes payable	4,000	
Notes receivable	1,000		Salaries payable	250	
Interest receivable	100		Total liabilities		$4,950
Supplies	2,325				
Equipment	6,600		**SHAREHOLDERS' EQUITY**		
Vehicle	3,800		Common shares	60,000	
Building	55,000		Retained earnings	71,375	
			Total shareholders' equity		131,375
			Total liabilities and shareholders'		
Total assets	$136,325		equity		$136,325

CHAPTER 2—PROCESSING ACCOUNTING INFORMATION

CHAPTER OVERVIEW

Chapter 2 uses the foundation established in the previous chapter and introduces you to the recording process for business transactions. A thorough understanding of this process is vital to your success in mastering topics in future chapters. The specific learning objectives for this chapter are to

1. **Analyze** business transactions
2. **Understand** how accounting works
3. **Record** business transactions
4. **Use** a trial balance
5. **Analyze** transactions for quick decisions

CHAPTER REVIEW

The terms used in accounting sometimes have meanings that differ from ordinary usage. Therefore, you must learn the accounting meaning of terms. Key terms to remember are: transactions, account, assets, liabilities, shareholders' (owners') equity, common shares, retained earnings, dividends, revenues, and expenses.

Transactions are any events that have a financial impact on the business and can be measured reliably.

An **account** is the basic summary device used to record changes that occur in a particular asset, liability, or shareholders' equity item.

Assets are those economic resources that will benefit the business in the future. Examples of asset accounts are Cash, Accounts Receivable, Inventory, Notes Receivable, Prepaid Expenses, Land, Buildings, Equipment, and Furniture and Fixtures.

Liabilities are obligations that a business owes. Examples of liability accounts include Notes Payable, Accounts Payable, and Accrued Liabilities.

Shareholders' (owners') equity is the claim that the shareholders have on the assets of the business. Examples of shareholders' equity accounts are Common Shares, Retained Earnings, and Dividends; of revenues, Service Revenue; and of expenses, Rent Expense.

Common shares (contributed capital) represent owners' (shareholders') investment in the business. When individuals invest in a corporation, they receive a stock certificate for the number of shares purchased.

Retained earnings represents the cumulative net income of the corporation less any dividends and less any net losses.

Dividends are distributions of assets by the corporation to the shareholders. Dividends decrease shareholders' equity.

Revenues represent the goods or services provided to customers. The Gap earns revenues when it sells merchandise (inventory) to customers, while a transportation company earns revenues when it provides a service to its customers. Revenues increase shareholders' equity.

Expenses are the costs of operating a business. Some examples of expenses are rent, cost of sales, insurance, supplies, and salaries. Expenses decrease shareholders' equity.

> **Study Tip:** When revenues are greater than expenses, the difference is net income. When revenues are less than expenses, the difference is net loss.

Objective 1 - Analyze business transactions

Every transaction will have a dual effect on the accounting equation. Therefore, the equation always remains in balance. Study carefully the eleven business transactions analyzed in the text, and reinforce your understanding by following the demonstration problems and explanations in this chapter of the Study Guide. You must have a thorough knowledge of how transactions affect the accounting equation to proceed further in this course.

See Exhibit 2-1 in the text. Transactions affect various balance sheet and income statement accounts. Some transactions will only affect two accounts, while others may affect more than two (multiple) accounts. You will see that some transactions affect only asset accounts (purchase of inventory for cash), while others affect both assets and liabilities (purchase inventory on account), and still others will affect assets and equity (performed services on account). Thus, you must analyze each transaction separately.

Transactions affecting shareholders' equity result in changes to either Common Shares or Retained Earnings. Common shares are affected when a corporation issues stock certificates to shareholders and receives assets in return (usually cash). Retained earnings are affected when the corporation records revenues, expenses, or authorizes the payment of dividends to the shareholders. Revenues increase retained earnings by bringing cash or other assets into the business in the form of earnings made by delivering goods or services to customers. Expenses are decreases in retained earnings that occur in the course of earning revenue.

After the transactions have been analyzed and recorded, the financial statements are used to summarize the business events. Recall the following from Chapter 1:
1. The cash flow statement summarizes the cash inflows and outflows and groups these cash flows into three categories.
2. The income statement summarizes the revenues and expenses and results in either net income or net loss.
3. The retained earnings statement summarizes the source and amounts of changes in retained earnings.
4. The balance sheet lists the details of the three elements in the accounting equation (assets, liabilities, shareholders' equity).

Exhibit 2-2 presents the financial statements using the transaction summary from Exhibit 2-1. (Note that there is no cash flow statement in that exhibit.)

Objective 2 - Understand how accounting works

Accounting is based on a **double-entry** system. Each transaction affects at least two accounts. **T-accounts** illustrate the dual effects of a transaction. The left side of the T-account is the **debit** side. The right side is the **credit** side.

> **Study Tip**: Remember: debit = left side and credit = right side, nothing more.

The account type determines how debits and credits are recorded. A debit increases the balance of an asset, and a credit decreases its balance. A credit increases the balance of a liability or shareholders' equity account, and a debit decreases its balance. **Exhibit 2-3 summarizes this information in a diagram. This is a very important diagram to memorize.**

(debit) Assets (credit)	=	(debit) Liability (credit)	+	(debit) Shareholders' Equity (credit)
increase | decrease		decrease | increase		decrease | increase

To illustrate, suppose that Clinton Corporation buys, on credit, office furniture of $35,000 for a consulting business. What debits and credits should be recorded? Debit Office Furniture, an asset, for $35,000. (Assets are increased by a debit.) Credit a liability for $35,000. (Liabilities are increased by a credit.)

> **Study Tip**: Refer to the basic accounting equation to understand the debit/credit rules. Increases in items on the *left side* of the equation are placed on the *left side* (debit) of the account. Increases in the items on the *right side* of the equation are placed on the *right side* (credit) of the account.

Exhibit 2-4 in your text shows the accounting equation and the first two transactions of Mackenzie Associates Inc., and Exhibits 2-5 and 2-6 summarize the debit/credit rules for the expanded accounting equation.

Objective 3 - Record business transactions

A **journal** is a chronological record of a corporation's transactions. It is the first place where a transaction is recorded. To record a transaction in the journal, follow these three steps:

1. Identify the transaction and specify each account affected by the transaction. Classify each account by type (asset, liability, shareholders' equity, revenue, or expense).
2. Determine whether each account balance is increased or decreased. Use the rules of debit and credit to determine whether to debit or credit the account.
3. Enter the transaction in the journal: first the debit, then the credit, and finally a brief explanation.

To illustrate, suppose that Gore Corporation borrows $150,000 from the bank to expand the business. What is the journal entry for this transaction?

Step 1 The source documents are a deposit slip for $150,000 and a loan agreement with the bank, both of which are dated March 20, 2007. The accounts affected are Cash (an asset) and Notes Payable (a liability).

Step 2 Both accounts will increase by $150,000. Debit Cash for $150,000 to increase Cash, and Credit Notes Payable for $150,000 to increase Notes Payable.

Step 3 Record the journal entry:

Date		Debit	Credit
Mar. 20	Cash	150,000	
	Notes Payable		150,000
	Bank loan for business expansion.		

> **Study Tip**: If one of the accounts affected is Cash, first determine whether Cash increases or decreases.

Examples of some typical journal entries are as follows:

Cash	25,000	
Common Shares		25,000
Issued shares of stock..		

Prepaid Insurance	3,000	
Cash		3,000
Purchased a 3-year insurance policy.		

Supplies	1,500	
Accounts Payable		1,500
Purchased supplies on account.		

Accounts Receivable	2,200	
Commissions Earned		2,200
Billed clients for services rendered.		

Salary Expense	800	
Cash		800
Paid salaries.		

Cash	1,400	
Accounts Receivable		1,400
Received payments from clients previously billed.		

Posting means transferring amounts from the journal to the appropriate accounts in the ledger. The journal entry for the bank loan in the previous example would be posted as follows:

Cash		Notes Payable	
150,000			150,000

Review Exhibit 2-7 in your text for an illustration of the ledger and Exhibit 2-8 for an illustration of journalizing and posting. Exhibit 2-9 shows the flow of accounting data.

Study Tip: Still having difficulty remembering how to increase a specific account? Memorize this acronym—DEAD CRLS (pronounced "dead curls"). Debits increase Expenses, Assets, and Dividends (DEAD) while Credits increase Revenues, Liabilities, and Shareholders' equity (CRLS).

Objective 4 - Use a trial balance

The **trial balance** is a list of all accounts with their balances. It tests whether total debits equal total credits. If total debits do not equal total credits, an error has been made. However, some errors may not be detected by a trial balance. One example is the posting of a transaction to the wrong account. Another is a transaction recorded at the wrong amount.

A **chart of accounts** consists of a list of all the accounts used in the business. Each account is assigned a unique number (this account number is used as a reference in the posting process). The order of the accounts in this list parallels the accounting equation. In other words, assets are listed first, followed by liability accounts and, lastly, shareholders' equity. Shareholders' equity is subdivided into common shares, retained earnings, dividends, revenue, and expense accounts. The numbers are assigned in ascending order so assets are assigned the lowest numbers while expenses carry the highest numbers. (Helpful hint: Exhibit 2-12 shows a company's chart of accounts).

The term **normal balance** refers to the type of balance (debit or credit) the account usually carries. The normal balance for any account is always the side of the account where increases are recorded. Therefore, the normal balances are

Account	Normal Balance
Assets	debit
Liabilities	credit
Common Shares	credit
Retained Earnings	credit
Dividends	debit
Revenues	credit
Expenses	debit

Exhibit 2-10 shows the Mackenzie Associates Inc. ledger accounts after posting and Exhibit 2-11 shows the company's trial balance.

Objective 5 - Analyze transactions for quick decisions

In general, the ledger is more useful than the journal in providing an overall model of a business. Therefore, when time is of the essence, accountants skip the journal and go directly to the ledger to compress transaction analysis, journalizing, and posting into a single step. This informal analysis permits decision makers to arrive at their decisions more quickly.

> **Study Tip**: Spend some time reading and thinking about the Decision Guidelines in your text. These should help you place the recording process in the proper context.

TEST YOURSELF

All the self-testing materials in this chapter focus on information and procedures that your instructor is likely to test in quizzes and examinations.

I. Matching   *Match each numbered term with its lettered definition.*

_____ 1. account
_____ 2. shareholders' equity
_____ 3. chart of accounts
_____ 4. transaction
_____ 5. credit
_____ 6. debit
_____ 7. double-entry system
_____ 8. journal

_____ 9. ledger
_____ 10. normal balance
_____ 11. posting
_____ 12. accrued liability
_____ 13. prepaid expenses
_____ 14. trial balance
_____ 15. dividends

A. detailed record of changes in a particular asset, liability, or shareholders' equity account during a period of time
B. costs recorded before being used
C. a liability incurred but not yet paid by the company
D. left side of an account
E. list of all the accounts and their account numbers
F. transferring information from the journal to the ledger
G. a list of all the accounts with their balances, which tests whether total debits equals total credits
H. the book of accounts
I. right side of an account
J. chronological record of an entity's transactions
K. the type of balance an account usually carries
L. the shareholders' claim to the business assets
M. payments of assets to shareholders
N. any event that both affects the financial position of a business entity and can be reliably recorded
O. recording the dual effects of transactions

II. Multiple Choice   *Circle the best answer.*

1. When inventory is paid with cash

   A. total assets increase
   B. total assets decrease
   C. total assets are unchanged
   D. total assets cannot be determined

2. A receivable is recorded when a business makes

   A. sales on account
   B. purchases on account
   C. sales for cash
   D. purchases for cash

3. An investment of equipment by a shareholder will result in

   A. an increase in both assets and liabilities
   B. an increase in both liabilities and shareholders' equity
   C. an increase in both assets and shareholders' equity
   D. no change in assets or shareholders' equity

4. A consultant performs services for which she receives cash. The correct entry for this transaction is

   A. debit Consulting Fees Revenue and credit Accounts Payable
   B. debit Consulting Fees Revenue and credit Cash
   C. debit Accounts Receivable and credit Consulting Fees Revenue
   D. debit Cash and credit Consulting Fees Revenue

5. An accountant debited Insurance Expense $4,600 and credited Cash $4,600 in error. The correct entry should have been to debit Prepaid Insurance for $4,600 and credit Cash for $4,600. As a result of this error

   A. assets are overstated by $4,600
   B. expenses are understated by $4,600
   C. the trial balance will not balance
   D. expenses are overstated by $4,600

6. Accounts Receivable had total debits for the month of $42,500 and total credits for the month of $31,700. If the beginning balance in Accounts Receivable was $21,200, what was the net change in Accounts Receivable?

   A. a decrease of $11,800
   B. an increase of $32,000
   C. an increase of $11,800
   D. a decrease of $32,000

7. Accounts Payable had a balance of $5,000 on March 1. During March, $750 of supplies were purchased on account. The March 31 balance was a credit of $2,850. How much were payments on Accounts Payable during March?

   A. $2,200
   B. $2,250
   C. $2,900
   D. $8,600

8. Which of the following accounts is a liability?

   A. Notes Payable
   B. Dividend
   C. Contributed Capital
   D. Note Receivable

9. The posting reference in the ledger tells

   A. the page of the ledger that the account is on
   B. the explanation of the transaction
   C. whether it is a debit or a credit entry
   D. the page of the journal where the entry can be found

10. The list of accounts and their account numbers is called the

   A. chart of accounts
   B. trial balance
   C. ledger
   D. accountants' reference

11. When the business pays cash to shareholders, the journal entry should include a

    A. debit to Accounts Payable
    B. credit to Capital
    C. debit to Cash
    D. debit to Dividends

12. When cash was received in payment for services rendered on account, the accountant debited Cash and credited Service Revenue. As a result there was

    A. an overstatement of Cash and understatement of Service Revenue
    B. an understatement of assets and overstatement of revenues
    C. an overstatement of assets and liabilities
    D. an overstatement of assets and an overstatement of revenues

13. Which is the appropriate transaction to recognize the receipt of $500 cash from a customer's accounts receivable?

A. Cash	$500	
Accounts payable		$500
B. Cash	$500	
Accounts receivable		$500
C. Accounts receivable	$500	
Cash		$500
D. Accounts payable	$500	
Cash		$500

14. Which of the following accounts usually has a debit balance?

    A. notes payable
    B. contributed capital
    C. dividends
    D. accrued liability

15. Which of the following is not an asset account?

    A. accounts receivable
    B. cash
    C. prepaid insurance
    D. contributed capital

III. Completion   *Complete each of the following statements.*

1. Put the following in proper sequence by numbering them from 1 to 4.

    _____ A. Journal entry
    _____ B. Post to ledger
    _____ C. Source document
    _____ D. Trial balance

2. Indicate whether debits increase or decrease each of the following accounts.

	Increase	Decrease
A. Cash	_____	_____
B. Accounts payable	_____	_____
C. Prepaid insurance	_____	_____
D. Notes receivable	_____	_____
E. Commissions Earned	_____	_____
F. Rent Expense	_____	_____

3. Indicate the normal balance for each of the following accounts.

	Debit	Credit
A. Accounts Receivable	_____	_____
B. Accounts Payable	_____	_____
C. Prepaid Rent	_____	_____
D. Vehicles	_____	_____
E. Common Shares	_____	_____
F. Notes Receivable	_____	_____
G. Salaries Expense	_____	_____
H. Fees Earned	_____	_____
I. Equipment	_____	_____
J. Dividends		

4. Indicate the type of account category each of the following accounts falls under.

	Asset	Liability	Equity
A. Accounts Receivable	_____	_____	_____
B. Accounts Payable	_____	_____	_____
C. Prepaid Rent	_____	_____	_____
D. Vehicles	_____	_____	_____
E. Common Shares	_____	_____	_____
F. Notes Receivable	_____	_____	_____
G. Salaries Expense	_____	_____	_____
H. Fees Earned	_____	_____	_____
I. Equipment	_____	_____	_____
J. Dividends	_____	_____	_____

IV. True/False   *For each of the following statements, circle* T *for true or* F *for false.*

1. T F Liabilities are the costs of doing business that decrease shareholders' equity.
2. T F The trial balance proves that no errors exist in the accounting records.
3. T F When a business records the receipt of cash from a customer paying an invoice, revenues will decrease.
4. T F When revenues exceed dividends, net income results.
5. T F A chart of accounts identifies all asset, liability, equity, revenue, and expense accounts.

6.   T F   When a corporation buys equipment and pays cash, total assets will increase by the cost of the new equipment.
7.   T F   Expenses carry normal debit balances.
8.   T F   Credit means left, debit means right.
9.   T F   Liability accounts are increased with credits.
10.   T F   Assets, expenses, and dividends are subdivisions of shareholders' equity.
11.   T F   The basic accounting equation will increase when the business borrows money from a bank.
12.   T F   When a client is billed for services rendered, both assets and shareholders' equity increase.
13.   T F   If a corporation pays dividends to the shareholders, the business records an expense.
14.   T F   The effect of paying a creditor is to record an expense.
15.   T F   Prepaid insurance is one type of asset account.

V. Exercises

1. Luchar Inc. operates a lighting business. During the first month of operations the following events occurred:

    A. Sold 10,000 common shares for $50,000.
    B. Paid rent of $2,250.
    C. Purchased $12,000 of equipment on account.
    D. Purchased $610 of supplies for cash.
    E. Performed services on account, $1,875.
    F. Paid $2,600 on the equipment purchased in C.
    G. Received $900 from customers on account.
    H. Performed $1,200 services, received cash.

    Prepare an analysis of transactions showing the effects of each event on the accounting equation.

	Cash	+	Accounts Receivable	+	Supplies	+	Equipment	=	Accounts Payable	+	Common Shares	+	Retained Earnings
A.													
B.													
C.													
D.													
E.													
F.													
G.													
H.													

ASSETS — LIABILITIES + SHAREHOLDERS' EQUITY

2. Diego Garcia, Inc. began business as a concept and design consulting corporation on May 1, 2006. During the first month of operations, the following transactions occurred:

May 1	Sold 5,000 common shares for $40,000.
May 2	Purchased office furniture for $28,000. Made a $7,000 cash down payment and gave the seller a note payable due in 120 days.
May 3	Paid $9,100 for one month's rent.
May 10	Collected $19,000 in cash for services rendered during the first 10 days of May.
May 19	Purchased $1,030 of supplies on account.
May 19	Paid the phone bill for the month, $412.
May 20	Billed clients for $17,800.
May 21	Received but did not pay the $282 utility bill for May.
May 25	Paid secretary a salary of $3,300.
May 28	Paid for the supplies purchased on May 19.
May 31	Performed $14,000 in services for the last third of May. Clients paid cash for all of these services.
May 31	Paid $1,800 dividends to shareholders.

Prepare the journal entries for each of these transactions. (Omit explanations.)

Date	Accounts	PR	Debit	Credit

3. The following are normal balances for the accounts of Linda's Limo Service, Inc. on July 31, 2006.

Accounts payable	$1,250
Accounts receivable	3,075
Advertising expense	115
Cash	7,380
Common shares	8,825
Fuel expense	775
Insurance expense	640
Prepaid rent	490
Salary expense	2,755
Salaries payable	215
Service revenue	5,545
Uniform cleaning expense	605

Prepare a trial balance based on the account balances above.

	Debit	Credit
Cash	_____	_____
Accounts receivable	_____	_____
Prepaid rent	_____	_____
Accounts payable	_____	_____
Salaries payable	_____	_____
Common shares	_____	_____
Service revenue	_____	_____
Advertising expense	_____	_____
Insurance expense	_____	_____
Fuel expense	_____	_____
Salary expense	_____	_____
Uniform cleaning expense	_____	_____
Total	=======	=======

4. Dragon Delivery Corporation had the following trial balance on June 30, 2006.

Cash	$ 56,000	
Accounts receivable	18,000	
Notes receivable	6,000	
Land	70,000	
Accounts payable		$ 8,400
Common shares		120,000
Delivery revenue		24,000
Salary expense		7,000
Insurance expense	3,000	
	$153,000	$ 159,400

The following items/errors caused the trial balance not to balance:

A. All accounts have a normal balance.
B. Recorded a $2,000 note payable as a note receivable.
C. Posted a $4,000 credit to Accounts Payable as $400.
D. Recorded Prepaid Insurance of $3,000 as Insurance Expense.
E. Recorded a cash revenue transaction by debiting Cash for $6,000 and crediting Accounts Receivable for $6,000.

Prepare a corrected trial balance as of June 30, 2006.

Dragon Delivery Corporation
Trial Balance
June 30, 2006

	Debit	Credit
Cash	_____	_____
Notes receivable	_____	_____
Prepaid insurance	_____	_____
Land	_____	_____
Accounts payable	_____	_____
Notes payable	_____	_____
Common shares	_____	_____
Delivery revenue	_____	_____
Salary expense	_____	_____
Insurance expense	_____	_____
Total	========	========

VI. Critical Thinking

The following errors occurred in posting transactions from the journal to the ledger:

1. A payment of $470 for insurance was posted as a $470 debit to Insurance Expense and a $740 credit to Cash.
2. The receipt of $300 from a customer on account was posted as a $300 debit to Cash and a $300 credit to Fees Earned.
3. The purchase of supplies on account for $140 was posted twice as a debit to Supplies and once as a credit to Accounts Payable.
4. The payment of $220 to a creditor on account was posted as a credit to Accounts Payable for $220 and a credit to Cash for $220.
5. The purchase of supplies for $100 was posted as a debit to supplies expense and a credit to cash.

For each of these errors, determine the following:
A. Is the trial balance out of balance?
B. If out of balance, what is the difference between the column totals?
C. Which column total is higher?
D. Which column total is correct?

Error	Out of balance?	Column total difference	Higher column total	Correct column total
1.				
2.				
3.				
4.				
5.				

DEMONSTRATION PROBLEMS

Demonstration Problem #1

Preston Leisure Services Corporation organizes and leads small group tours to Antarctica. During the month of January, 2006 (the first month of operations), the following transactions occurred:

Jan. 1   Sold 3,000 common shares for $50,000.
Jan. 1   An office was located in town and rent of $2,000 was paid for the first month.
Jan. 3   Office supplies were purchased for cash at a cost of $400.
Jan. 5   A computer and a laser printer to be used in the business were purchased on account for
             $3,200.
Jan. 8   Additional office supplies costing $1,200 were purchased on account.
Jan. 10   Commissions of $4,250 were billed on account to clients.
Jan. 15   Additional fees totaling $1,800 were collected from clients during the first 15 days of the
             month and were deposited into the business chequing account.
Jan. 16   Cash of $2,300 was received from clients billed on Jan. 10.
Jan. 18   Paid for the office supplies purchased on Jan. 8.
Jan. 21   Dividends of $2,500 were paid.
Jan. 31   Commissions totaling $3,100 were collected from clients during the second half of the month.
             These fees were deposited into the business chequing account.

Required:

1. Prepare an analysis of transactions of Preston Leisure Services Corporation. Use Exhibit 2-1 in the text as a guide and the format on the next page for your answers.
2. Prepare the income statement, statement of retained earnings, balance sheet, and cash flow statement for the business after recording the January transactions.

Requirement 1 (Analysis of transactions)

Cash	+	ASSETS Accounts Receivable	+	Office Supplies	+	Equipment	=	LIABILITIES Accounts Payable	+	SHAREHOLDERS' EQUITY Common Shares	+	Retained Earnings

Requirement 2 (Income Statement, Statement of Retained Earnings, Balance Sheet, and Cash Flow Statement)

Demonstration Problem #2

The trial balance of River Rafting, Inc. on May 1, 2006, lists the entity's assets, liabilities, and shareholders' equity.

	Balance	
Account Title	Debit	Credit
Cash	$ 8,000	
Equipment	24,000	
Accounts Payable		$ 5,000
Common Shares		27,000

During May, the business performed the following transactions:

a. In anticipation of expanding the business in the near future, the company borrowed $65,000 from a local bank. A note payable was signed.
b. A small parcel of land was acquired for $25,000 cash. The land is expected to be used as the future location of the business.
c. Rafting trips were provided for clients. Cash totaling $4,000 was received for these trips.
d. Supplies costing $800 were purchased on account.
e. Rafting trips were provided for clients. Earned revenue on account totaling $4,500.
f. The following expenses were paid in cash:
   1. Salary expense, $3,000
   2. Rent expense, $1,400
   3. Advertising expense, $1,150
   4. Interest expense, $650
g. Declared and paid dividends of $2,200.
h. Paid $3,600 owed on account.
i. Received $3,100 cash on account for services previously rendered.

Required:

1. Using the T-account format, open the following ledger accounts for River Rafting, Inc. with the balances as indicated.

   ASSETS
   Cash, $8,000
   Accounts receivable, no balance
   Supplies, no balance
   Equipment, $24,000
   Land, no balance

   LIABILITIES
   Accounts payable, $5,000
   Notes payable, no balance

   SHAREHOLDERS' EQUITY
   Common shares, $27,000
   Dividends, no balance

   REVENUE
   Rafting revenue, no balance

   EXPENSES
   Salary expense, no balance
   Rent expense, no balance
   Interest expense, no balance
   Advertising expense, no balance

2. Journalize the transactions. Key each journal entry by its transaction letter.
3. Post to the T-accounts. Key all amounts by letter and compute a balance for each account.
4. Prepare the trial balance as of May 31, 2006.
5. Prepare the income statement, statement of retained earnings, and balance sheet.

Requirements 1 and 3: (Open ledger accounts and post journal entries)

ASSETS

LIABILITIES

SHAREHOLDERS' EQUITY

REVENUE

EXPENSES

```
┌────────────┬────────────          ┌────────────┬────────────
             │                                   │
             │                                   │
             │                                   │
             │                                   │

┌────────────┬────────────          ┌────────────┬────────────
             │                                   │
             │                                   │
             │                                   │
             │                                   │
```

Requirement 2 (Journal entries)

Date	Accounts and Explanation	PR	Debit	Credit

Requirement 4 (Trial Balance)

ACCOUNTS	DEBITS	CREDITS
Cash		
Accounts receivable		
Supplies		
Equipment		
Land		
Accounts payable		
Notes payable		
Common shares		
Dividends		
Rafting revenue		
Salary expense		
Rent expense		
Interest expense		
Advertising expense		

Requirement 5 (Income Statement, Statement of Retained Earnings, Balance Sheet)

SOLUTIONS

A. TEST YOURSELF

I. Matching

1. A	4. N	7. O	10. K	13. B
2. L	5. I	8. J	11. F	14. G
3. E	6. D	9. H	12. C	15. M

II. Multiple Choice

1.   C   When cash is received on an account receivable, two assets are affected: cash is increased and accounts receivable is decreased. Since the increase in cash is equal to the decrease in accounts receivable, total assets are unchanged.

2.   A   Only sales on account cause a receivable to be recorded. Purchases on account cause a payable to be recorded; sales for cash and purchases for cash do not affect receivables.

3.   C   The sale of common shares for the value of the equipment invested causes an increase in the assets of the business. Since the owners have claim to those assets they invested in the business, there is also an increase in shareholders' equity.

4.   D   The receipt of cash, an asset, for the performance of services causes an increase in equity. This increase in equity from providing services is called revenue. Cash is increased with a debit and revenue is increased with a credit.

5.   D   The recorded entry incorrectly increased expenses by $4,600. Accordingly, expenses are overstated. Since the entry should have debited Prepaid Insurance, but did not, assets are *understated*. Even though the entry is erroneous, it included both a debit and credit and the trial balance will balance.

6.   C   The $42,500 of debits to Accounts Receivable increased the balance, while the $31,700 of credits to Accounts Receivable decreased the balance. The net effect of the debits and the credits is $42,500 - $31,700 = $10,800 increase.

7.   C   The following equation is used to solve this problem:

        Beginning balance
+   increase   (new accounts)
-   <u>decrease</u>   (payments)
=   <u>ending balance</u>

Rearranged to solve for payments the equation is:

Payments = beginning balance + new accounts - ending balance
Payments = $5,000 + 750 - $2,850 = $2,900

8.   A   Notes payable is an amount the business must pay because it signed a promissory note that requires future payment.

9.   D   The posting reference provides a "trail" through the accounting records for future reference.

10.   A   A list of accounts and account numbers is called the chart of accounts.

11.   D   Dividends decrease the Cash account balance and increase the balance in the Dividends account. To decrease the cash balance it is necessary to credit the Cash account; to increase the dividends account balance it is necessary to debit the Dividends account.

12.   D   The journal entry made incorrectly credited (increased) the Service Revenue account balance. The correct entry should have been to credit (decrease) Accounts Receivable. As a result, assets (Accounts Receivable) are overstated and revenue (Service Revenue) is overstated.

13.   B   Cash $500
           Accounts receivable $500
           The cash received is an increase to the asset account, thus debiting cash, and the accounts receivable is decreasing (a credit) as it has been paid.

14   C   Dividends are decreases to shareholders' equity and thus a debit.

15.   D   Contributed capital is an equity account.

III. Completion

1. A. 2.   B. 3.   C. 1   D. 4
    (Source documents provide the information necessary to prepare journal entries. Journal entries are posted to the ledger. The trial balance is prepared from ledger balances.)

2. A. increase   B. decrease   C. increase   D. increase   E. decrease   F. increase
    (Debits increase accounts with a normal debit balance and decrease accounts with a normal credit balance. Assets, dividends, and expenses have normal debit balances, while liabilities, shareholders' equity, and revenue have normal credit balances.)

Study Tip: Remember DEAD CRLS, the study tip given earlier?

3. A. debit   B. credit   C. debit   D. debit   E. credit   F. debit   G. debit   H. credit
    I. debit   J. debit
    (Assets, expenses, and dividends have normal debit balances. Liabilities, shareholders' equity, and revenue have normal credit balances.)

4. A. Accounts Receivable   Asset
    B. Accounts Payable   Liability
    C. Prepaid Rent   Asset
    D. Vehicles   Asset
    E. Common Shares   Equity
    F. Notes Receivable   Asset
    G. Salaries Expense   Equity
    H. Fees Earned   Equity
    I. Equipment   Asset
    J. Dividends   Equity

IV. True/False

1.   F   Liabilities are obligations of the business; expenses are the costs of doing business.
2.   F   The trial balance only proves the equality of debits and credits in the ledger; it does not prove that no errors were made.
3.   F   Revenues will increase at the time the services/goods are sold, not at the time the invoice is paid by the customer.
4.   F   Net income is the excess of revenues over expenses. Dividends have no effect on net income.
5.   T
6.   F   Because the amount of increase in equipment is equal to the amount of decrease in cash, total assets will not change.
7.   T
8.   F   Debit is the left side and credit is the right side of a T-account.
9.   T
10. F   Expenses and dividends are subdivisions of shareholders' equity (along with common shares, retained earnings, and revenues); assets are the economic resources available for future use.
11. T
12. T
13. F   Dividends are not a cost of doing business; they are the distribution of assets to shareholders.
14. F   When paying a creditor, both assets (cash) and liabilities (accounts payable) decrease. Expenses are not affected.
15. T

V. Exercises

	Cash	+	Accounts Receivable	+	Supplies	+	Equipment	=	Accounts Payable	+	Common Shares	+	Retained Earnings
					ASSETS				**LIABILITIES + SHAREHOLDERS' EQUITY**				
A.	$50,000							=			$50,000		
B.	-2,250							=					$-2,250
	$47,750							=			$50,000		$-2,250
C.							$12,000	=	$12,000				
	$47,750					+	$12,000	=	$12,000	+	$50,000		$-2,250
D.	-610			+	$ 610			=					
	$47,140			+	$ 610	+	$12,000	=	$12,000	+	$50,000		$-2,250
E.			$ 1,875					=					$ 1,875
	$47,140	+	$ 1,875	+	$ 610	+	$12,000	=	$12,000	+	$50,000		$-375
F.	-2,600							=	- 2,600				
	$44,540	+	$ 1,875	+	$ 610	+	$12,000	=	$9,400	+	$50,000		$-375
G.	900		-900					=					
	$45,440	+	$ 975	+	$ 610	+	$12,000	=	$9,400	+	$50,000		$-375
H.	1,200							=					$1,200
	$46,640	+	$975	+	$610	+	$12,000	=	$9,400	+	$50,000	+	$825

2.

Date	Account	PR	Debit	Credit
May 1	Cash		40,000	
	Common Shares			40,000
May 2	Furniture		28,000	
	Cash			7,000
	Notes Payable			21,000
May 3	Rent Expense		9,100	
	Cash			9,100
May 10	Cash		19,000	
	Consulting Revenues			19,000
May 19	Supplies		1,030	
	Accounts Payable			1,030
May 19	Telephone Expense		412	
	Cash			412
May 20	Accounts Receivable		17,800	
	Consulting Revenues			17,800

May 21	Utility Expense		282	
	Accounts Payable			282
May 25	Salary Expense		3,300	
	Cash			3,300
May 28	Accounts Payable		1,030	
	Cash			1,030
May 31	Cash		14,000	
	Consulting Revenues			14,000
May 31	Dividends		1,800	
	Cash			1,800

3.

Linda's Limo Service, Inc.
Trial Balance
July 31, 2006

	Debit	Credit
Cash	$ 7,380	
Accounts receivable	3,075	
Prepaid rent	490	
Accounts payable		$ 1,250
Salaries payable		215
Common shares		8,825
Service revenue		5,545
Advertising expense	115	
Insurance expense	640	
Fuel expense	775	
Salary expense	2,755	
Uniform cleaning expense	605	
Total	$15,835	$15,835

4.

Dragon Delivery Corporation
Trial Balance
June 30, 2006

	Debit	Credit
Cash	$ 56,000	
Accounts receivable	24,000	
Notes receivable	4,000	
Prepaid insurance	3,000	
Land	70,000	
Accounts payable		$ 12,000
Notes payable		2,000
Common shares		120,000
Delivery revenue		30,000
Salary expense	7,000	
Insurance expense	0	
Total	$164,000	$164,000

VI. Critical Thinking

Error	Out of balance?	Column total difference	Higher column total	Correct column total
1.	yes	$270	credit	credit
2.	no			
3.	yes	$140	debit	credit
4.	yes	$440	credit	debit
5.	no			

DEMONSTRATION PROBLEMS

Demonstration Problem #1 Solved and Explained

Requirement 1

Jan. 1 The sale of common shares for $50,000 increased equity in the business by the same amount. Thus:

Assets	=	Liabilities	+	Shareholders' Equity
Cash				Common Shares
+50,000		no change		+50,000

Jan. 1   Monthly rent of $2,000 was paid, so Cash decreased by $2,000. In return for the rent, the business received the right to use the office space. However, the corporation still owns no part of the office; its right to use the office cannot be considered an asset. Since it has paid $2,000 cash but has not received an asset in return, nor paid a liability, the equity in the business has decreased by $2,000.

Assets	=	Liabilities	+	Shareholders' Equity
Cash				Retained Earnings
-2,000		no change		-2,000

Jan. 3 $400 was paid for office supplies. In return for the cash, the business received ownership of the office supplies. When a business owns a resource to be used in the business, that resource is an asset. Since the $400 cash was exchanged for $400 worth of assets, shareholders' equity was not affected. Remember: When cash is exchanged for an asset, shareholders' equity is unaffected.

Assets		=	Liabilities	+	Shareholders' Equity
Cash	Office Supplies				
-400	+400		no change		no change

Jan. 5   A computer and laser printer were purchased for $3,200 on account. The business now owns the equipment, which is an asset. However, payment was not made, but promised. The promise of payment is a debt, a liability. By promising the computer sales company $3,200, the business has added $3,200 to its liabilities, which until this point were zero.

Assets	=	Liabilities	+	Shareholders' Equity
Equipment				
+3,200		+3,200		no change

Jan. 8   Office supplies costing $1,200 were purchased on account. As we saw in the Jan. 5 debt transaction, when a business incurs a debt in exchange for an asset, the business has added the asset but it has also added a corresponding liability.

Assets	=	Liabilities	+	Shareholders' Equity
Supplies		Accounts Payable		
+1,200		+1,200		no change

Jan. 10   Commissions of $4,250 were earned on account. When a client promises to pay for services rendered, the promise represents an asset to the business. A business earns revenue when it performs a service, whether it receives cash immediately or expects to collect the cash later. Revenue transactions cause the business to grow, as shown by the increase in total assets and equities. Note that both the assets and the shareholders' equity in the business have increased.

	Assets	=	Liabilities	+	Shareholders' Equity
	Accounts Receivable				Retained Earnings
	+4,250		no change		+4,250

Jan. 15 Fees totaling $1,800 were earned and collected. When services are rendered and cash is collected, the asset Cash increases by the amount collected and the retained earnings of the business increase as well.

	Assets	=	Liabilities	+	Shareholders' Equity
	Cash				Retained Earnings
	+1,800		no change		+1,800

Jan. 16 Collected $2,300 cash on the account receivable created on Jan. 10. The asset Cash is increased and the asset Accounts Receivable is decreased by the same amount. Note that revenue is unaffected by the actual receipt of the cash since the firm has already recorded the revenue when it was earned on Jan. 10.

	Assets		=	Liabilities	+	Shareholders' Equity
	Cash	Accounts Receivable				
	+2,300	-2,300		no change		no change

Jan. 18 Paid for the supplies purchased on Jan. 8. The payment of cash on account does not affect the asset Office Supplies because the payment does not increase or decrease the supplies available to the business. The effect on the accounting equation is a decrease in the asset Cash and a decrease in the liability Accounts Payable.

	Assets	=	Liabilities	+	Shareholders' Equity
	Cash		Accounts Payable		
	-1,200		-1,200		no change

Jan. 21 Dividends of $2,500 were paid. The cash dividends decrease the asset Cash and reduce the shareholders' equity in the business. Note that the dividends do not represent a business expense.

	Assets	=	Liabilities	+	Shareholders' Equity
	Cash				Retained Earnings
	-2,500		no change		-2,500

Jan. 31 Fees totaling $3,100 were collected. When services are rendered and immediately collected, the asset Cash increases by the amount received, and the retained earnings of the business increase as well.

	Assets	=	Liabilities	+	Shareholders' Equity
	Cash				Retained Earnings
	+3,100		no change		+3,100

PRESTON LEISURE SERVICES CORPORATION

	ASSETS				=	LIABILITIES + SHAREHOLDERS' EQUITY			
	Cash +	Accounts Receivable +	Office Supplies +	Equipment	=	Accounts Payable +	Common Shares +	Retained Earnings	Type of shareholders' equity transaction
Jan. 1	+50,000						+50,000		Investment by shareholders
Jan. 1	-2,000							-2,000	Rent expense
Jan. 3	-400		+400						
Jan. 5				+3,200		+3,200			
Jan. 8			+1,200			+1,200			
Jan. 10		+4,250						+4,250	Commissions earned
Jan. 15	+1,800							+1,800	Commissions earned
Jan. 16	+2,300	-2,300							
Jan. 18	-1,200					-1,200			
Jan. 21	-2,500							-2,500	Dividends
Jan. 31	+3,100							+3,100	Commissions earned
	$51,100	$1,950	$1,600	$3,200		$3,200	$50,000	$4,650	
	$57,850					$57,850			

Requirement 2 (Income Statement, Statement of Retained Earnings, Balance Sheet, and Cash Flow Statement)

Preston Leisure Services Corporation
Income Statement
For the Month Ended January 31, 2006

Commissions earned		$9,150
Less: Expenses		
Rent		2,000
Net income		$7,150

Preston Leisure Services Corporation
Statement of Retained Earnings
For the Month Ended January 31, 2006

Retained earnings, January 1, 2006		-0-
Add: Net income	$7,150	
Less: Dividends	2,500	4,650
Retained earnings, January 31, 2006		$4,650

Preston Leisure Services Corporation
Balance Sheet
January 31, 2006

ASSETS		**LIABILITIES**		
Cash	$51,100	Accounts payable		$ 3,200
Accounts receivable	1,950			
Office supplies	1,600	**SHAREHOLDERS' EQUITY**		
Equipment	3,200	Common shares	$50,000	
		Retained earnings	4,650	54,650
Total assets	$57,850	Total liabilities & shareholders' equity		$57,850

Preston Leisure Services Corporation
Cash Flow Statement
For the Month Ended January 31, 2006

Cash flows from operating activities:		
Cash received from customers	$7,200˙	
Cash paid to suppliers	(3,600)	
Net cash flows from operating activities		$ 3,600
Cash flows from financing activities:		
Proceeds from sale of shares	50,000	
Cash paid for dividends	(2,500)	
Net cash flows from financing activities		47,500
Net cash increase during the month		51,100
Add: beginning cash balance		0
Cash balance, January 31, 2006		$51,100

˙ The business earned commissions of $9,150; however, only $7,200 was received in cash. Note the ending Accounts Receivable balance of $1,950.

Demonstration Problem #2 Solved

Requirement 1 (Open ledger accounts)

ASSETS

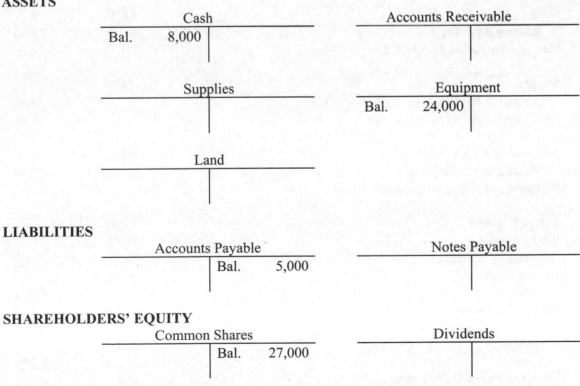

LIABILITIES

SHAREHOLDERS' EQUITY

REVENUE

Rafting Revenue

EXPENSES

Salary Expense

Rent Expense

Interest Expense

Advertising Expense

Requirement 2 (Journal entries)

Date	Accounts and Explanation	PR	Debit	Credit
a.	Cash		65,000	
	Notes Payable			65,000
	Borrowed cash and signed note payable.			
b.	Land		25,000	
	Cash			25,000
	Purchased land for future office location.			
c.	Cash		4,000	
	Rafting Revenue			4,000
	Revenue earned and collected.			
d.	Supplies		800	
	Accounts Payable			800
	Purchased supplies on account.			
e.	Accounts Receivable		4,500	
	Rafting Revenue			4,500
	Performed services on account.			
f.	Salary Expense		3,000	
	Rent Expense		1,400	
	Advertising Expense		1,150	
	Interest Expense		650	
	Cash			6,200
	Paid cash expenses.			
g.	Dividends		2,200	
	Cash			2,200
	Declared and paid dividends.			

h.	Accounts Payable	3,600	
	Cash		3,600
	Paid on account.		

i.	Cash	3,100	
	Accounts Receivable.		3,100
	Received on account.		

Requirement 3 (Posting)

ASSETS

Cash

Bal.	8,000			
(a)	65,000	(b)	25,000	
(c)	4,000	(f)	6,200	
(i)	3,100	(g)	2,200	
		(h)	3,600	
Bal.	43,100			

Accounts Receivable

(e)	4,500	(i)	3,100
Bal.	1,400		

Supplies

(d)	800	
Bal.	800	

Equipment

Bal.	24,000	
Bal.	24,000	

Land

(b)	25,000	
Bal.	25,000	

LIABILITIES

Accounts Payable

		Bal.	5,000
(h)	3,600	(d)	800
		Bal.	2,200

Notes Payable

(a)	65,000	
Bal.	65,000	

SHAREHOLDERS' EQUITY

Common Shares

Bal.	27,000	
Bal.	27,000	

Dividends

(g)	2,200	
Bal.	2,200	

REVENUE

Rafting Revenue

(c)	4,000	
(e)	4,500	
Bal.	8,500	

EXPENSES

Salary Expense		
(f)	3,000	
Bal.	3,000	

Rent Expense		
(f)	1,400	
Bal.	1,400	

Interest Expense		
(f)	650	
Bal.	650	

Advertising Expense		
(f)	1,150	
Bal.	1,150	

Requirement 4 (Trial Balance)

Account	Debit	Credit
Cash	$43,100	
Accounts receivable	1,400	
Supplies	800	
Equipment	24,000	
Land	25,000	
Accounts payable		$2,200
Notes payable		65,000
Common shares		27,000
Dividends	2,200	
Rafting revenue		8,500
Salary expense	3,000	
Rent expense	1,400	
Interest expense	650	
Advertising expense	1,150	
Total	$102,700	$102,700

Total debits = total credits. The accounts appear to be in balance. If the trial balance did not balance, we would look for an error in recording or posting.

Requirement 5

River Rafting, Inc
Income Statement
For the Month Ended May 31, 2006

Revenues: Rafting revenue		$8,500
Less: Expenses		
Salary expense	$3,000	
Rent expense	1,400	
Interest expense	650	
Advertising expense	1,150	
Total expenses		6,200
Net income		$2,300

River Rafting, Inc.
Statement of Retained Earnings
For the Month Ended May 31, 2006

Retained earnings, May 1, 2006		$ 0
Add: Net income	$2,300	
Less: Dividends	2,200	
Net increase in retained earnings		100
Retained earnings, May 31, 2006		$100

River Rafting, Inc.
Balance Sheet
May 31, 2006

ASSETS		LIABILITIES		
Cash	$43,100	Accounts payable	$ 2,200	
Accounts receivable	1,400	Notes payable	65,000	
Supplies	800	Total liabilities		$67,200
Equipment	24,000	**SHAREHOLDERS' EQUITY**		
Land	25,000	Common shares	$27,000	
		Retained earnings	100	27,100
Total assets	$94,300	Total liabilities & shareholders' equity		$94,300

CHAPTER 3—ACCRUAL ACCOUNTING AND THE FINANCIAL STATEMENTS

CHAPTER OVERVIEW

Chapter 3 continues the discussion begun in Chapter 2 concerning the recording of business transactions using debit and credit analysis. Therefore, you should feel comfortable with the debit and credit rules when you begin. In this chapter, you will learn about the adjusting process that takes place prior to the preparation of the financial statements. In addition, you are introduced to the closing process. The specific learning objectives for this chapter are to

1. **Relate** accrual accounting and cash flows
2. **Apply** the revenue and matching principles
3. **Update** the financial statements by adjusting the accounts
4. **Prepare** the financial statements
5. **Close** the books
6. **Use** the current ratio and the debt ratio to evaluate a business

CHAPTER REVIEW

Objective 1 – Relate accrual accounting and cash flows

In **cash-basis accounting**, transactions are recorded only when cash is received or paid. In **accrual-basis accounting**, a business records transactions as they occur, without regard to when cash changes hands. GAAP requires that businesses use the accrual basis so that financial statements will not be misleading. Revenues are considered earned when services have been performed or merchandise is sold because the provider has a legal right to receive payment. Expenses are considered incurred when merchandise or services have been used. Financial statements would understate revenue if they did not include all revenues earned during the accounting period and would understate expenses if they did not include all expenses incurred during the accounting period.

Accountants prepare financial statements at specific intervals called **accounting periods**. The basic interval is a year, and nearly all businesses prepare annual financial statements. Usually, however, businesses need financial statements more frequently at quarterly or monthly intervals. Statements prepared at intervals other than the one-year interval are called **interim statements**.

Whether financial statements are prepared on an annual basis or on an interim basis, the **time-period concept** ensures that accounting information is prepared at regular intervals. The cutoff date is the last day of the time interval for which financial statements are prepared. All transactions that occur up to the cutoff date should be included in the accounts. Thus, if financial statements are prepared for January, all transactions occurring on or before January 31 should be recorded. (Helpful hint: review Exhibit 3-1 in your text.)

Objective 2 - Apply the revenue and matching principles

The **revenue principle** guides the accountant as to 1) when to record revenue and 2) the amount of revenue to record. Revenue is recorded when it is earned, that is, when a business has delivered a completed good or service. The amount of revenue to record is generally the cash value of the goods delivered or the services performed. Helpful hint: review Exhibit 3-2 in your text.)

The **matching principle** guides the accountant in recording expenses. The objectives of the matching principle are 1) to identify the expenses that have been incurred in an accounting period; 2) to measure the expenses and to match them against revenues earned during the same period. (Matching does NOT mean matching revenues against expenses). There is a natural association between revenues and some types of expenses. If a business pays its salespeople commissions based on amounts sold, there is a relationship between sales revenue and commission expense. Other expenses, such as rent, do not have a strong association with revenues. These types of expenses are generally associated with a period of time, such as a month or a year. (Helpful hint: review Exhibit 3-3 in your text.) See the discussion relating to earnings management and ethical issues of accrual accounting.

Objective 3 - Update the financial statements by adjusting the accounts

Accrual-basis accounting requires adjustments at the end of the accounting period. Accountants use adjusting entries to obtain an accurate measure of the period's income, to bring the accounts up to date for the preparation of financial statements, and to properly record the effect of transactions that span more than one accounting period. End-of-period processing begins with the preparation of a trial balance, which is sometimes referred to as an **unadjusted trial balance.**

Adjusting entries fall into three basic categories: 1) **deferrals**, 2) **amortization**, and 3) **accruals. Deferrals** adjust asset or liability accounts. Frequently, a business will pay for goods and services in advance. Examples are supplies, insurance, and rent. Because these have been paid for before being used, they are recorded as assets. As time passes, these are used and the asset needs to be adjusted to reflect an accurate balance on the financial statements. The adjustment transfers an amount from the asset account to an expense account. The amount transferred represents the amount of the asset consumed. Many businesses receive payments from customers before the service has been provided (or the goods sold). For example, in order to fly to visit a relative you need a ticket. To get the ticket you have to pay the airline (or travel agent) in advance. At the time you purchase your ticket, the airline receives the cash but has not yet provided the service to earn the cash received. This is another example of deferral. Because the airline has accepted your money they have a liability (an obligation) to provide you with a service in the future. Once the service has been provided, the airline needs to transfer an amount from a liability account to a revenue account. These two examples illustrate the more common types of deferral adjustments—prepaid expenses and unearned revenues.

Amortization is a process that systematically allocates (spreads) the cost of a capital asset to an expense account over the useful life of the capital asset. All capital assets (except land) are subject to amortization. The effect of adjusting for amortization is to reduce the value (called book value) of the plant asset over its life. This reduction in value also affects the income statement because amortization expense is an additional cost to the business.

In a sense, **accruals** are the opposite of deferrals. Accruals refer to expenses and revenues that are not recorded in advance. Rather, they are recorded when the cash has been paid (for an expense) or received (for revenues). The most common example of an accrued expense is salary because most employees receive their wages some time after they have performed the work. An example of accrued revenue is interest earned on the savings account. Although the interest is being earned as each day passes, it is only recorded when received.

However, waiting until the cash has been paid (for an expense) or received (for revenues) could mean the expense or revenue is not correctly matched with its corresponding revenue or expense. The expense or revenue is therefore accrued (provided for) in the correct period.

1) **Prepaid expenses** are expenses that are paid in advance. They are assets because the future benefits are expected to extend beyond the present accounting period. If we pay insurance premiums of $24,000 ($2,000 per month for the next twelve months) on December 31, then on December 31 we will have Prepaid Insurance of $24,000. None of the $24,000 payment is an expense during December because the payment benefits future periods. Insurance expense will be recorded each month as a portion of the $24,000 payment expires. Remember that the amount of a prepaid asset that has expired is an expense. Other examples of prepaid expenses are supplies, rent, and sometimes advertising. At the end of January, $2,000 will be expensed as insurance expense, with the remaining $22,000 being prepaid insurance.

> **Study Tip:** Adjustments will be easier if you become familiar with the natural relationships that exist for each type of adjustment. For instance, the adjusting entry for a prepaid expense always affects an asset account and an expense account.

2) **Amortization** is recorded to account for the fact that capital assets decline in usefulness as time passes. Examples of capital assets include buildings, office equipment, and vehicles. One distinguishing feature of capital assets, compared with prepaid expenses, is that capital assets are usually useful for longer periods. Land is the only capital asset that is not amortized.

   The reduction in the usefulness of capital assets is recorded in a contra account called **Accumulated Amortization**. **Contra accounts** always have companion accounts and have account balances opposite from the account balances of the companion accounts. For accumulated amortization, the companion account is a capital asset account. The plant asset account has a debit balance, and the contra account, Accumulated Amortization, has a credit balance. The difference between these two amounts is called the asset's **book value**.

> **Study Tip:** The adjusting entry for amortization always debits Amortization Expense and credits an Accumulated Amortization account.

3) An **accrued expense** is an expense that a business has incurred but has not yet paid. Therefore, an accrued expense is also a liability. Accrued expenses include salary expense for employees. If you are working or have worked a summer job, then you know that there may be an interval of several days or even a week between the end of your pay period and the date that you receive your paycheque. If an accounting period ends during such an interval, then your employer's salary expense would be accrued for the salary that you have earned but have not yet been paid. (For example, if you get paid every second Friday and the last paycheque was on June 25, then after the weekend three days would expire for which you worked by the end of the accounting period and would represent an accrued expense for those three days.) Other examples of accrued expenses are interest and sales commissions.

> **Study Tip:** The adjusting entry for an accrued expense always debits an expense and credits a liability (payable) account.

4) **Accrued revenues** have been earned, but payment in cash has not been received nor has the client been billed. If a corporation earns $750 of revenue on January 28 but does not bill the client until February 3, then accrued revenue of $750 would be recorded on January 31.

Study Tip: The adjusting entry for accrued revenue always debits an asset (receivable) account and credits a revenue account.

5) **Unearned revenues** occur when cash is received from a customer before work is performed. Suppose that on March 15 you pay $80 for two tickets to a concert scheduled for April 7. The concert hall will not earn the $80 until April 7. Therefore, on March 15, the concert hall will debit Cash and credit Unearned Revenue. Unearned revenue is a liability account. In April, when the concert occurs, the concert hall earns the revenue and will debit Unearned Revenue and credit Revenue.

Study Tip: The adjusting entry for unearned revenue always involves a liability (unearned) account and a revenue account.

Note that each type of adjusting entry affects at least one income statement account and at least one balance sheet account. Also note that none of the adjusting entries has an effect on Cash. Adjusting entries are noncash transactions required by accrual accounting. (Helpful hint: review Exhibits 3-7 to 3-9 in your text for a concise summary of these adjustments.)

The adjusted trial balance lists all the accounts and balances after the adjustments have been prepared. The general sequence for preparing an adjusted trial balance is

1) Prepare an unadjusted trial balance.
2) Assemble the information for adjusting entries.
3) Journalize and post adjusting entries.
4) Compute the adjusted account balances.

Study Exhibits 3-10 and 3-11 in your text to become familiar with the adjusted trial balance.

Objective 4 - Prepare the financial statements

The **adjusted trial balance** provides the data needed to prepare the financial statements. The financial statements should always be prepared in the following order:

1) Income Statement
2) Statement of Retained Earnings
3) Balance Sheet

The reason for this order is quite simple: The income statement computes the amount of net income. Net income is needed for the statement of retained earnings. The statement of retained earnings computes the amount of ending retained earnings. Ending retained earnings is needed for the balance sheet. Exhibits 3-12, 3-13, and 3-14 in your text illustrate the flow of data from the income statement.

The income statement starts with revenues for the period and subtracts total expenses for the period. A positive result is net income; a negative result is net loss.

The statement of retained earnings starts with the amount of retained earnings at the beginning of the period, adds net income or subtracts net loss, and subtracts dividends. The result is the ending retained earnings balance.

The balance sheet uses the asset and liability balances from the adjusted trial balance and the retained earnings balance from the statement of retained earnings.

Note that none of the financial statements will balance back to the total debits and total credits on the adjusted trial balance. This is because the financial statements group accounts differently from the debit and credit totals listed on the adjusted trial balance. For example, the new balance for retained earnings on the balance sheet is a summary of the beginning retained earnings balance, the revenue and expense accounts used to obtain net income, and dividends paid during the period.

Objective 5 – Close the books

Closing the accounts refers to the process of preparing the accounts for the next accounting period. Closing involves journalizing and posting the **closing entries**. Closing the accounts sets the balances of revenues, expenses, and dividends to zero. Remember that when the balance sheet is prepared, the retained earnings balance includes the summary effect of the revenue, expense, and dividend accounts. These accounts are **temporary (nominal) accounts**—they measure the effect on shareholders' equity for a single accounting period. This is in contrast to balance sheet accounts, which are **permanent (real) accounts**—they do not affect retained earnings.

The steps taken to close the accounts of an entity are

1. Transfer the credit balances from the revenue accounts to the Retained Earnings account. This is accomplished by debiting the accounts for the amount of their credit balances and crediting the Retained Earnings account for the total amount of the debits.

2. Transfer the debit balances from the expense accounts to the Retained Earnings account. This is accomplished by crediting the expense accounts for the amount of their debit balances and debiting the Retained Earnings account for the total amount of the credits.

After these first two closing entries have been journalized and posted, all the revenue and expense accounts should have zero balances.

3. Transfer the balance in the Dividends account to Retained Earnings. This is accomplished by crediting the Dividends account for the amount of its debit balance and debiting Retained Earnings.

Exhibit 3-15 in your text illustrates the closing process. Note that when the closing entries are posted, the balance in Retained Earnings should be the same as the amount reported on the balance sheet.

Assets and liabilities are classified according to their liquidity. **Liquidity** is a measure of how quickly an item can be converted into cash. The balance sheet lists assets and liabilities in the order of their relative liquidity, with Cash listed first as the most liquid asset .

Current assets are those assets that are expected to be converted into cash, sold, or consumed within one year or within the business's normal operating cycle if longer than a year. Current assets include: 1) cash, 2) accounts receivable, 3) notes receivable, 4) inventory, and 5) prepaid expenses.

Long-term assets are all assets that are not current assets. Long-term assets include capital assets such as: 1) land, 2) buildings, and 3) equipment.

Current liabilities are obligations due within one year or one operating cycle if the cycle is longer than one year. Current liabilities include: 1) accounts payable, 2) notes payable due within one year, 3) salary payable, 4) unearned revenue, 5) interest payable, 6) current portion of bonds payable and mortgage payable.

Long-term liabilities are obligations due in future years. Long-term liabilities include: the portion of 1) notes payable, 2) bonds payable, and 3) mortgages payable due in more than a year.

Exhibit 3-16 in your text is an example of a **classified balance sheet,** which shows current assets separate from long-term assets and current liabilities separate from long-term liabilities. The **multi-step income statement** contains subtotals that highlight important relationships between revenues and expenses.

Objective 6 - Use the current ratio and the debt ratio to evaluate a business

Before a loan is made, creditors like to be able to predict whether a borrower can repay the loan. Ratios of various items drawn from a company's financial statements can help creditors assess the likelihood that a loan can be repaid.

The **current ratio** measures the ability of a company to pay current liabilities (short-term debt) with current assets.

$$\text{Current ratio} = \frac{\text{Total current assets}}{\text{Total current liabilities}}$$

The debt ratio measures the relationship between total liabilities and total assets. The debt ratio is an indication of a company's ability to pay both current and long-term debt.

$$\text{Debt ratio} = \frac{\text{Total liabilities}}{\text{Total assets}}$$

Review the decision guidelines on using the current ratio and the debt ratio.

TEST YOURSELF

All the self-testing materials in this chapter focus on information and procedures that your instructor is likely to test in quizzes and examinations.

I. Matching

1. *Match each numbered term with its lettered definition.*

_____ 1. contra asset	_____ 13. accrued expenses
_____ 2. matching principle	_____ 14. liquidation
_____ 3. prepaid expenses	_____ 15. accrued revenues
_____ 4. unearned revenue	_____ 16. closing the accounts
_____ 5. amortization	_____ 17. current liability
_____ 6. capital asset	_____ 18. liquidity
_____ 7. revenue principle	_____ 19. long-term asset
_____ 8. book value	_____ 20. closing entries
_____ 9. deferrals	_____ 21. Retained Earnings
_____ 10. accruals	_____ 22. long-term liability
_____ 11. accumulated amortization	_____ 23. permanent accounts
_____ 12. valuation account	_____ 24. temporary accounts

A. a category of miscellaneous assets that typically expire in the near future
B. a liability created when a business collects cash from customers in advance of doing work for the customer
C. an asset account with a credit balance and a companion account
D. an expense associated with spreading (allocating) the cost of a capital asset over its useful life
E. long-lived assets, such as land, buildings, and equipment, that are used in the operations of the business
F. the basis for recording revenues that tells accountants when to record revenues and the amount of revenue to record
G. the basis for recording expenses that directs accountants to identify all expenses incurred during the period, to measure the expenses, and to match them against the revenues earned during that same period
H. a process of discontinuing operations and going out of business
I. revenues that have been earned but not recorded
J. an account used to determine the value of a related account
K. a collective term for accrued expenses and accrued revenues
L. expenses that have been incurred but not yet recorded
M. a balance sheet account credited when adjusting for amortization
N. the difference between a capital asset account balance and its companion account balance
O. a collective term for prepaid expenses and unearned revenues
P. a debt due to be paid within one year or within one of the entity's operating cycles if the cycle is longer than a year
Q. a liability other than a current liability
R. a measure of how quickly an item may be converted to cash
S. a permanent account into which revenues, expenses, and dividends are transferred at the end of the accounting period
T. accounts that are not closed at the end of the accounting period
U. an asset other than a current asset
V. entries that transfer the revenue, expense, and dividend balances from these accounts to the shareholders' equity account
W. revenue accounts, expense accounts, and dividends
X. the step in the accounting cycle that prepares the accounts for recording the transactions of the next period

2. *Match each numbered term with its lettered definition.*

_____ 1. cash-basis accounting   _____ 5. debt ratio
_____ 2. time-period concept   _____ 6. multi-step income statement
_____ 3. operating cycle   _____ 7. current ratio
_____ 4. classified balance sheet   _____ 8. adjusted trial balance

A. a listing of accounts debits and credits once all adjustments have been made
B. accounting information can be reported at regular intervals
C. transactions are recorded only when cash is paid or received
D. current assets are separated from long-term assets and current liabilities are separated from long-term liabilities
E. current assets divided by current liabilities
F. time span during which cash is paid for goods and services that are sold to customers and the business receives payment
G. a document that highlights the important relationships between revenues and expenses
H. total liabilities divided by total assets

II. Multiple Choice   *Circle the best answer.*

1. Fransisco Inc. takes an order in October, manufactures it in November, ships and bills it in December, and receives payment in January. They don't recognize revenue until January if they are using

   A. accrual-basis accounting
   B. cash-basis accounting
   C. income tax accounting
   D. actual-basis accounting

2. An example of accrual-basis accounting is

   A. recording the purchase of land for cash
   B. recording utility expense when the bill is paid
   C. recording revenue when merchandise is sold on account
   D. recording salary expense when wages arc paid

3. Which of the following is considered an adjusting entry category?

   A. accruals
   B. deferrals
   C. amortization
   D. all of the above

4. All of the following have normal credit balances *except*

   A. Accumulated Amortization
   B. Wages Payable
   C. Prepaid Insurance
   D. Unearned Fees

5. The first financial statement prepared from the adjusted trial balance is the

   A. income statement
   B. balance sheet
   C. statement of retained earnings
   D. cash flow statement

6. Which of the following statements regarding the link between the financial statements is correct?

   A. net income from the income statement goes to the balance sheet
   B. shareholders' equity from the balance sheet goes to the statement of retained earnings
   C. net income from the balance sheet goes to the income statement
   D. retained earnings from the statement of retained earnings goes to the balance sheet

7. Jackson Co. paid 12 months' insurance on January 1 and appropriately debited Prepaid Insurance for $3,000. On January 31, Jackson should

   A. credit Prepaid Insurance for $2,750
   B. debit Insurance Expense for $250
   C. debit Prepaid Insurance for $2,750
   D. credit Insurance Expense for $2,750

8. A company has a beginning balance in Supplies of $2,100. It purchases $2,200 of supplies during the period and uses $1,800 of supplies. If the accountant does not make an adjusting entry for supplies at the end of the period, then

   A. assets will be understated by $2,500
   B. assets will be overstated by $1,800
   C. expenses will be overstated by $1,800
   D. expenses will be understated by $2,500

9. During November, a company received $15,000 cash for services rendered. It also performed $7,500 of services on account and received $5,200 cash for services to be performed in December. The amount of revenue to be included on the November income statement using accrual accounting is

   A. $12,700
   B. $22,500
   C. $15,000
   D. $17,300

10. A company correctly made an adjusting entry on December 31, 2006, and credited Prepaid Advertising for $900. During 2006, it paid $2,250 for advertising. The December 31, 2006, balance in Prepaid Advertising was $1,500. What was the balance in the Prepaid Advertising account on January 1, 2006?

    A. $3,500
    B. $ 150
    C. $4,650
    D. $2,400

11. Which of the following accounts will appear on the classified balance sheet as a current asset?

    A. Supplies
    B. Salary Expense
    C. Interest earned
    D. Dividends

12. Which of the following is a permanent account?

    A. Supplies Expense
    B. Commissions Earned
    C. Advertising Expense
    D. Retained Earnings

13. Suppose a company has posted its first two closing entries to the Retained Earnings account. The amount of the debit is greater than the amount of the credit. This means that the company had

A. net income
B. a net loss
C. net income only if there were no dividends
D. a net loss only if there were no dividends

14. Dividends have a balance of $14,000 before closing. What is the correct entry to close the Dividends account?

A. debit Retained Earnings and credit Dividends, $14,000
B. debit Dividends and credit Common Shares, $14,000
C. debit Dividends and credit Retained Earnings, $14,000
D. debit Common Shares and credit Dividends, $14,000

15. Which of the following accounts would not be classified as a current asset?

A. Cash
B. Accounts Receivable
C. Prepaid Insurance
D. Vehicles

16. The current ratio compares

A. current assets to long-term assets
B. current assets to current liabilities
C. current liabilities to long-term liabilities
D. total liabilities to total assets

III. Completion   *Complete each of the following statements.*

1. _____basis accounting recognizes revenue when it is earned and expenses when they are incurred.

2. Adjusting entry categories include _____ , _____ , _____ , _____ , and _____ .

3. The end-of-period process of updating the accounts is called _____.

4. Accumulated Amortization is an example of a(n) _____ account.

5. The revenue principle provides guidance to accountants as to _____ and _____.

6. The objectives of the matching principle are: _____, _____, and _____.

7. Financial statements should be prepared in the following order: 1)_____,
   2)_____, and 3)_____.

8. The basic interval for financial statements is _____, while statements prepared at other times and for shorter intervals of time are called _____.

9. Revenue and expense accounts are _____ accounts.

10. The accounts that are never closed at the end of an accounting period are called _____accounts.

11. The Dividends account is closed to the_____ account.

12. _____refers to how quickly an asset can be converted into cash.

13. The two types of deferrals are _____ and _____.

14. The debt ratio compares _____ to _____.

15. The _____ is a measure of short-term liquidity.

IV. True/False   *For each of the following statements, circle* T *for true or* F *for false.*

1.   T F   The operating cycle ensures that accounting information is reported at regular intervals.
2.   T F   Adjusting entries affect both the income statement and the balance sheet.
3.   T F   An example of a deferral is prepaid insurance.
4.   T F   The adjustment for supplies transfers part of the account balance to a liability account.
5.   T F   Book value is the difference between cost and amortization expense.
6.   T F   When an expense accrues, a liability is also accruing.
7.   T F   When adjusting for accrued revenue, an asset is being increased.
8.   T F   The amounts appearing on an adjusted trial balance are the same amounts that will appear on the income statement.
9.   T F   The amounts appearing on an adjusted trial balance are the same amounts that will appear on the balance sheet.
10. T F   Revenue, expense, and the Dividends accounts are all temporary accounts.
11. T F   The Retained Earnings account will increase if there has been net income for the period.
12. T F   The balance in the Dividends account is closed to the Common Shares account.
13. T F   The Retained Earnings account is closed to the Common Shares account.
14. T F   To calculate the current ratio, current assets are divided by current liabilities.
15. T F   After the closing process is complete, all real accounts will have zero balances.

V. Exercises

1. The accounting records of Casa Rojas Pancake Emporium include the following unadjusted normal balances on April 30:

Accounts Receivable	$ 1,800
Supplies	610
Salary Payable	0
Unearned Revenue	900
Service Revenue	5,100
Salary Expense	1,225
Supplies Expense	0
Amortization Expense	0
Accumulated Amortization	1,100

The following information is available for the April 30 adjusting entries:

a. Supplies on hand, $360
b. Salaries owed to employees, $470
c. Service revenue earned but not billed, $1,505
d. Services performed which had been paid for in advance, $245
e. Amortization, $750

Required:

1. Open the T-accounts. See the format below.
2. Record the adjustments directly to the T-accounts. (Key each entry by letter.)
3. Compute the adjusted balance for each account.

Accounts Receivable	Supplies	Salary Payable

Unearned Revenue	Service Revenue	Salary Expense

Supplies Expense	Amortization Expense	Accumulated Amortization

2. The balance sheets for Fanny's Salon had the following balances after adjusting entries:

	2005	2006
Supplies	$2,700	$1,075
Prepaid insurance	3,400	800
Taxes payable	2,100	200
Unearned revenue	4,150	4,100

Cash payments and receipts for 2006 included

Payments for supplies	$6,200
Payments for insurance	4,800
Payments of taxes	2,400
Receipts from customers	91,000

How much supplies expense, insurance expense, tax expense, and revenue were reported in the 2006 income statement?

3. Record the December 31 adjusting entries for each of the following in the space provided below.

A. On Jan. 1, the Prepaid Rent account has a balance of $15,000 representing six months' rent through June 30. On June 30, a two-year lease was signed for a total cost of $36,000 and a cheque was issued for that amount.

B. On Dec. 31, the balance in the Unearned Subscriptions account was $11,700, which represented advance payments from customers for subscriptions (52 issues) to a newsletter. As of Dec. 31, 22 issues of the newsletter had been published.

C. The company had an $18,000 note receivable on the books at year end. The six-month note was dated Nov. 1 and carried a 9% interest rate.

D. A total of $3,150 wages and salaries had accrued on Dec. 31.

A.   GENERAL JOURNAL

Date	Accounts and Explanation	PR	Debit	Credit

B.   GENERAL JOURNAL

Date	Accounts and Explanation	PR	Debit	Credit

C.

GENERAL JOURNAL

Date	Accounts and Explanation	PR	Debit	Credit

D.

GENERAL JOURNAL

Date	Accounts and Explanation	PR	Debit	Credit

4. Minder Inc. had the following trial balance at December 31, 2006:

Minder Inc.
Trial Balance
December 31, 2006

Cash	$ 19,000	
Accounts receivable	8,000	
Prepaid advertising	3,600	
Supplies	4,200	
Notes payable		$11,400
Unearned revenue		5,400
Common shares		10,000
Retained earnings		2,200
Dividends	900	
Fees earned		18,000
Salaries expense	6,600	
Rent expense	3,000	
Utilities expense	1,700	
	$47,000	$47,000

Additional information:

A. Supplies at year end totaled $1,500.
B. $2,200 of the prepaid advertising was expired at year end.

Required:

1. Prepare the appropriate adjusting entries.
2. Prepare closing entries.
3. Compute Minder Inc.'s ending retained earnings balance.

Requirement 1 (Adjusting entries)

GENERAL JOURNAL

Date	Accounts and Explanation	PR	Debit	Credit

Requirement 2 (Closing entries)

GENERAL JOURNAL

Date	Accounts and Explanation	PR	Debit	Credit

Requirement 3 (Ending Retained Earnings balance)

Beginning Retained Earnings	$
Plus: Net Income	
Less: Dividends	
Ending Retained Earnings	$

VI. Critical Thinking

1. If a business is using cash-basis accounting, what is the amount listed on the balance sheet for accounts receivable, assuming clients have been billed $118,500 during the year and sent in payments totaling $93,000 by the end of the year?

2. What would be the impact to a company of not performing a closing process?

DEMONSTRATION PROBLEMS

Demonstration Problem #1

Videos Delivered, Inc. is in the business of renting videos. The trial balance for Videos Delivered, Inc. at December 31, 2006, and the data needed for year-end adjustments are as follows:

Trial Balance
December 31, 2006

Cash	$19,415	
Accounts receivable	90	
Prepaid rent	1,200	
Supplies	400	
Rental tape library	24,000	
Accumulated amortization—tape library		$12,000
Furniture	9,500	
Accumulated amortization—furniture		3,800
Accounts payable		1,450
Salaries payable		
Unearned tape rental revenue		1,300
Common shares		15,000
Retained earnings		7,150
Dividends	3,000	
Tape rental revenue		43,365
Salaries expense	14,400	
Rent expense	6,600	
Utilities expense	2,800	
Amortization expense—tape library		
Amortization expense—furniture		
Advertising expense	2,660	
Supplies expense		
Total	$84,065	$84,065

Adjustment data:

    a.   Amortization for the year:
          - on the rental tape library, $4,000
          - on the furniture, $1,900
    b.   Accrued salaries expense at December 31, $120.
    c.   Prepaid rent expired, $500.
    d.   Unearned tape rental revenues that remain unearned as of December 31, $625.
    e.   Supplies on hand at December 31, $310
    f.   Accrued advertising expense at December 31, $115. (Credit Accounts Payable)

Required:

1. Prepare T-accounts for those accounts listed on the trial balance that are affected by the adjusting entries. Enter their December 31 unadjusted balances, then prepare and post the adjusting journal entries in the accounts. Key adjustment amounts by letter as shown in the text.
2. Using the form provided, enter the adjusting entries in the Adjustment columns, and prepare an adjusted trial balance, as shown in Exhibit 3-10 of the text. Be sure that each account balance affected by an adjusting entry agrees with the adjusted T-account balances as calculated in Requirement 1.

Requirement 1 (T-accounts; adjusting journal entries; posting to ledger)

a.

Date	Accounts	PR	Debit	Credit
Dec. 31				

b.

Date	Accounts	PR	Debit	Credit
Dec. 31				

c.

Date	Accounts	PR	Debit	Credit
Dec. 31				

d.

Date	Accounts	PR	Debit	Credit
Dec. 31				

e.

Date	Accounts	PR	Debit	Credit
Dec. 31				

f.

Date	Accounts	PR	Debit	Credit
Dec. 31				

Requirement 2 (Adjusted trial balance)

Videos Delivered, Inc.
Preparation of Adjusted Trial Balance
For the Year Ended December 31, 2006

Accounts	Trial Balance		Adjustments		Adjusted Trial Balance	
	Debit	Credit	Debit	Credit	Debit	Credit
Cash	$19,415					
Accounts receivable	90					
Prepaid rent	1,200					
Supplies	400					
Rental tape library	24,000					
Accumulated amortization— tape library		$12,000				
Furniture	9,500					
Accumulated amortization— furniture		3,800				
Accounts payable		1,450				
Salaries payable						
Unearned tape rental revenue		1,300				
Common shares		15,000				
Retained earnings		7,150				
Dividends	3,000					
Tape rental revenue		43,365				
Salaries expense	14,400					
Rent expense	6,600					
Utilities expense	2,800					
Amortization expense—tape library						
Amortization expense— furniture						
Advertising expense	2,660					
Supplies expense						
	$84,065	$84,065				

Demonstration Problem #2

Refer to the adjusted trial balance in Demonstration Problem #1 and complete the following:

1. An income statement
2. A statement of retained earnings
3. A balance sheet
4. The necessary closing entries

Income Statement

Statement of Retained Earnings

Balance Sheet

Closing Entries

Date	Accounts	PR	Debit	Credit

SOLUTIONS

A. TEST YOURSELF

I. Matching

1.

1. C	6. E	11. M	16. X	21. S
2. G	7. F	12. J	17. P	22. Q
3. A	8. N	13. L	18. R	23. T
4. B	9. O	14. H	19. U	24. W
5. D	10. K	15. I	20. V	

2. Matching

1. C	2. B	3. F	4. D
5. H	6. G	7. E	8. A

II. Multiple Choice

1. B In cash-basis accounting, the accountant does not record a transaction until cash is received or paid. In accrual-basis accounting, the accountant records a transaction when it occurs. Income tax accounting is appropriate for the preparation of income tax returns, and actual-basis accounting has no meaning.

2. C Recording revenue when the merchandise is sold is the only event listed that does not involve the receipt or payment of cash. Accordingly, it would not be recorded using cash-basis accounting and is the only item that would be recorded under accrual-basis accounting.

3. D Adjusting entries assign revenues to the period in which they are earned and expenses to the period in which they are incurred. The categories of adjusting entries are 1) deferrals, 2) amortization, and 3) accruals.

4. C Prepaid insurance is an asset account with a normal debit balance. The other items listed have normal credit balances.

5. A Since net income is required to prepare the statement of retained earnings, the income statement should be prepared first.

6. D The correct sequence is
1) net income from the income statement goes to the statement of retained earnings
2) retained earnings from the statement of retained earnings goes to the balance sheet

7.   B   One month of insurance will expire during January. Therefore, 1/12 × $3,000 (or $250) will
           be expensed by the following journal entry:
               Insurance Expense   250
                   Prepaid Insurance   250

8.   B   The entry that should be made is:
               Supplies Expense   1,800
                   Supplies   1,800
           Failure to credit the Supplies account for $1,800 means that assets will be overstated by
           $1,800.

9.   B   With accrual accounting, total revenues in June will be $15,000 of revenues received in cash
           plus $7,500 of revenues that have been billed but not received.

10.   B   This problem requires you to work backwards to find the solution.
               Adjusted balance (given) $1,500
               Adjustment (given)   900
               Unadjusted balance $2,400
           The unadjusted trial balance amount of $2,400 consists of the beginning balance and
           purchases made during the year. Since the purchases were $2,250 (given), the beginning
           balance must have been $150.

           > **Study Tip**: Once again, remember this important formula:
           >   Beginning balance + Additions - Reductions = Ending balance

11.   A   Supplies will be used within one year and is a current asset.

12.   D   Revenue, expenses, and Dividends are temporary accounts. They are closed at the end of each
           accounting period. Retained Earnings is a permanent account.

13.   B   Closing has the effect of transferring all revenues to the credit side of Retained Earnings and
           all expenses to the debit side. If revenues are larger than expenses, the difference reflects net
           income. If expenses are greater than revenue, the difference reflects a net loss.

14.   A   The entry to close dividends is
               Retained Earnings $14,000
                   Dividends $14,000

15.   D   Current assets are assets that are expected to be converted to cash, sold, or consumed during
           the next 12 months or within the business's normal operating cycle if longer than a year.
           Vehicles would not fit this description, while the other accounts listed would.

16.   B   The current ratio is current assets ÷ current liabilities.

III. Completion

1.   Accrual
2.   prepaid expenses, amortization, accrued expenses, unearned revenue, accrued revenues (order not important)
3.   adjusting the accounts
4.   contra asset

Study Tip: A contra account has two distinguishing characteristics: (1) it always has a companion account, and (2) its normal balance is opposite that of the companion account. Accumulated Amortization's companion account is a long-term asset account, such as Building or Equipment.

5. when to record revenue, the amount of revenue to record
6. to identify expenses which have been incurred, to measure the expenses, to match the expenses with revenues earned during the same time period
7. income statement, statement of retained earnings, balance sheet (order is important)
8. one year, interim statements
9. temporary (revenue, expenses, and Dividends are temporary accounts. They are closed at the end of each accounting period)
10. permanent (permanent accounts, i.e., assets, liabilities, and shareholders' equity, are not used to measure income for a period and are not closed at the end of the period)
11. Retained Earnings (The entry to close dividends is always:

    Retained Earnings   XX

        Dividends   XX)

12. Liquidity (balance sheets list assets and liabilities in the order of their relative liquidity)
13. prepaid expenses and unearned revenues
14. total liabilities, total assets
15. current ratio (current assets ÷ current liabilities)

IV. True/False

1. F   The time-period concept ensures that accounting information is reported at regular intervals.
2. T
3. T
4. F   When adjusting for supplies (a prepaid expense), an expense account and an asset account are affected.
5. F   Book value is the difference between cost and accumulated amortization.
6   T
7. T
8. T
9. F   The balance in retained earnings on the adjusted trial balance will not be the same as the amount reported on the balance sheet because the ending retained earnings balance carried forward from the retained earnings statement has been updated to include net income (or loss) and dividends.
10. T
11. T
12. F   The Dividends account is closed to Retained Earnings.
13. F   The Retained Earnings account is a permanent account, not a temporary account; therefore, it is not closed at the end of the accounting period.
14. T
15. F   After closing, the temporary accounts have zero balances. The real (permanent) accounts are not closed at the end of the accounting period.

IV. Exercises

1.

Accounts Receivable	
Bal. 1,800	
(c) 1,505	
Bal. 3,305	

Supplies	
Bal. 610	
	(a) 250
Bal. 360	

Salary Payable	
	(b) 470
	Bal. 470

Unearned Revenue	
	Bal. 900
(d) 245	
	Bal. 655

Service Revenue	
	Bal. 5,100
	(c) 1,505
	(d) 245
	Bal. 6,850

Salary Expense	
Bal. 1,225	
(b) 470	
Bal. 1,695	

Supplies Expense	
(a) 350	
Bal. 350	

Amortization Expense	
(e) 750	
Bal. 750	

Accumulated Amortization	
	Bal. 1,100
	(e) 750
	Bal. 1,850

2. Remember that Beginning balance + Additions - Reductions = Ending balance

For Supplies:

Beginning balance	+	Supplies purchased for cash	-	Supplies expense	=	Ending balance
$2,700	+	$6,200	-	?	=	$1,075

Supplies expense = $7,825

For Insurance:

Beginning balance	+	Insurance Paid	-	Insurance expense	=	Ending balance
$3,400	+	$4,800	-	?	=	$800

Insurance expense = $7,400

For Taxes payable:

Beginning balance	+	Tax expense	-	Cash paid for taxes	=	Ending balance
$2,100	+	?	-	$2,400	=	$200

Tax expense = $500

For Unearned revenue:

Beginning balance	+	Receipts from customers	-	Revenue earned	=	Ending balance
$4,150	+	$91,000	-	?	=	$4,100

Revenue = $91,050

3.

Date	Accounts and Explanation	PR	Debit	Credit
A.	Rent Expense		24,000	
	Prepaid Rent			24,000
	($15,000 + 6 months at $1,500 per month)			
B.	Unearned Subscriptions		4,950	
	Subscriptions Revenue			4,950
	($11,700 / 52 = $225; $225 × 22 = $4,950)			
C.	Interest Receivable		270	
	Interest Earned			270
	($18,000 × 0.09 × 2 / 12)			
D.	Wages and Salaries Expense		3,150	
	Wages and Salaries Payable			3,150

4.

Requirement 1

Date	Accounts and Explanation	PR	Debit	Credit
A.	Supplies Expense		2,700	
	Supplies			2,700
	If ending supplies are $1,500, then $2,700 of supplies were used.			
B.	Advertising Expense		2,200	
	Prepaid Advertising			2,200
	To record expired advertising.			

Requirement 2

Date	Accounts and Explanation	PR	Debit	Credit
Dec. 31	Fees Earned		18,000	
	Retained Earnings			18,000
Dec. 31	Retained Earnings		16,200	
	Salaries Expense			6,600
	Rent Expense			3,000
	Utilities Expense			1,700
	Supplies Expense			2,700
	Advertising Expense			2,200
	Supplies Expense and Advertising Expense from Requirement 1 must be included.			
Dec. 31	Retained Earnings		900	
	Dividends			900

Requirement 3

Beginning Retained Earnings	$2,200
Plus: Net Income	1,800
	4,000
Less: Dividends	900
Ending Retained Earnings	$3,100

VI. Critical Thinking

1. The answer is 0. Why? Because cash-basis accounting does not record revenue when a client is billed, only when the business receives payment. Therefore, while the business may send bills to clients, they are not recorded.

2. A company that does not perform the closing process would have revenue, expense, and dividend account balances not closed to retained earnings, which would then cause the balance sheet to be out of balance. We accumulate revenues and expenses separately to aid in the preparation of the income statement, but then are required to close these accounts to retained earnings to determine the total earnings retained in the business since its inception, less the amount redistributed to shareholders or owners. It would also be difficult to prepare the following year's income statement if the books are not closed at the year end.

DEMONSTRATION PROBLEMS

Demonstration Problem #1 Solved and Explained

Requirement 1 (T-accounts; adjusting entries; posting to ledger)

a.

Amortization Expense—Tape Library

(a) 4,000	
Bal. 4,000	

Accumulated Amortization—Tape Library

	Bal. 12,000
	(a) 4,000
	Bal. 16,000

Amortization Expense—Furniture

(a) 1,900	
Bal. 1,900	

Accumulated Amortization—Furniture

	Bal. 3,800
	(a) 1,900
	Bal. 5,700

Date	Accounts	PR	Debit	Credit
Dec. 31	Amortization Expense—Tape Library		4,000	
	Accumulated Amortization—Tape Library			4,000
	To record amortization expense on tape library			

Amortization Expense—Furniture	1,900	
Accumulated Amortization—Furniture		1,900
To record amortization expense on furniture		

Explanation of Adjustment (a)

As a capital asset (such as a building, furniture, machinery, or equipment) becomes less useful, its cost is gradually transferred from the asset account to an amortization expense account. The recording of amortization expense for Videos Delivered, Inc. requires a debit of $5,900 ($4,000 on the rental tape library and $1,900 on furniture) to Amortization Expense (expenses are increased with debits) and credits to the contra accounts of $4,000 to Accumulated Amortization—Tape Library and $1,900 to Accumulated Amortization—Furniture (assets are decreased with credits). Note that the original cost of the asset remains unchanged on the books of Videos Delivered, Inc. The reduction in book value of each asset is accomplished by increasing the asset's accumulated amortization account.

Example: Change in book value of furniture.

Capital Assets	Before Adjustment	Change	After Adjustment
Furniture	$9,500	0	$9,500
Less accumulated amortization	3,800	+1,900	5,700
Book value	$5,700	-$1,900	$3,800

b.

Salaries Expense		Salaries Payable	
Bal. 14,400			(b) 120
(b) 120			
Bal. 14,520			Bal. 120

Date	Accounts	PR	Debit	Credit
Dec. 31	Salaries Expense		120	
	Salaries Payable			120
	To accrue salaries expense			

Explanation of Adjustment (b)

Amounts owed to employees for salaries and wages unpaid as of the close of an accounting period must be accrued. The facts indicate that $120 must be accrued to record salaries expense and the related liability. As a result, Salaries Expense is debited $120 (expenses are increased by debits), and Salaries Payable is credited $120 (liabilities are increased by credits).

c.

Rent Expense		Prepaid Rent	
Bal. 6,600		Bal. 1,200	(c) 600
(c) 600			
Bal. 7,200		Bal. 600	

Date	Accounts	PR	Debit	Credit
Dec. 31	Rent Expense		600	
	Prepaid Rent			600
	To record rent expense			

Explanation of Adjustment (c)

Videos Delivered, Inc. paid two months' rent in advance early in December. This prepayment created an asset (Prepaid Rent) for Videos Delivered, Inc. in the form of a purchased future right to use the rental space. At the end of the year, the prepaid asset account must be adjusted for the amount of the prepayment that has expired. During December, one month's worth of the prepayment was used up. As a result, one month's prepaid rent of $600 is transferred to expense by crediting (assets are reduced by credits) the Prepaid Rent account and debiting (expenses are recorded as debits) the Rent Expense account. Note that one month's rent remains in the Prepaid Rent account.

d.

Tape Rental Revenue			Unearned Revenue	
	Bal. 43,365			Bal. 1,300
	(d) 675	(d) 675		
	Bal. 44,040			Bal. 625

Date	Accounts	PR	Debit	Credit
Dec. 31	Unearned Rent Revenue		675	
	Tape Rental Revenue			675
	To record revenue collected in advance.			

Explanation of Adjustment (d)

When cash is collected from customers before the agreed-upon product or service is provided, a liability is created. If $625 of the $1,300 of unearned rental revenue remains unearned, then $675 has become earned revenue. The liability account Unearned Rental Revenue should be debited (a liability is reduced by a debit) and Tape Rental Revenue should be credited (a revenue is increased by a credit).

e.

Supplies Expense			Supplies		
(e)	90		Bal.	400	(e) 90
Bal.	90		Bal.	310	

Date	Accounts	PR	Debit	Credit
Dec. 31	Supplies Expense		90	
	Supplies			90
	To record supplies expense.			

Explanation of Adjustment (e)

Supplies purchased for business use represent an asset until they are used. The Supplies account must be adjusted periodically to reflect supplies no longer on hand. Supplies of $310 remain on hand at December 31. Since $400 of supplies were on hand initially, it is clear that $90 of supplies have been used up ($400 - $310 = $90). Reduce the Supplies account by crediting it $170 (assets are decreased by credits) and record the $90 supplies expense by debiting Supplies Expense (expenses are recorded by debits).

f.

Advertising Expense				Accounts Payable		
Bal.	2,660				Bal.	1,450
(f)	115				(f)	115
Bal.	2,775				Bal.	1,565

Date	Accounts	PR	Debit	Credit
Dec. 31	Advertising Expense		115	
	Accounts Payable			115
	To record accrued advertising expense.			

Explanation of Adjustment (f)

The rationale for this entry is similar to that for the adjusting entry that accrued salary expense. Advertising Expense is increased by debiting the account (expenses are recorded by debits) and Accounts Payable is credited (liabilities are recorded by credits) to reflect the debt owed by Videos Delivered, Inc.

Requirement 2 (Adjusted trial balance)

Videos Delivered, Inc.
Preparation of Adjusted Trial Balance
For the Year Ended December 31, 2006

Accounts	Trial Balance		Adjustments		Adjusted Trial Balance	
	Debit	Credit	Debit	Credit	Debit	Credit
Cash	$19,415				$19,415	
Accounts receivable	90				90	
Prepaid rent	1,200			(c) 600	600	
Supplies	400			(e) 90	310	
Rental tape library	24,000				24,000	
Accumulated amortization— tape library		$12,000		(a) 4,000		$16,000
Furniture	9,500				9,500	
Accumulated amortization— furniture		3,800		(a) 1,900		5,700
Accounts payable		1,450		(f) 115		1,565
Salaries payable				(b) 120		120

Unearned tape rental revenue		1,300	(d) 675			625
Common shares		15,000				15,000
Retained earnings		7,150				7,150
Dividends	3,000				3,000	
Tape rental revenue		43,365		(d) 675		44,040
Salaries expense	14,400		(b) 120		14,520	
Rent expense	6,600		(c) 600		7,200	
Utilities expense	2,800				2,800	
Amortization expense—tape library			(a) 4,000		4,000	
Amortization expense—furniture			(a) 1,900		1,900	
Advertising expense	2,660		(f) 115		2,775	
Supplies expense			(e) 90		90	
	$84,065	$84,065	$7,500	$7,500	$90,200	$90,200

Demonstration Problem #2 Solved

Requirement 1

Videos Delivered, Inc.
Income Statement
For the Year Ended December 31, 2006

Revenues:
    Tape rental revenue $44,040
Expenses:
    Salaries expense $14,520
    Rent expense   7,200
    Utilities expense   2,800
    Amortization expense   5,900
    Advertising expense   2,775
    Supplies expense   90
Total expenses   33,285
Net income $ 10,755

Requirement 2

Videos Delivered, Inc.
Statement of Retained Earnings
For the Year Ended December 31, 2006

Retained earnings January 1, 2004 $ 7,150
   Add: Net Income   10,755
     17,905
   Less: Dividends   3,000
Retained earnings December 31, 2004 $14,905

Requirement 3

Videos Delivered, Inc.
Balance Sheet
December 31, 2006

ASSETS			LIABILITIES		
Cash		$19,415	Accounts payable		$ 1,565
Accounts receivable		90	Salaries payable		120
Prepaid rent		600	Unearned tape rental revenue		625
Supplies		310	Total liabilities		2,310
Tape rental library	24,000				
Less: Acc. amort.—library	16,000	8,000	**SHAREHOLDERS' EQUITY**		
Furniture	9,500		Common shares	15,000	
Less: Acc. amort.—furniture	5,700	3,800	Retained earnings	14,905	
			Total shareholders' equity		29,905
			Total liabilities and		
Total assets		$32,215	shareholders' equity		$32,215

Requirement 4

Date	Accounts	PR	Debit	Credit
Dec. 31	Tape Rental Revenue		44,040	
	Retained Earnings			44,040
Dec. 31	Retained Earnings		33,285	
	Salaries Expense			14,520
	Rent Expense			7,200
	Utilities Expense			2,800
	Amortization Expense—Tape Library			4,000
	Amortization Expense—Furniture			1,900
	Advertising Expense			2,775
	Supplies Expense			90
Dec. 31	Retained Earnings		3,000	
	Dividends			3,000

CHAPTER 4—INTERNAL CONTROL AND CASH

CHAPTER OVERVIEW

This chapter introduces you to internal control and the processes that a business follows to control the organization's assets. As cash is the most liquid asset, this chapter applies internal control concepts to cash. However, internal control applies to all assets—topics covered in upcoming chapters. The specific learning objectives for this chapter are to

1. **Set up** an effective system of internal control
2. **Use** a bank reconciliation as a control device
3. **Apply** internal controls to cash receipts and cash payments
4. **Use** a budget to manage cash
5. **Weigh** ethical judgments in business

CHAPTER REVIEW

Internal control is the organizational plan and all related measures designed to 1) optimize the use of resources, 2) prevent and detect error and fraud, 3) safeguard assets and records, and 4) ensure accurate and reliable accounting records.

The *Sarbanes-Oxley Act* (SOX) was passed by congress in the United States as a result of the accounting scandals involving such companies as Enron and WorldCom. The Act was designed to revamp corporate governance and has been considered by many accounting bodies around the world, including Canada. Measures introduced include requiring CEO's and CFO's to certify the financial statements and evaluate the effectiveness of the internal controls.

Objective 1 – Set up an effective system of internal control

An effective system of internal control has the following characteristics:

1. **Competent, reliable, and ethical personnel**. Paying competitive salaries, training people thoroughly, and providing adequate supervision help to promote competence.
2. **Assignment of responsibilities**. All duties to be performed must be identified, and responsibility for the performance of those duties must be assigned to appropriate people.
3. **Proper authorization**. An organization generally has a written set of rules that outline approved procedures. Proper authorization must be obtained for deviations from standard policies.
4. **Supervision of employees**. Even the most trusted employees can be tempted to steal or defraud a company.
5. **Separation of duties**. Separation of duties is designed to limit the possibility of fraud or theft in the handling of assets. The company must have
   a) separation of operations from accounting
   b) separation of the custody of assets from accounting
6. **External and internal audits.** An examination of both the system of internal control and the financial statements by both the internal and external auditors; the goal is to provide assurance to users.

Auditors evaluate the system of internal control to estimate the reliability of the accounting system. Auditors also help to spot areas where improvements in internal control can be made. **Internal auditors** are employees of the company. **External auditors** are employed by public accounting firms and are hired by a business to audit its books.

Business documents and records are designed according to each company's needs. Source documents and records include sales invoices, purchase orders, and special journals. Good internal control requires documents to be pre-numbered. A gap in the numbered sequence will call attention to a missing document.

Additional controls include electronic sensors (for inventory), fireproof vaults (for cash), point-of-sale terminals (also for cash), and fidelity bonds (for employee theft).

As more and more companies use **e-commerce** to transact some of their business, additional internal control issues arise to ensure that access to assets is restricted to only those with the proper authority. To prevent **e.fr@ud**, information technology experts have added several layers of protection to secure hardware, software, and data, called the onion model (see Exhibit 4-4). Examples of these additional layers are **encryption**, **firewalls**, **intrusion detection devices**, **incident response procedures**, and audits by external specialists. Encryption transforms data into a form that makes it unreadable by anyone not possessing authorized access to it (see Exhibit 4-5 in your text). Firewalls attempt to limit access by unauthorized persons (see Exhibit 4-6 in your text). However, unauthorized individuals may still succeed in getting through, or around, the firewall. Intrusion detection devices are designed to identify when this occurs, while incident response procedures are designed to identify hackers and take them out of the system. Audits by external specialists are frequently used to validate a system's security and integrity.

The **limitations** of an internal control system are determined by the opportunities available for collusion and the resources that management devotes to the system. Collusion between two or more people working together to defraud the firm may go undetected by the system of internal control. Internal control must be designed and judged in light of the costs and the benefits.

Using a **bank account** promotes internal control over cash. For accounting purposes, cash includes currency, coins, cheques, money orders, and bank accounts. Banks safeguard cash and provide detailed records of transactions. Cash is the most common means of exchange, and it is also the most tempting asset for theft.

Documents used to control bank accounts include cheques and bank statements. Banks usually send monthly statements to depositors. The bank statement shows the beginning balance in the account, all transactions recorded during the month, and the ending balance. The bank also returns canceled cheques with the statement.

Electronic Funds Transfer (EFT) is a system that relies on electronic impulses to account for cash transactions. EFT systems reduce the cost of processing cash transactions by reducing the documentary evidence of transactions. This lack of documentation poses a challenge to managers and auditors to enforce the internal control system.

Objective 2 - Use a bank reconciliation as a control device

Bank reconciliations are necessary because there are usually differences between the time that transactions are recorded on a business's books and the time that those transactions are recorded by the bank. For example, if you mail a cheque to a supplier on the last day of the month, you will record it on that day. However, the cheque will not clear your bank until the supplier has received it and deposited it in its bank several days later.

The general format for a bank reconciliation is:

BANK		**BOOKS**	
	Balance, last day of month		Balance, last day of month (trial balance of general ledger)
+	Deposits in transit		
-	Outstanding cheques	+	Bank collections
±	Correction of bank errors	+	Interest paid on deposits
		-	Service charges
		±	Correction of book errors
	Adjusted bank balance =		Adjusted book balance

Adjustments to the bank balance never require preparation of journal entries. Adjustments to the bank balance include the following items:

1. Deposits in transit have been recorded by the company, but not by the bank. There is often a time lag of a day or two until the deposit is sent to the bank and posted by the bank.
2. Outstanding cheques are cheques issued by the company and recorded on its books but which have not yet been paid by the bank. There is a time lag of several days until the cheques are cashed or deposited by the payee and sent to the business's bank to be paid.
3. Corrections of bank errors are the responsibility of the bank. The bank should be notified and the corrections should appear on the next statement.

Adjustments to the books always require preparation of journal entries. Adjustments to the book balance include the following items:

1. The bank collects money on behalf of depositors (either cash, cheque, or electronic funds transfer). Examples are a lock-box system where customers pay directly to the bank accounts. A bank may also collect on a note receivable for the depositor. The bank will notify the depositor of these collections on the bank statement. The journal entry for the collection of a note receivable and the related interest is

Cash	XXX	
Note Receivable		XXX
Interest Revenue (if applicable)		XXX

2. Interest revenue is sometimes paid on the chequing account. The journal entry to record the interest is

Cash	XX	
Interest Revenue		XX

3. Service charges are the bank's fees for processing transactions. The journal entry for a service charge is

Miscellaneous Expense	X	
Cash		X

4. Nonsufficient funds (NSF) cheques are customer cheques that have been returned by the customer's bank because the customer's account did not contain sufficient funds to cover the amount of the cheque. Cheques may also be returned if the maker's account has closed, the date is stale, the signature is not authorized, the cheque has been altered, or the cheque form is improper. The amount of returned cheques is subtracted from the book balance and the following journal entry is made:

Accounts Receivable	XX	
Cash		XX

5. The cost of printing cheques is handled like a service charge. The journal entry is

Miscellaneous Expense	XX	
Cash		XX

6. Errors on the books must be handled on a case by case basis. If cheques are recorded on the books for the wrong amount, then an entry must be prepared to correct the original entry.

Study Exhibits 4-9 and 4-10 carefully. Be sure you understand the components of a bank reconciliation and the journal entries needed to correct the Cash account balance.

Objective 3 - Apply internal controls to cash receipts and cash payments

The objective of internal control over cash receipts is to ensure that all cash is deposited in the bank and recorded correctly in the company's accounting records.

A point-of-sale terminal is a good device for management control over cash received in a store. Positioning the machine so that customers see the amounts rung up discourages cashiers from overcharging customers and pocketing the excess over actual prices. Issuing receipts requires cashiers to record the sale. Comparing actual receipts to control tapes maintained by the terminal discourages theft.

For payments received from customers by mail, separation of duties among different people promotes good internal control. The mailroom clerk should open all mail and record incoming payments. The mailroom should deliver cheques to the cashier for deposit and send remittance advices to the accounting department for posting. Comparison of mailroom totals, cashier totals, and accounting totals should be made daily.

Some companies use a lock-box system as another means of internal control. Customers mail payments to an address, which is actually the company's bank. This also increases efficiency because the funds can be put to use immediately.

Payment by cheque is a good control over cash payments. However, before a cheque can be issued, additional control procedures have occurred. For instance, companies require approved purchase orders before goods or services can be acquired, receiving reports verifying that goods received conform to the purchase order, an invoice that agrees with both the purchase order and receiving report, and, finally, an authorized cheque in payment of the invoice. Additionally, many companies require two signatures before a cheque can be sent. (Helpful hint: review Exhibits 4-12 to 4-16 in your text.)

Businesses keep a **petty cash** account to have cash on hand for minor expenses that do not warrant preparing a cheque. Such expenses include taxi fares, local delivery costs, and small amounts of office supplies.

Suppose a petty cash fund of $200 is established. The cash is placed under the control of a custodian and the following entry is made:

Petty Cash	200	
Cash		200

This type of entry is also used to increase the amount in the fund, say from $200 to $300:

Petty Cash	100	
Cash		100

> **Study Tip**: Note that once the fund is established, no entry is made to the Petty Cash account except to change the total amount in the fund.

Petty cash is disbursed using petty cash tickets, which document the disbursements. Cash on hand plus the total of the petty cash tickets should always equal the fund balance. This is referred to as an **imprest fund**.

A petty cash fund must be periodically replenished, particularly on the balance sheet date. A cheque is drawn for the amount of the replenishment. An entry is made as follows:

Various accounts listed on petty cash tickets	XX	
Cash		XX

Note that the expenses on the petty cash tickets are recorded in the general journal when the fund is replenished.

Objective 4 - Use a budget to manage cash

A **budget** is a quantitative expression of a plan that helps managers coordinate the organization. Cash budgeting, therefore, is a way to manage cash. This is accomplished by developing a plan for future cash receipts and disbursements. The cash budget starts with the amount of cash on hand at the beginning of the period. To this is added the budgeted cash receipts. Sources of cash receipts will include revenue transactions, the sale of assets, and proceeds from borrowing money and/or selling shares. Budgeted cash disbursements will include expenditures for operating activities, acquisition of assets, dividends, and payments of debt. Once these budgeted receipts and disbursements have been determined, they can be compared with the expected receipts and disbursements. If the results of the expected cash activity exceed the budgeted activity, the managers will have the opportunity to invest the excess and generate additional revenue (the interest earned on the invested cash). If the budgeted activity exceeds the expected cash activity, the company will need to arrange financing to maintain the desired amount of cash. Exhibit 4-17 illustrates a typical format for a cash budget.

When reported on the balance sheet, most companies list "Cash and cash equivalents"—this includes cash and other items similar enough to be included with cash (such as petty cash, short-term time deposits, and certificates of deposit).

Objective 5 - Weigh ethical judgments in business

Most businesses have codes of ethics to which their employees are expected to conform. Most professional accountants are members of the Canadian Institute of Chartered Accountants, the Certified General Accountants Association of Canada, or the Society of Management Accountants of Canada. They are bound by the rules of professional conduct of their respective organization. In many situations, the ethical course of action is clear. However, when this is not the case, the following questions and guidelines may prove helpful:

Questions	Decision Guidelines
1. What are the ethical issues, if any?	Identify the ethical issues.
2. What are the options?	Specify the alternatives.
3. Who is involved in the situation?	Identify the people involved.
4. What are the possible consequences?	Assess the possible outcomes.
5. What shall I do?	Make the decisions.

TEST YOURSELF

All the self-testing materials in this chapter focus on information and procedures that your instructor is likely to test in quizzes and examinations.

I. Matching *Match each numbered term with its lettered definition.*

_____ 1. external auditors
_____ 2. lock-box system
_____ 3. bank statement
_____ 4. encryption
_____ 5. Electronic Funds Transfer
_____ 6. nonsufficient funds cheque
_____ 7. outstanding cheque
_____ 8. service charge
_____ 9. firewall

_____ 10. imprest system
_____ 11. bank reconciliation
_____ 12. cheque
_____ 13. deposit in transit
_____ 14. incident response procedure
_____ 15. internal control
_____ 16. petty cash
_____ 17. budget

A. a deposit recorded by the company but not by its bank
B. a cheque for which the payer's bank account has insufficient money to pay the cheque
C. a cheque issued by a company and recorded on its books but not yet paid by its bank
D. the quantitative expression of a plan that helps managers coordinate the organization
E. a document for a particular bank account that shows its beginning and ending balances and lists the month's transactions that affect the account
F. a document that instructs the bank to pay a designated person or business a specified amount of money
G. a fund containing a small amount of cash that is used to pay minor expenditures
H. transforming data to make it unreadable
I. means to limit access to electronic data
J. a system that accounts for cash transactions by electronic impulses rather than paper documents
K. identifying hackers and taking them out of the system
L. a bank's fee for processing transactions
M. a method of accounting for petty cash
N. employed by public accounting firms; hired to audit a client's books
O. a method of internal control over cash receipts where customers send payments directly to the company's bank
P. process of explaining the reasons for the difference between a depositor's records and the bank's records of the depositor's bank account
Q. the organizational plan and all related measures adopted by an entity to safeguard assets, ensure accurate and reliable accounting records, promote operational efficiency, and encourage adherence to company policies

II. Multiple Choice *Circle the best answer.*

1. Jana Fox handles cash receipts and has the authority to write off accounts receivable. This violates separation of

   A. custody of assets from accounting
   B. operations from accounting
   C. duties within the accounting function
   D. authorization of transactions from custody of related assets

2. Max Dillon records both cash receipts and cash payments. This violates separation of

   A. custody of assets from accounting
   B. operations from accounting
   C. duties within the accounting function
   D. authorization of transactions from custody of related assets

3. Which of the following items does not require a journal entry?

   A. interest paid on a chequing account
   B. deposits in transit
   C. collection by the bank of a note receivable
   D. bank service charge

4. The journal entry to record an NSF cheque returned by the bank is

   A. debit Cash, credit Accounts Receivable
   B. debit Accounts Payable, credit Cash
   C. debit Accounts Receivable, credit Cash
   D. debit Miscellaneous Expense, credit Cash

5. Which of the following is not an internal control procedure for cash receipts?

   A. comparing actual cash to cash register tape totals
   B. point-of-sale terminals
   C. paying bills by cheque
   D. enabling customers to see amounts entered on cash receipts

6. If you discover a bank error while completing a reconciliation, you

   A. debit Cash if the error is in your favour
   B. credit Cash if the error is in the bank's favour
   C. debit (or credit) Bank Expense for the amount of the error
   D. none of the above

7. Which of the following documents is prepared first?

   A. purchase requisition
   B. receiving report
   C. purchase order
   D. cheque

8. If an outstanding cheque from July is not cashed at the end of August and a company performs monthly bank reconciliations, the accountant should

   A. add an amount to the balance per book
   B. deduct an amount from the balance per book
   C. add an amount to the balance per bank
   D. deduct an amount from the balance per bank

9. If the cash balance at the beginning of the month is $9,200, cash receipts during the month are $41,250, and the ending cash balance is $8,325, what were cash payments during the month?

   A. $50,450
   B. $58,775
   C. $42,125
   D. $33,800

10. Which of the following is not an internal control for cash?

    A. fidelity bonds
    B. point-of-sale terminals
    C. electronic sensors
    D. fireproof vault

11. If a bank service charge for $20 shows up on the bank statement, the adjusting entry would include

    A. a debit to cash on company books only, $20
    B. a credit to cash on company books only, $20
    C. a credit to cash on both company and bank books for $20
    D. no entry is necessary, just adjust it on bank reconciliation statement.

12. If a cheque written for $374 for utilities is entered in the books as $734, then the correcting entry would include

    A. a debit to utilities expense for $374 and a credit to cash of $374
    B. a credit to utilities expense for $360 and a debit to cash of $360
    C. a debit to utilities expense for $360 and a credit to cash for $360
    D. no entry is necessary, just a note to the financial statements

13. A good system of internal control should do all of the following *except*

    A. minimize the use of resources
    B. prevent and detect errors and fraud
    C. safeguard assets and records
    D. all of the above are characteristics of a good system of internal controls.

14. Which of the following is not an example of a control procedure?

    A. separation of duties
    B. proper authorization
    C. collusion of employees
    D. all of the above are good examples of control procedures.

15. Which of the following is not a part of the onion model of e-commerce systems security?

    A. encryption
    B. incident response procedure
    C. intrusion detection devices
    D. all are part of an effective onion model

III. Completion *Complete each of the following statements.*

1. _____is a means of making small cash disbursements quickly.

2. _____auditors are regular employees of a business; _____auditors are independent of the business.

3. In a good internal control system, the following functions are separated:

    a)_____

    b)_____

    c)_____

4. _____is the transformation of data by a mathematical process into a form unreadable by anyone without the appropriate secret key.

5. Indicate how each of the following items is treated in a bank reconciliation. Use: AB for additions to the bank balance; AF for additions to the firm's balance; DB for deductions from the bank balance; and DF for deductions from the firm's balance.

    _____ A.   A deposit for $143 was not recorded in the books

    _____ B.   A cheque for $34 was entered in the books as $43

    _____ C.   Bank collection of a note receivable

    _____ D.   Bank service charges

    _____ E.   A deposit was credited by the bank to the firm's account in error

    _____ F.   Deposits in transit

_____ G. Interest earned on a chequing account

_____ H. Outstanding cheques

_____ I. NSF cheques

6. What account is debited for 5F above? _____

7. What will be the amount of the adjustment in 5B above? _____

8. What account(s) is (are) debited when petty cash is replenished? _____

9. _____ insure a company against theft by an employee.

10. Cash, petty cash, short-term time deposits, and certificates of deposits are referred to collectively as _____.

11. _____ was developed to enhance corporate governance resulting from accounting scandals.

12. The purpose of an audit is to _____.

13. A _____ attempts to limit access to electronic data by unauthorized persons.

14. The quantitative expression of a plan that helps managers coordinate the entity's activities is called a _____.

15. A _____ helps a company manage its cash by developing a plan for _____ and _____.

IV. True/False   *For each of the following statements, circle* T *for true or* F *for false.*

1.   T F   NSF cheques are reconciled by deducting them from the balance per book.
2.   T F   The vice president for accounting is the chief accounting officer in a corporation.
3.   T F   Internal auditors are employees of the corporation.
4.   T F   The most liquid asset is cash.
5.   T F   When preparing a bank reconciliation, outstanding cheques are deducted from the balance per book.
6.   T F   The bank reconciliation is one method of internal control.
7.   T F   The responsibility for internal controls rests with internal auditors.
8.   T F   No employee should be exempt from supervision.
9.   T F   Persons who authorize transactions should not handle the related asset.
10. T F   NSF cheques are recorded as accounts payables.
11. T F   Internal audits examine company transactions for agreement with management policies.
12. T F   The purchase order is prepared before a purchase requisition.
13. T F   The Petty Cash account is a revenue account and carries a normal credit balance.
14. T F   Certificates of deposit are classified as cash equivalents.
15. T F   A cash budget and the cash flow statement present the same information, just in different formats.

V. Exercises

1. Henry's bank statement gave an ending balance of $3,578.00. Reconciling items include: deposit in transit, $825.00; service charge, $9.00; outstanding cheques, $449.00; and interest earned on his chequing account, $7.50. What is the adjusted bank balance after the bank reconciliation is prepared?

2. Using the information in Exercise 1 above, what was the unadjusted ending balance in Henry's chequebook?

3. During the month of April, Smallville Industries had the following transactions in its Petty Cash fund:

   April 1   Established petty cash fund, $400
   April 6   Paid postage, $19
   April 8   Paid freight charges on supplies purchased, $43
   April 11   Purchased office supplies, $77
   April 22   Paid miscellaneous expenses, $28
   April 30   Replenished the petty cash fund ($231 in actual cash was in the lock-box)

   Prepare the journal entries required by each of the above transactions.

Date	Accounts and Explanation	PR	Debit	Credit

4. From the following information, present a Cash Budget for the year ended September 30, 2006.

Proceeds from note receivable	$150,000
Purchases for inventory	110,000
Receipts from customers	285,000
Payments for dividends	55,000
Proceeds from sale of equipment	21,500
Payments for interest and taxes	108,000
Cash required for operating expenses	92,250
Debt payments	81,700

The cash balance as of October 1, 2005, is $95,500. The budgeted cash balance for September 30, 2006, is $100,000.

Cash Budget
For the Year Ended September 30, 2006

VI. Critical Thinking

1. At the Fat Lady Sings Opera House, you notice that there is a box office at the entrance where the cashier receives cash from customers and, with a press of a button, a machine ejects serially numbered tickets. To enter the opera house, a customer must present his or her ticket to the door attendant. The attendant tears the ticket in half and returns the stub to the customer. The other half of the ticket is dropped into a locked box.

   A. What internal controls are present in this scenario?

   B. What should management do to make these controls more effective?

   C. How can these controls be rendered ineffective?

2. Explain how the new *Sarbanes-Oxley Act* may improve corporate governance.

DEMONSTRATION PROBLEMS

Demonstration Problem #1

The following petty cash transactions occurred in July:

July 1		Management decided to establish a petty cash fund. A cheque for $200 was written and cashed with the proceeds given to Cheryl Haynes, who was designated custodian of the fund.
	1	The president of the business immediately took $25 for lunch money.
	4	$12.95 was disbursed to reimburse an employee for an air-express package paid for with personal funds.
	6	COD freight charges on supplies were paid, $22.
	9	$29 was spent on postage stamps while the postage metre was being repaired.
	11	The president "borrowed" another $35 from the fund.
	12	COD freight charges on supplies were paid, $31.
	13	Because the fund was running low, Ms. Haynes requested a cheque to replenish it for the disbursements made. As there was $45.05 on hand, Ms. Haynes requested a cheque for $154.95. However, her supervisor authorized a cheque for $354.95 so sufficient funds would be on hand and only require monthly replenishment.
	16	The monthly charge for the office newspaper was paid, $18.
	19	COD charges on supplies were paid, $47.
	20	The president took $55 from the fund.
	22	Ms. Haynes took $12 from the fund to purchase coffee and supplies for the office coffee room.
	25	The president's spouse arrived by taxi. The fare of $19 plus a $3 tip was paid from the petty cash fund.
	26	$35 was paid from the fund to have the front windows washed.
	28	A coworker did not have lunch money. Ms. Haynes gave the coworker $15 from the fund and took a postdated cheque for that amount.
	31	The company decided to replenish the fund on the last working day each month. There was $196.00 left in the fund.

Required:

1. Record the appropriate transactions in the General Journal.
2. Post any entries to the Petty Cash account.

Requirement 1 (General Journal entries)

GENERAL JOURNAL

Date	Accounts and Explanation	PR	Debit	Credit

Requirement 2 (Post entries to Petty Cash Fund)

Petty Cash Fund

Demonstration Problem #2

The cash account for Gary's Gardening shows the following information on August 31, 2006:

Cash

Balance	$9,682	Aug. 2	$ 232
Aug. 3	242	Aug. 5	2,114
Aug. 7	1,701	Aug. 9	745
Aug. 12	408	Aug. 14	756
Aug. 14	900	Aug. 15	905
Aug. 24	2,715	Aug. 18	305
Aug. 31	382	Aug. 22	781
		Aug. 29	828
Balance	$9,364		

Gary's Gardening received the following bank statement on August 31, 2006.

Bank Statement for Gary's Gardening

Beginning balance			$9,682
Deposits and other credits:			
Aug. 4		242	
8		1,701	
11		2,630	BC
13		408	
15		900	
25		2,715	
31		16	INT
			8,612
Cheques and other debits:			
Aug. 3		$725	
7		223	
11		2,114	
12		745	
15		756	
20		175	NSF
24		905	
30		781	
31		29	SC
			6,453
Ending balance:			$11,841

Legend:
BC = Bank Collection   NSF = Nonsufficient Funds Cheque
SC = Service Charge   INT = Interest Earned

Additional data for the bank reconciliation is as follows:

1. The $2,630 bank collection on Aug. 11 includes $130 interest revenue. The balance was attributable to the collection of a note receivable.
2. The correct amount of the Aug. 2 transaction is $223, a payment on account. The bookkeeper mistakenly recorded the cheque as $232.
3. The NSF cheque was received from Ray's Pet Store.
4. The bank statement includes a $725 deduction for a cheque drawn by Larry's Gardening (Gary's biggest competitor). The bank has been notified of its error by Gary.
5. The service charge consists of two charges: $4 for the monthly account charge and $25 for the NSF cheque.
6. A deposit was made on Aug. 31 after the bank was closed.

Required:

1. Prepare the bank reconciliation of Gary's Gardening on August 31, 2006. Use the form provided.
2. Record the entries based on the bank reconciliation. Include explanations. Use the form provided.

Requirement 1 (Bank reconciliation)

Gary's Gardening
Bank Reconciliation
August 31, 2006

Requirement 2 (Entries based on bank reconciliation)

Date	Accounts and Explanation	PR	Debit	Credit

SOLUTIONS

A. TEST YOURSELF

I. Matching

1. N	5. J	9. I	13. A	17. D
2. O	6. B	10. M	14. K	
3. E	7. C	11. P	15. Q	
4. H	8. L	12. F	16. G	

II. Multiple Choice

1.   D   Handling cash receipts and having authority to write off accounts receivable puts the person in a position to illegitimately write off an account on which payment has been received. This is a violation of separation of the authorization of transactions from custody of related assets.

2.   C   Independent performance of various phases of accounting helps to minimize errors and the opportunities for fraud.

3.   B   Deposits in transit are cash receipts that have been recorded in the journal of the business but have not yet been recorded by the bank. The other items listed are items that will be reflected in the bank's records but have not yet been recorded on the books of the business.

4.   C   An NSF cheque represents a previously recorded cash receipt that has no substance and, accordingly, must be reversed; reduce Cash (credit) and re-establish the receivable (debit).

5.   C   Paying bills by cheque is an internal control procedure for cash payments, not cash receipts. The other items listed are internal control procedures for cash receipts.

6.   D   Bank errors are not recorded in the company's records. They are reported to the bank.

7.   A   The purchasing process starts when the sales department identifies the need for merchandise and prepares a purchase requisition. The purchase order, receiving report, and cheque follow in that order.

8.   D   This amount needs to be deducted from the balance per bank as the company has already deducted it from cash when the cheque was written.

9.   C   The formula is Beginning balance + Receipts – Payments = Ending balance.

10.   C   Electronic sensors attempt to control inventory, not cash.

11.   B   The adjusting entry includes a credit to cash of $20 on the company's books.

12.   C   The adjusting entry would be for $360 = $734 - $374 reversing entry.
Debit cash $360 and credit utilities expense $360

13. A   The internal control system should optimize the use of resources, which may not be to minimize the resources. In some cases, you would want to maximize the use of resources.

14. C   Collusion is a method used to get around effective controls by employees trying to defraud a company.

15. D. All of the above are parts of the onion model.

III. Completion

1. Petty Cash fund
2. Internal; external (Internal auditors report directly to the company's president or audit committee of the board of directors. External auditors audit the entity as a whole and usually report to the shareholders.)
3. custody of assets from accounting, authorization of transactions from custody of related assets, operations from accounting
4. Encryption
5. A) AF   B) AF   C) AF   D) DF   E) DB   F) AB   G) AF   H) DB   I) DF
6. None—the business has already recorded them.
7. $9, the difference between $34 and $43
8. Various expense accounts (Note that the Petty Cash account is debited or credited only when the amount of the fund is changed.)
9. Fidelity bonds
10. Cash and cash equivalents
11. *Sarbanes-Oxley Act* (SOX)
12. examine financial statements, accounting systems, and controls
13. firewall
14. budget
15. cash budget; cash receipts; cash payments

IV. True/False

1.   T
2.   F   The controller is the chief accounting officer in the corporation.
3.   T
4.   T
5.   F   Outstanding cheques have already been deducted from the books. When preparing the bank reconciliation they are deducted from the balance per bank.
6.   T
7.   F   The responsibility rests with top management.
8.   T
9.   T
10. F   NSF cheques are recorded as an accounts receivable.
11. T
12. F   The requisition is prepared before the order.
13. F   Petty Cash is an asset account and carries a debit balance.
14. T
15. F   A cash budget looks to the future whereas the cash flow statement reflects the past.

V. Exercises

1.

Balance per bank statement		$3,578
Add:		
	Deposit in transit	825
		$4,403
Deduct:		
	Outstanding cheques	449
	Adjusted bank balance	$3,954

Note: the bank has already adjusted the service charge and interest in the bank balance shown.

2. This requires you to work backwards. Start by setting up what is known and then solve for the unknown balance. Remember that the adjusted balance in the chequebook will equal the adjusted bank balance on the bank reconciliation.

Balance per chequebook		?
Add:		
	Interest earned	7.50
		?
Deduct:		
	Service charge	9.00
	Adjusted bank balance	$3,954

Adjusted bank balance from part 1.
Book balance + $7.50 - $9.00 = $3,954
Book balance = $3,955.50

3.

Date	Accounts and Explanation	PR	Debit	Credit
April 1	Petty Cash		400	
	Cash			400
April 30	Miscellaneous Expense		28	
	Postage Expense		19	
	Supplies		77	
	Freight		43	
	Cash Short and Over		2	
	Cash			169

Note that you make an entry to record the various expenses only when the Petty Cash fund is replenished. The $2 difference represents cash short and over.

4.

Cash Budget
For the Year Ended September 30, 2006

Cash balance, October 1, 2005		$ 95,500
Estimated cash receipts		
Receipts from customers	$285,000	
Proceeds from sale of equipment	21,500	
Proceeds from note receivable	150,000	456,500
		$552,000
Estimated cash disbursements		
Purchases of inventory	110,000	
Payments for dividends	55,000	
Payments for interest and taxes	108,000	
Operating expenses	92,250	
Payments for debt	81,700	446,950
Cash available (needed) before new financing		105,050
Budgeted cash balance, September 30, 2006		100,000
Cash available for additional investments		$ 5,050

VI. Critical Thinking

1. A. Notice that there is separation of duties—one person issues the ticket and collects the money and the other person oversees the admission to the opera house. Thus, a ticket is necessary to gain entrance.

   The tickets are serially numbered. Management can determine the amount of cash that should be in the drawer by multiplying the price of each ticket by the number of tickets issued.

   B. To make the controls more effective, management should 1) record the serial number of the first and last ticket sold on each cashier's shift, 2) maintain control over the unsold tickets, and 3) count the cash at the beginning and end of each shift.

   C. The controls are ineffective if there is collusion by the cashier and the door attendant. The door attendant may choose to keep the entire ticket instead of tearing it in half. The ticket is then given to the cashier to be sold again. The cashier can then pocket the cash received for the "used" tickets. Remember, internal controls are ineffective if everyone colludes.

2. The new *Sarbanes-Oxley Act* may improve corporate governance by having senior managers be more responsible for the information contained within the financial statements, by requiring the CEO and CFO to certify the financial statements and evaluate the effectiveness of the internal controls, thereby putting more importance on internal controls. This will help users of the financial statements be able to put more reliability on the financial statements. Note, however, that collusion can still exist.

DEMONSTRATION PROBLEMS

Demonstration Problem #1 Solved and Explained

Requirement 1

Only three entries were required in this problem! Remember, the purpose of a petty cash fund is to make small disbursements while avoiding the time and cost of writing cheques. Therefore, entries are only recorded when a fund is established, when the fund balance is changed, and when the fund is replenished.

| July 1 | Petty Cash Fund | 200 | |
| | Cash | | 200 |

July 13	Accounts Receivable (President)	60.00	
	Postage	41.95	
	Supplies	53.00	
	Petty Cash Fund	200.00	
	Cash		354.95

Freight charges on assets are debited to the asset account because they represent an additional cost incurred to acquire the asset. The amounts taken by the president are debited to accounts receivable because they represent an amount the president owes the fund. However, the purpose of a petty cash fund is NOT to provide "pocket money" for an officer of the corporation. This practice should not continue.

July 31	Supplies	47	
	Accounts Receivable (President)	77	
	Accounts Receivable (Employee)	15	
	Miscellaneous Expense	65	
	Cash		204

The newspaper, coffee money, and window washing were all charged to Miscellaneous Expense although they could be debited to separate accounts. The postdated cheque is charged to Accounts Receivable because it represents an amount the employee owes the business. Allowing an employee to "borrow" from the petty cash fund violates effective internal control procedures and should be stopped immediately. If permitted to continue, the petty cash fund will contain nothing but a stack of postdated cheques!

Requirement 2

	Petty Cash Fund	
July 1	200	
July 13	200	
Bal.	400	

Assuming the company is correct in its estimates that a $400 balance is sufficient for the petty cash fund, the general ledger account (Petty Cash Fund) will remain as presented above with the $400 balance undisturbed.

Demonstration Problem #2 Solved and Explained

Requirement 1

Gary's Gardening
Bank Reconciliation
August 31, 2006

BANK:		
Balance August 31, 2006		$11,841
Add:		
Deposit in transit of August 31, 2006		382
Correction of bank error		725
		12,948
Less:		
Outstanding cheques		
Aug. 18 Cheque	305	
Aug. 29 Cheque	828	1,133
Adjusted bank balance August 31, 2006		$11,815
BOOKS:		
Balance August 31, 2006		$9,364
Add:		
Bank collection of note receivable,		
including interest of $130		2,630
Interest earned on bank balance		16
Error—Aug. 2 Cheque		9
		12,019
Less:		
Service charge		29
NSF cheque		175
Adjusted bank balance August 31, 2006		$11,815

Explanation: bank reconciliation

1. A bank reconciliation prepared on a timely basis provides good internal control over a company's cash accounts. Comparing the cash balance in the general ledger with the cash balance maintained by the bank makes errors easy to detect.

2. The month-end balance shown in the general ledger rarely agrees with the month-end balance shown on the bank statement. The difference generally occurs for one of two reasons:

   a. Timing differences: These occur because of the time lag that occurs when one record keeper records a transaction before the other. Typical timing differences include
      - Deposits in transit (the bank has yet to record)
      - Outstanding cheques (the bank has yet to record)
      - Bank service charges (the company has yet to record)

- Notes collected by the bank (the company has yet to record)
- Interest earned on account (the company has yet to record)
- NSF cheques (the company has yet to record)

b. Errors: An error must result in an adjustment by the record keeping party that made the error. If the error is made by the company, a general journal entry is made. The correcting entry will include an increase or decrease to the Cash account. Note that if the bank has made the error, the proper procedure is to notify the bank promptly. Since the company's records are accurate, no journal entry is needed.

Requirement 2

Date	Accounts and Explanation	PR	Debit	Credit
a.	Cash		2,630	
	Note Receivable			2,500
	Interest Revenue			130
	Note Receivable collected by the bank.			
b.	Cash		16	
	Interest Revenue			16
	Interest earned on bank balance.			
c.	Miscellaneous Expense		4	
	Cash			4
	Bank service charge.			
d.	Accounts Receivable – Ray's Pet Store		200	
	Cash			200
	NSF cheque returned by bank plus service charge.			
e.	Cash		9	
	Accounts Payable			9
	To correct error in recording Cheque #115.			

Explanations: Journal Entries (Note: ONLY entries to adjust the companies books need to be performed).

Entries (a) and (b) are necessary to record the increase in the cash account attributable to 1) the collection of interest and principal on the note receivable, and 2) interest earned on the account paid by the depository bank. These are timing differences that occur because of the time lag between the recording of an item on the bank's books and the books of the company. The bank has already recorded these items in its records (as evidenced by the bank statement), and the company must do so when it learns of the transaction(s).

Entries (c) and (d), which are similar to entries a and b, reduce cash on the company's books. These timing differences have already been recorded by the bank. Entry (c) reduces cash for chequing account (or other) service charges for the monthly period and brings the account up to date. The entry for the NSF cheque is necessary to establish an account receivable for Ray's Pet Store. It had paid the company with a cheque that was deposited in the Cash account. Because the cheque was returned unpaid for nonsufficient funds, the company must pursue collection of the debt and record on its books that $200 ($175 + $25 service charge) is still owed.

Entry (e) represents the correction of an error when a cheque was recorded as a reduction to Cash of $232 instead of $223.

Note: No entry is required for the bank error. Once notified, the bank needs to correct its books.

CHAPTER 5—TEMPORARY INVESTMENTS AND RECEIVABLES

CHAPTER OVERVIEW

In Chapter 4, you learned about the importance of internal control and the application of internal control procedures to cash. Chapter 5 expands this discussion to include other current assets, specifically temporary investments and receivables. The specific learning objectives for this chapter are to

1. **Understand** temporary investments
2. **Apply** internal controls to receivables
3. **Use** the allowance method for uncollectible receivables
4. **Account** for notes receivable
5. **Use** days' sales in receivables and the acid-test ratio to evaluate financial position

CHAPTER REVIEW

Study Tip: Much of the discussion in this chapter will be easier to understand if you become familiar with the following terms: creditor, debt instrument, debtor, equity securities, maturity, securities, and term.

Objective 1 – Understand temporary investments

The three most liquid assets companies have are cash and cash equivalents, temporary investments, and accounts receivables. **Temporary investments**, (also called **marketable securities**) are investments that the company plans to hold for one year or less. Temporary investments can be interest-bearing securities, such as bonds, or shares of another company.

Temporary investments fall into one of four categories:

1) Loans and receivables—financial assets with fixed or determinable payments that are not quoted actively and are created by the entity by providing money, goods, or services directly to a debtor. Valuation—measured at amortized cost less reductions for impairment or uncollectability.
2) Held to maturity—financial assets with fixed or determinable payments and fixed maturity, such as debt securities and mandatory redeemable preferred shares, that an entity intends and is able to hold to maturity. Valuation—measured at amortized cost, less reductions for impairment or uncollectability.
3) Trading—financial assets acquired for the purpose of generating a profit from short-term fluctuations in price. Valuation—measured at fair value, with changes in fair value reported in net profit or loss for the period.
4) Available for sale (covered in Chapter 10)—financial assets that are not in one of the above three categories. Includes all investment in equity instruments that are not held for trading. Valuation—fair value changes are recognized directly in equity until the financial asset is sold, at which time the realized gain or loss is reported in net profit or loss.

Trading investments are recorded at cost when purchased:

| Temporary Investment | XX | |
| Cash | | XX |

The receipt of interest from temporary investments in interest-bearing securities is recorded as follows:

| Cash | XX | |
| Interest Income | | XX |

The receipt of dividends paid on shares held as temporary investments is recorded as follows:

| Cash | XX | |
| Dividend Revenue | | XX |

GAAP requires companies to value trading investments on the annual financial statements at their current market value. An *unrealized* gain occurs when the trading asset has increased above the cost:

| Temporary Investment | XX | |
| Unrealized Gain on Investment | | XX |

An *unrealized* loss is recorded as follows:

| Unrealized Loss on Temporary Investments | XX | |
| Temporary Investments | | XX |

Temporary investments on the balance sheet are recorded at the lower of cost or market. Interest revenue, dividend revenue, and gains and losses arising from temporary investments are reported as other revenue, gains, and losses on the income statement. (Helpful hint: review Exhibit 5-1 in the text.)

A *realized* gain or loss occurs when the temporary investment is sold. For a loss, the journal entry would be:

Cash	XX	
Loss on Sale of Temporary Investment	XX	
Temporary Investment		XX

Accounts and Notes Receivable

Receivables arise when goods or services are sold on credit. The basic types of receivables are **accounts receivable** and **notes receivable**.

Accounts receivable are amounts that customers owe a business for purchases made on credit. They should be collectible according to a firm's normal terms of sale, such as net 30 days. Accounts receivable are sometimes called **trade receivables**, and are current assets.

Notes receivable occur when customers sign formal agreements to pay for their purchases. These agreements are called **promissory notes**, and usually extend for periods of 60 days or longer. The portion of notes receivable scheduled to be collected within a year is a current asset; the remaining amount is a long-term asset.

Other receivables include miscellaneous items such as loans to employees and subsidiary companies.

Objective 2 - Apply internal controls to receivables

The main issues in controlling and managing the collection of receivables are:

1. What are the benefits of extending credit to customers? What is the cost?
2. Extend credit only to creditworthy customers
3. Separate cash-handling and accounting duties
4. Pursue collection from customers to maximize cash flow

It is imperative that cash-handling and cash accounting duties be separated; otherwise, too many opportunities exist for employees to steal cash from the company. This is true in both the receivables department and the credit department.

The main issues in accounting for receivables are:

1. Measuring and reporting receivables at the net realizable value (the amount we expect to collect)
2. Measuring and reporting the expense associated with uncollectible accounts

Extending credit to customers involves the risk that some customers will not pay their obligations. Uncollectible-Account Expense (also called Doubtful-Account Expense or Bad-Debt Expense) occurs when a business is unable to collect from some credit customers. This expense is a cost of doing business, and should be measured, recorded, and reported. Two methods used by accountants are the **allowance method** and the **direct write-off method**.

Objective 3 - Use the allowance method for uncollectible receivables

The **allowance method** is the preferred way to account for Uncollectible-Account Expense (it is better for matching the expense with revenue earned). This method estimates and records collection losses before specific uncollectible accounts are identified.

Allowance for Uncollectible Accounts is a contra account to Accounts Receivable. Remember, contra accounts are subtracted from a related account. An example from an earlier chapter is Accumulated Amortization (which is subtracted from a related capital asset).

The allowance method records estimated Uncollectible-Account Expense. The entry to the contra account has the effect of reducing the net balance in Accounts Receivable:

> Accounts Receivable
> - Allowance for Uncollectible Accounts
> = Net Accounts Receivable (also called **net realizable value**)

Recording estimated bad debts has the effect of reducing net Accounts Receivable and matching Uncollectible-Account Expense with its related Sales Revenue.

Using the allowance method requires an estimate of uncollectible accounts.

The **percentage-of-sales method** (also called the **income-statement approach**) estimates uncollectible accounts as a percentage of sales, using past experience to set the percentage. The amount of the journal entry is equal to credit sales times the bad-debt percentage, and is recorded as:

Uncollectible-Account Expense	XX	
Allowance for Uncollectible Accounts		XX

The **aging-of-accounts-receivable method** (also called the **balance-sheet approach)** involves grouping accounts receivable according to the length of time they have been outstanding. Accounts are usually grouped into 30-day increments, such as 1-30, 31-60, 61-90, and over 90 days. Different percentages of the total receivables in each group are estimated to be uncollectible. The amount for each group is equal to the total receivables in that group times the estimated uncollectible percentage for that group.

The amount of the journal entry will be what is needed to bring the Allowance account to the estimated amount calculated using the aging method. Therefore, if the existing balance in the Allowance for Uncollectible Accounts is a credit, the amount of the journal entry will be less than the estimate. If the existing balance in the Allowance for Uncollectible Accounts is a debit, the amount of the journal entry will be greater than the estimate.

The expense is recorded as:

Uncollectible-Account Expense	XX	
Allowance for Uncollectible Accounts		XX

> **Study Tip**: When using an estimate based on sales, adjust *for* the estimate; when using an estimate based on accounts receivable, adjust *to* the estimate.

When using the allowance method, specific accounts receivable are written off when the credit department determines that the receivable is not collectible. Specific accounts are written off with this journal entry:

Allowance for Uncollectible Accounts	XX	
Accounts Receivable		XX

Note that this entry does not affect expense because the estimated expense has already been recorded. (See Exhibit 5-3 for a comparison of the percentage-of-sales and aging methods for estimating uncollectibles.)

Using the **direct write-off method**, the company writes off an account receivable directly to an expense account. In other words, the Allowance account is not used.

The journal entry for a direct write off is:

Uncollectible-Account Expense	XX	
Accounts Receivable		XX

The direct write-off method is easy to use; however, it suffers from two defects. First, it does not set up an Allowance for Uncollectibles account and therefore overstates the value of accounts receivable on the balance sheet. Second, it may not match the uncollectible-account expense with the revenue that generated the account receivable.

Objective 4 - Account for notes receivable

Notes receivables are more formal than accounts receivables. Usually, the maker (debtor) will sign a promissory note and must pay the principal amount plus interest to the payee (creditor) on the maturity date. The maturity value is the sum of the principal amount plus the interest.

Review Exhibit 5-4 in your text to be certain you are familiar with the following terms:

Promissory note	Interest period (note period or note term)
Maker (debtor)	Maturity date (due date)
Payee (creditor)	Interest rate
Principal	

The formula for computing interest is:

Principal × Interest Rate × Time = Interest Amount

Study the examples in the text. It is important to be able to compute interest based on years, months, and days (time factor is the portion of the year the note is in force).

Generally, notes arise from two events, as follows:

Notes Receivable	XX	
Sales		XX

Sold goods and received a promissory note.

Notes Receivable	XX	
Accounts Receivable		XX

Receipt of a note from a customer in payment of the account.

Interest revenue is earned as time passes, and not just when cash is collected. If the interest period of the note extends beyond the current accounting period, then part of the interest revenue is earned in the current accounting period and part is earned in the next accounting period.

A note receivable is a negotiable instrument. Frequently, a business will sell a note receivable to a bank to raise cash. Selling a note receivable before its maturity date is called **discounting a note receivable**. The seller receives less than the maturity value (that is, gives up some of the interest revenue) in exchange for receiving cash. The discounted value, called the proceeds, is the amount the seller (business) receives from the purchaser (bank).

Factoring accounts receivables is another way companies use receivables to finance operations. Similar to discounting notes receivables, factoring refers to selling the accounts receivables to a financial institution (called a factor). The factor earns money by purchasing them at less than face value and collecting them at the total amount due. The difference between the selling price of the receivable and the face value is recorded as financing expense on the books of the seller.

Objective 5 – Use days' sales in receivables and the acid-test ratio to evaluate financial position

Days' sales in receivables (also called the average collection period) measures the average days an account receivable is outstanding.

$$\text{One day's sales} = \frac{\text{Net Revenues}}{365}$$

$$\text{Average Net Accounts Receivable} = \frac{\text{Beginning Accounts Receivable} + \text{Ending Accounts Receivable}}{2}$$

$$\text{Days' sales in average accounts receivable} = \frac{\text{Average Net Accounts Receivable}}{\text{One day's sales}}$$

A related ratio is **accounts receivable turnover**, computed as follows:

$$\frac{\text{Net Sales}}{\text{Average Net Accounts Receivable}}$$

Because temporary investments and receivables affect cash, the cash flow statement will report these effects. When cash is collected from accounts receivables, the amount is reflected in the operating activities section of the cash flow statement. The purchase (or sale) of temporary investments is reported as an investing activity on the cash flow statement. The collection of a note receivable would also be reported as an investing activity.

The **acid-test (quick) ratio** measures the ability of a business to pay all of its current liabilities if they become due immediately.

$$\text{Acid-test Ratio} = \frac{\text{Cash} + \text{Temporary investments} + \text{Net current receivables}}{\text{Total Current Liabilities}}$$

Remember that inventory, supplies, and prepaid expenses are not used to compute the acid-test ratio.

TEST YOURSELF

All the self-testing materials in this chapter focus on information and procedures that your instructor is likely to test in quizzes and examinations.

I. Matching

1. *Match each numbered term with its lettered definition.*

_____ 1. aging-of-accounts-receivable method
_____ 2. temporary investments
_____ 3. accounts receivable turnover
_____ 4. direct write-off method
_____ 5. factor
_____ 6. term
_____ 7. maturity
_____ 8. payee
_____ 9. promissory note
_____ 10. Uncollectible Account Expense

_____ 11. allowance method
_____ 12. securities
_____ 13. acid-test ratio
_____ 14. percentage-of-sales approach
_____ 15. equity securities
_____ 16. trading securities
_____ 17. debt instruments
_____ 18. principal
_____ 19. receivable
_____ 20. interest

A. net sales divided by average net accounts receivable
B. notes payable or share certificates that entitle the owner to the benefits of an investment
C. tells whether the entity could pay all its current liabilities if they came due immediately
D. a method of estimating uncollectible receivables as a percentage of net sales

E. a method of accounting for bad debts in which the company records uncollectible-account expense and credits the customer's account receivable when the credit department decides that a customer's account receivable is uncollectible

F. a business that earns revenues by purchasing the accounts receivable of another business at a discount and then collecting the full amount from the customer

G. the length of time until a debt instrument matures

H. investments that are to be sold in the near future with the intent of generating a profit on the sale

I. the date on which a debt instrument matures

J. the person who receives promised future payment on a note

K. the amount loaned out or borrowed

L. a written promise to pay a specified amount of money on a particular future date

M. a monetary claim against a business or an individual that is acquired by selling goods and services on credit or by lending money

N. a way to estimate bad debts by analyzing individual accounts receivable according to the length of time they have been due

O. investments that a company plans to hold for one year or less

P. a method of recording collection losses based on estimates made prior to determining that specific accounts are uncollectible

Q. the borrower's cost of renting money from a lender

R. share certificates that represent the investor's ownership of shares in a corporation

S. a payable, usually some form of note or bond payable

T. cost of extending credit that arises from the failure to collect from credit customers

2. *Match each numbered term with its lettered definition.*

_____ 1. allowance for doubtful accounts
_____ 2. creditor
_____ 3. debtor
_____ 4. held-to-maturity securities

_____ 5. acid-test or quick ratio
_____ 6. balance-sheet approach
_____ 7. days' sales in receivables
_____ 8. income-statement approach

A. the party to whom money is owed
B. (cash + short-term investment + net current receivables) / total current liabilities
C. contra account to accounts receivable
D. the party who owes money
E. ratio of average net accounts receivables to one day's sales
F. the method used to compute the percentage-of-sales method
G. financial assets that a company does not intend to sell prior to maturity
H. the method used to estimate bad debts focusing on accounts receivable balances

II. Multiple Choice   *Circle the best answer.*

1. Using the allowance method, writing off a specific account receivable will

A. increase net income
B. decrease net income
C. not affect net income
D. affect net income in an undetermined manner

2. Temporary investments are accounted for at

   A. historical cost
   B. fair market value
   C. cost less allowance for decline
   D. maturity value

3. Which of the following will occur if Uncollectible-Account Expense is not recorded at the end of the year?

   A. expenses will be overstated.
   B. net income will be understated
   C. liabilities will be understated
   D. assets will be overstated

4. Net Accounts Receivable is equal to

   A. Accounts Receivable - Allowance for Uncollectible Accounts
   B. Accounts Receivable + Allowance for Uncollectible Accounts
   C. Accounts Receivable - Uncollectible-Account Expense
   D. Accounts Receivable + Uncollectible-Account Expense

5. Accounts Receivable has a debit balance of $14,200 and the Allowance for Uncollectible Accounts has a credit balance of $700. A specific account of $400 is written off. What is the amount of net receivables after the write off?

   A. $13,500
   B. $14,200
   C. $13,800
   D. $13,900

6. Allowance for Uncollectible Accounts is

   A. an expense account
   B. a contra liability account
   C. a contra asset account
   D. a liability account

7. A four-month note receivable reported on the balance sheet is classified as a

   A. current asset
   B. long-term asset
   C. current liability
   D. long-term liability

8. Interest is equal to

   A. Principal × Time
   B. Principal ÷ Rate ÷ Time
   C. Principal × Rate ÷ Time
   D. Principal × Rate × Time

9. Assets listed as temporary investments on the balance sheet are

   A. only liquid
   B. listed on the national stock exchange
   C. only intended to be converted to cash within one year
   D. liquid and intended to be converted to cash within one year

10. An analysis of the current accounts receivable shows there is $14,000 of accounts receivables, $6,000 not yet due, $4,000 within 30 days overdue and $4,000 more than 30 days overdue. Historically, 2% of accounts receivable not yet due will be uncollectible, 10% of accounts less than 30 days overdue and 30% of accounts over 30 days due will be uncollectible. If the balance of the allowance for doubtful accounts is a $100 credit, what amount will be necessary to make the adjusting entry to the allowance for doubtful accounts?

    A. $1,720
    B. $1,620
    C. $1,820
    D. $13,280

11. The Gray's Company purchased investment securities at a cost of $22,000. At the end of the accounting period the securities had a market value of $19,500. Which of the following statements is *true* if the investment is classified as a trading temporary investment?

    A. the unrealized loss would not be recognized in the financial statements
    B. the securities would be reported on the balance sheet at $19,500
    C. the securities would be reported on the balance sheet at $22,000
    D. the unrealized loss would cause an increase in equity

12. The Gray's Company purchased investment securities at a cost of $22,000. At the end of the accounting period the securities had a market value of $23,500. Which of the following journal entries would be required if the investment is classified as a trading temporary investment?

    A. debit unrealized loss on investment, $1,500
    B. credit unrealized gain on investment, $1,500
    C. debit temporary investments, $23,500
    D. no entry would be necessary

13. All of the following current assets are included in the acid-test ratio *except*

    A. cash
    B. inventory
    C. temporary investments
    D. net current receivables

14. Temporary investments transactions are reported on the cash flow statement as

    A. operating activities
    B. investing activities
    C. financing activities
    D. both operating and investing activities

15. Receivable transactions (cash receipts) are reported on the cash flow statement as

    A. operating activities
    B. investing activities
    C. financing activities
    D. none of the above

III. Completion *Complete each of the following statements.*

1. _____ are investments that the company plans to hold for one year or less.

2. Trading temporary investments are valued on the annual financial statements at the _____ _____ .

3. _____ occurs when the year-end value of the trading temporary investment is higher than the original cost of the investment.

4. The maker of a debt instrument is the _____. The holder of a debt instrument is the _____ .

5. Temporary investments are recorded at _____ when acquired, but reported on the balance sheet at _____ .

6. The difference between an unrealized loss and a realized loss is _____ _____ .

7. The direct write-off method of accounting for bad debt violates the _____ principle.

8. The method of estimating bad debts that focuses on the balance sheet is the _____ _____ method.

9. The method of estimating bad debts that focuses on the income statement is the _____ _____ method.

10. The _____ measures the ability of a business to pay all its current liabilities if they become due immediately.

11. To calculate the average days an account receivable is outstanding, average net accounts receivable is divided by _____ .

IV. True/False   *For each of the following statements, circle* T *for true or* F *for false.*

1.   T F   Interest earned on temporary investments is reported in the operating activities section of the cash flow statement.
2.   T F   Receipts from accounts receivables are reported as investing activities on the cash flow statement.
3.   T F   Collections on notes receivables are reported as operating activities on the cash flow statement.
4.   T F   Days' sales in receivables indicate how long, on average, it takes to collect accounts receivables.
5.   T F   When computing the acid-test ratio, inventory is included in the numerator.
6.   T F   Temporary investments can be either equity securities or debt instruments.
7.   T F   A creditor is the party who owes money.
8.   T F   Temporary investments are reported on the balance sheet at the lower of cost or market value.
9.   T F   Temporary investments are always reported on the balance sheet at their market value.
10. T F   Unrealized gains and losses on temporary investments are reported on the income statement.
11. T F   The maturity value of a note receivable is the sum of the principal and interest.
12. T F   The direct write-off method violates the disclosure principle.
13. T F   Net realizable value equals total accounts receivable less uncollectible-accounts expense.
14. T F   When using the allowance method, the write off on an uncollectible account will reduce total assets by the amount of the account receivable written off.
15. T F   Discounting notes receivables and factoring accounts receivables are two methods of financing receivables.

V. Exercises

1.   Sunshine Studios uses the Allowance method to account for bad debts. Indicate the effect that each of the following transactions will have on gross Accounts Receivable, the Allowance for Uncollectible Accounts, net Accounts Receivable, and Uncollectible-Accounts Expense. Use + for increases and - for decreases, and 0 for no effect.

	Gross Accounts Receivable	Allowance for Uncollectible Accounts	Net Accounts Receivable	Uncollectible-Accounts Expense
An account receivable is written off	_____	_____	_____	_____
An account receivable is reinstated	_____	_____	_____	_____
A customer pays his account receivable	_____	_____	_____	_____
1.5% of $950,000 in sales is estimated to be uncollectible	_____	_____	_____	_____
4% of $95,000 in accounts receivable is estimated to be uncollectible (the balance in the allowance account is a credit of $550)	_____	_____	_____	_____

2. Compute the missing amounts. Use a 365-day year where applicable.

	Principal	Interest rate	Duration	Interest	Maturity Value
A.	$9,000	8%	2 months	_____	_____
B.	$10,000	9%	120 days	_____	_____
C.	_____	12%	30 days	_____	$15,147.95
D.	$6,000	_____	10 months	$300	_____

3. Phillip's Fitness has a $185,000 balance in Accounts Receivable on December 31, 2006. The Allowance for Uncollectible Accounts has a $200 credit balance. Credit sales totaled $825,000 for the year.

Part A

a. If Phillip's Fitness uses the percentage-of-sales method and estimates that 1.0% of sales may be uncollectible, what is the Uncollectible-Account Expense for 2006?

b. What is the ending balance in the Allowance for Uncollectible Accounts after adjustments?

c. Would your answers be different if the Allowance for Uncollectible Accounts had a $200 debit balance?

Part B

a. If Phillip's Fitness uses the aging-of-accounts-receivable method and has determined that $7,200 of Accounts Receivable is uncollectible, what is the Uncollectible-Account Expense for 2006?

b. What is the ending balance in the Allowance for Uncollectible Accounts after adjustments?

c. Would your answers be different if the Allowance for Uncollectible Accounts had a $200 debit balance?

4. Prepare journal entries for the following temporary investments transactions. Management considered these trading securities:

March 12   Purchased 2,500 shares of Scott Corporation at $33.50. The commission was $35.00.
June 18   Received a $0.50 per share cash dividend.
Aug. 28   Sold 100 shares of Scott Corporation for $40 per share. The commission was $35.
Dec. 31   The market value of the shares is $31.00 as of today.

Date	Account and Explanation	Debit	Credit

5. On April 30, 2006, Stewart Corporation paid $900,000 for 7% commercial paper of Star Inc. as a temporary investment. The commercial paper pays interest on April 30 and October 31.

Record Stewart's purchase of the commercial paper, the receipt of semiannual interest on October 31, and the accrual of interest revenue on December 31.

Date	Account and Explanation	Debit	Credit

VI. Critical Thinking

At November 31, 2006, Red Cup Inc. holds temporary investments costing $360,000.

1. Assume the market value of the investments at December 31, 2006 has fallen to $345,000. What value will Red Cup Inc. report for these investments on the balance sheet and what will be the effect on the income statement?

2. Assume Red Cup Inc. still holds the same investments at December 31, 2007, and that the value has risen to $475,000 at that date. What value will Red Cup Inc. now report on the balance sheet and what effect will this recovery in value have on the company's reported net income?

DEMONSTRATION PROBLEMS

Demonstration Problem #1

Huynh Inc. manufactures machine parts. The company's year-end trial balance for 2006 reported the following:

Accounts Receivable	$5,125,200
Less: Allowance for Uncollectible Accounts	51,770
	$5,073,430

Assume that net credit sales for 2006 amounted to $12,300,000 and Allowance for Uncollectible Accounts has not yet been adjusted for 2006.

Required:

1. At the end of 2006, the following accounts receivable were deemed uncollectible:

Boyce Inc.	$ 9,150
Caster Corporation	8,007
Shaw Products	6,823
UST Wholesalers	13,090
Total	$37,070

   Prepare the 2006 journal entry necessary to write off the above accounts.

2. Assume that the company uses the percentage-of-sales method to estimate Uncollectible-Account Expense. After analyzing industry averages and prior years' activity, Huynh's management has determined that Uncollectible-Account Expense for 2006 should be 1.5% of net credit sales. Prepare the journal entry to record and adjust Uncollectible-Account Expense.

3. Assume that the company uses the aging-of-accounts-receivable method. The aging schedule prepared by the company's credit manager indicated that an allowance of $202,000 for uncollectible accounts is appropriate. Prepare the appropriate journal entry.

4. Calculate net realizable value of accounts receivable assuming (a) the percentage-of-sales method was used and (b) the aging-of-accounts-receivable method was used.

Requirement 1 (Write off of uncollectible accounts)

GENERAL JOURNAL

Date	Accounts and Explanation	PR	Debit	Credit

Requirement 2 (Adjustment to record Uncollectible-Account Expense using the percentage-of-sales method)

GENERAL JOURNAL

Date	Accounts and Explanation	PR	Debit	Credit

Requirement 3 (Adjustment to record Uncollectible-Account Expense using the aging-of-accounts-receivable method)

GENERAL JOURNAL

Date	Accounts and Explanation	PR	Debit	Credit

Requirement 4

(a) $_____

(b) $_____

Demonstration Problem #2

At the beginning of the year, Leicester Inc. held the following temporary investments:

	Book Value
500 shares Atlas Inc.	$41.13 ea.
Money market funds	$45,000
1,200 shares EZ Inc.	$34.25 ea.
400 shares Valu.com	$26.38 ea.
820 shares Wal-Way Corporation	$104.75 ea.

During the current year, the following occurred:

On February 10 Leicester Inc. received a 26¢/share dividend on the Atlas shares. Shortly thereafter, Atlas shares increased to $48.50, so the security was sold on March 1 less a brokerage commission of $325.

The money market funds earned 0.5% interest monthly (6% annual interest), payable at the end of the month. Interest cheques were received and used for other purposes.

Quarterly dividends of 17.5¢/share were received on the EZ shares on March 24 and June 24. On July 8, the shares were sold for $29.50 per share less a brokerage commission of $485.

On August 31, Leicester Inc. purchased a $100,000, six-month Treasury Bill (T-bill). The T-bill earns 7.1% annual interest, payable at maturity.

The Valu.com shares remained in the portfolio throughout the year; no dividends were received during the year, and the shares were trading at $25 per share at year end.

The Wal-Way shares also remained in the company's portfolio throughout the year. Quarterly dividends of $1.06 were received throughout the year. On December 31 the shares were trading at $121.

Required:

1. For each security, record journal entries to reflect interest or dividends received during the year.
2. Present journal entries to record the sale of the Atlas and EZ shares.
3. For the remaining securities (money market funds, T-bills, Valu.com, and Wal-Way), present any necessary year-end adjusting journal entries.

Requirement 1

Date	Accounts and Explanation	PR	Debit	Credit

Requirement 2

Date	Accounts and Explanation	PR	Debit	Credit

Requirement 3

Date	Accounts and Explanation	PR	Debit	Credit

SOLUTIONS

A. TEST YOURSELF

I. Matching

1.

1. N	5. F	9. L	13. C	17. S
2. O	6. G	10. T	14. D	18. K
3. A	7. I	11. P	15. R	19. M
4. E	8. J	12. B	16. H	20. Q

2.

1. C	2. A	3. D	4. G
5. B	6. H	7. E	8. F

II. Multiple Choice

1. C Writing off a specific account receivable using the allowance method takes the form of:
    Allowance for Uncollectible Accounts   XX
        Accounts Receivable   XX
    Both accounts involved are balance sheet accounts; accordingly, net income is not affected.

2. B Temporary investments are accounted for at fair market value.

3. D Failing to record the Uncollectible-Accounts Expense also means that no increase in the Allowance for Uncollectible Accounts (contra accounts receivable) was recorded. Accordingly, expenses are understated and assets are overstated.

4. A Net Accounts Receivable is the result of netting the Accounts Receivable balance against its contra account, Allowance for Uncollectible Accounts.

5. A When Accounts Receivable and the Allowance account are both reduced by $13,500, Net Accounts Receivable will be unchanged.
    [$14,200 - $700 = ($14,200 - $400) - ($700 - $400)]

6. C Allowance for Uncollectible Accounts is a companion account to Accounts Receivable and has a normal credit balance while Accounts Receivable has a normal debit balance. A contra account has two distinguishing characteristics: 1) it always has a companion account, and 2) its normal balance is opposite that of the companion account.

7. A A note receivable is an asset. An asset that will be converted to cash within one year is a current asset.

8.   D   Interest is a function of the amount advanced to the borrower, the interest rate, and the term of the loan.

9.   D   Note that besides the determinable liquidity of the investment, the intent of management determines an investment's classification as a temporary investment.

10. B   ($6,000 × 2% + $4,000 × 10% + $4,000 × 30%) - $100 = $1,620. The amount of the allowance is adjusted *to* the aging schedule amount.

11. B   GAAP requires that temporary investments be reported at the current market value.

12. B   GAAP requires that temporary investments be reported at the current market value, thus a credit to Unrealized Gain on Investment for $1,500 would be made.

13. B   Inventory is not included in the acid-test ratio because it may not be easy to sell the goods.

14. D   The purchase and sale of temporary investments are investing activities, whereas the interest and dividends received on temporary investments are reported as operating activities.

15. A   Collections from customers are cash receipts from operating activities.

III. Completion

1. Temporary investments (or marketable securities)
2. current market value
3. Unrealized gain
4. debtor, creditor
5. cost, the lower of cost or market value
6. unrealized losses are not the result of a sales transaction, whereas realized losses do result from sales transactions
7. matching (The direct write-off method fails to match the business's cost of extending credit to customers who do not pay with the revenue generating the expense.)
8. aging-of-accounts-receivable (Aging the accounts focuses on estimating the appropriate balance in the contra account receivable account, Allowance for Uncollectible Accounts.)
9. percentage-of-sales (The percentage-of-sales method focuses on calculating the appropriate cost to match against sales in the current period as Uncollectible-Accounts Expense.)
10. acid-test (quick) ratio
11. one day's sales

IV. True/False

1.   T
2.   F   Receipt of accounts receivables is an operating activity.
3.   F   Collections on notes receivables are investing activities, not operating activities.
4.   T
5.   F   Generally, inventory does not convert to cash quickly enough and is therefore excluded from the acid-test ratio.
6.   T
7.   F   The creditor is the party to whom money is owed.
8.   F   Temporary investments are reported at their current market value.

9.	T
10.	T
11.	T
12.	F	Violates the matching principle, not the disclosure principle.
13.	F	Net realizable value equals total accounts receivable less Allowance for Uncollectible Accounts.
14.	F	One advantage of the allowance method is that the write off of an account receivable does not affect the net realizable value of accounts receivables.
15.	T

V. Exercises

1.

	Gross Accounts Receivable	Allowance for Uncollectible Accounts	Net Accounts Receivable	Uncollec-tible-Accounts Expense
An account receivable is written off	-	-	0	0
An account receivable is reinstated	+	+	0	0
A customer pays his account receivable	-	0	-	0
1.5% of $950,000 in sales is estimated to be uncollectible	0	+	-	+
4% of $95,000 in accounts receivable is estimated to be uncollectible (the balance in the allowance account is a credit of $550)	0	+	-	+

2.

A.	interest = $9,000 × 0.08 × 2/12 = $120
maturity value = $9,000 + $120 = $9,120

B.	interest = $10,000 × 0.09 × 120/365 = $295.89
maturity value = $10,000 + $295.89 = $10,295.89

C.	maturity value = principal + interest
interest = principal × rate × time
$15,147.95 = P + (P × 0.12 × 30/365)
P = $15,000
interest = $147.95

D. interest = principal × rate × time
$300 = \$6{,}000 \times R \times 10/12$
$R = 6\%$
maturity value = principal + interest
maturity value = $\$6{,}000 + \$300 = \$6{,}300$

3. A. a. Uncollectible-Account Expense = $0.01 \times \$825{,}000 = \$8{,}250$
   b. Ending balance in Allowance for Uncollectible Accounts = $\$200 + \$8{,}250 = \$8{,}450$
   c. Yes. The amount of Uncollectible-Account Expense would be the same. However, the balance in the Allowance for Uncollectible Accounts would be different ($\$8{,}250 - \$200 = \$8{,}050$).

   B. a. The current balance in the Allowance account is a $200 credit, and the desired balance in the Allowance account is a $7,200 credit. The Uncollectible-Account Expense will be $7,200 - $200 = $7,000.
   b. The ending balance will be $7,200.
   c. Yes. It would require a credit of $7,400 to bring the balance in the Allowance account to a credit of $7,200; the corresponding debit is to the Uncollectible-Account Expense. The ending balance in the Allowance account will be the same, $7,200.

4.

Mar. 12	Temporary Investment—Scott Corp.	83,785	
	Cash [(2,500 shares × $33.50) + $35.00]		83,785
	Per share cost = $47.75		
June 18	Cash	1,250	
	Dividend Revenue		1,250
Aug. 28	Cash [(1,000 shares × $40) - $35]	39,965	
	Temporary Investment—Scott Corp. (1,000 shares × $40)		33,500
	Gain on Sale of Investment		6,465
Dec. 31	Unrealized Loss on Temporary Investment	3,750	
	Temporary Investment—Scott Corp.		3,750
	The remaining 1,500 shares after the sale have lost $2.50 ($33.50 - $31) × 1,500 = $3,750 unrealized loss.		

5.

Apr. 30	Temporary Investment—Star Inc.	900,000	
	Cash		900,000
Oct. 31	Cash	31,500	
	Interest Revenue		31,500
	($900,000 × 0.07 × 6/12 = $31,500)		
Dec. 31	Temporary Investment—Star Inc.	10,500	
	Interest Revenue		10,500
	($900,000 × 0.07 × 2/12 = $10,500)		

VI. Critical Thinking

1. The investments should be reported on the balance sheet at $345,000, the current market value. The write down of the investment will result in an unrealized loss of $15,000 ($360,000 - $345,000). The reported income before income tax for the year will be reduced by this amount.

2. GAAP requires that the investment be reported at the current market value, thus the temporary investment would be increased with a resulting unrealized holding gain of $130,000 ($475,000 - $345,000). The reported income tax would be increased by this amount.

DEMONSTRATION PROBLEMS

Demonstration Problem #1 Solved and Explained

Requirement 1

GENERAL JOURNAL

Date	Accounts and Explanation	PR	Debit	Credit
Dec. 31, 2006	Allowance for Uncollectible Accounts		37,070	
	Accounts Receivable—Boyce Inc.			9,150
	Accounts Receivable—Caster Corporation			8,007
	Accounts Receivable—Shaw Products			6,823
	Accounts Receivable—UST Wholesalers			13,090
	To write off uncollectible accounts.			

Requirement 2

Uncollectible-Account Expense	184,500	
Allowance for Uncollectible Accounts		184,500

Net credit sales of 2006 were $12,300,000. Uncollectible-Account Expense for 2006 is therefore $184,500 ($12,300,000 × 1.5% = $184,500). An examination of the activity to date in the Uncollectible-Account Expense and Allowance for Uncollectible Accounts reveals the effect of the entries made in Requirements 1 and 2.

Uncollectible-Account Expense		Allowance for Uncollectible Accounts		Accounts Receivable	
(2) 184,500		(1) 37,070	Bal. 51,770	Bal. 5,125,200	(1) 37,070
Bal. 184,500			(2) 184,500	Bal. 5,088,130	
			Bal. 199,200		

Note that the Allowance account started at $51,770. In Requirement 1, it was reduced by $37,070 when the uncollectible accounts were written off against the Allowance account. Note that prior to the 2006 adjustment, the Allowance was down to $14,700 ($51,770 - $37,070 = $14,700). The Allowance was then adjusted upward to $199,200 in Entry 2, when the company recorded 2006 Uncollectible-Account Expense of $184,500.

Requirement 3

Uncollectible-Account Expense	187,300	
Allowance for Uncollectible Accounts		187,300

When the aging-of-accounts-receivable method is used, the adjustment brings Allowance for Uncollectible Accounts to the balance indicated by the aging schedule. Before adjustment, the balance in the Allowance account was $14,700. The facts reveal that the desired balance in the Allowance account should be set at $202,000. The difference between the unadjusted balance and the desired balance ($202,000 - $14,700= $187,300) represents the amount of the adjustment and the amount of expense.

> **Study Tip**: When using the percentage-of-sales method, adjust *for* the estimate. When using accounts receivable as a basis, adjust *to* the estimate (that is, the estimate should be the balance in the Allowance account after the adjusting entry is posted).

Requirement 4

(a) $4,888,930

Net realizable value is the difference between total accounts receivable and the balance in the allowance account after adjustment. It represents the amount we expect to receive from those accounts. After adjustment in Requirement 2 above, the balance in Accounts Receivable is $5,088,130 and the balance in the Allowance account is $199,200.

(b) $4,886,130

After adjustment in Requirement 3 above, the balance in the Allowance account is $202,000. The balance in Accounts Receivable remains $5,088,130.

> **Study Tip**: The two approaches to estimating uncollectible accounts will always result in different amounts for net realizable value. If each approach resulted in the same value, there wouldn't be any need for alternative approaches! Remember: the percentage-of-sales method emphasizes the revenue/expense relationship on the income statement, while the aging-of-accounts-receivable method emphasizes asset value on the balance sheet.

Demonstration Problem #2 Solved and Explained

Requirement 1

Atlas Inc.

Feb. 10	Cash	130	
	Dividend Revenue		130
	(500 shares × $0.26 per share)		

Money Market Funds

	Cash	225	
	Interest Revenue		225
	($45,000 × 0.5%)		

This entry would be recorded monthly. The annual amount of interest revenue would be $2,700 ($225 × 12).

EZ Inc.

March 24	Cash	210	
	Dividend Revenue		210

(1,200 shares × $0.175 per share)

June 24	Cash	210	
	Dividend Revenue		210

(as above)

T-Bill
No entry as interest is payable at maturity.

Valu.com
No entry—no dividends received.

Wal-Way Corporation

	Cash	869.20	
	Dividend Revenue		869.20

(820 shares × $1.06/share)
This entry would be recorded four times, for an annual total of $3,476.80 ($869.20 × 4).

Requirement 2

Atlas Inc.

March 1	Cash	23,925	
	Temporary Investment—Atlas Inc.		20,565
	Gain on Sale of Investment		3,360

($48.50 × 500 shares less $325 commission)

EZ Inc.

July 8	Cash	34,915	
	Loss on Sale of Investment	6,185	
	Temporary Investment—EZ Inc.		41,100

The security was valued at $41,100 (1,200 shares × $34.25/per share). It sold for $35,400 (1,200 shares × $29.50/per share) less a commission of $485, resulting in a loss of $6,185.

Requirement 3

Money market funds
No year-end entry required. Because interest was received throughout the year, the year-end amortized cost is the same as the carrying value, $45,000.

T-Bill

Dec. 31	Temporary Investment—T-bill	2,367	
	Interest Revenue		2,367

($100,000 × 7.1% × 4/12)

The interest income earned but not yet received must be reported in the period earned.

Valu.com

Dec. 31	Unrealized Loss on Temporary Investment	552	
	Temporary Investment—Valu.com		552
	($26.38 - $25) × 400 shares		

Valu.com is a temporary investment. As such, the account should be valued at current market value as of the balance sheet date. The current market value is $1.38 less ($26.38 - $25) than the book value.

Wal-Way Corporation

| Dec. 31 | Temporary Investment—Wal-Way Corp. | 13,325 | |
| | Unrealized Gain on Temporary Investment | | 13,325 |

The unrealized gain of $13,325 [($121.00 - $104.75) × 820 shares] is reported on the financial statements at the current market value as of the balance sheet date.

CHAPTER 6—MERCHANDISE INVENTORY, COST OF GOODS SOLD, AND GROSS MARGIN

CHAPTER OVERVIEW

In Chapters 4 and 5, you learned more about current assets (cash, temporary investments, receivables, etc.) and procedures to control them. In this chapter you are introduced to merchandising businesses and some topics unique to them. One of the most important is merchandise inventory, including procedures to account for and control this current asset. The specific learning objectives for this chapter are to

1. **Account** for inventory transactions
2. **Analyze** the various inventory methods
3. **Identify** the income tax effects of the inventory methods
4. **Use** the gross profit percentage and inventory turnover to evaluate a business
5. **Estimate** inventory by the gross margin method and the retail method
6. **Show** how inventory errors affect cost of goods sold and income

CHAPTER REVIEW

Inventory—The merchandise that a company holds with the intent to sell to customers.

Cost of Goods Sold—The cost of the inventory that the business has sold to customers. Also called *cost of sales*.

Use the cost of goods sold model

For the past five chapters we have examined financial accounting principles as they apply to service businesses. We now turn our attention to merchandising businesses. This type of business generates revenue by purchasing goods (called inventory) and selling the products to customers. The difference between the selling price of an item and its cost is called the gross margin or gross profit. The term "gross" is used because the formula does not take into consideration the operating expenses of the period. Operating expenses are deducted from the gross margin to determine the net income, as follows (see Exhibit 6-1 in the text):

Sales - Cost of Goods Sold = Gross Margin

Gross Margin - Operating Expenses = Net Income

The cost of goods sold model is a term used to describe the relationship between inventories at the beginning and end of each accounting period and the net additions to inventory during the period. The model describes the following relationships:

Goods Available for Sale = Beginning Inventory + Net purchases

Cost of Goods Sold = Goods Available for Sale - Ending Inventory

(Helpful hint: review Exhibits 6-2 and 6-3 in the text.)

A merchandiser cannot run out of inventory, so a crucial question is "How much inventory should I keep on hand?" Managers use both a cost of goods sold budget and an ending inventory budget to accurately assess the business's inventory needs.

Two of the topics that need to be addressed for merchandising businesses are related to inventory: specifically, how many units of inventory are on hand, and what is the cost of each of those units?

Quantity on hand is determined by a physical count of all the items of inventory the business owns. Determining unit cost, however, can be more complicated.

Objective 1 - Account for inventory transactions

The two main types of inventory accounting systems are the periodic system and the perpetual system. Both systems require a physical count prior to the preparation of the annual financial statements. However, only the perpetual system maintains a running record of the quantities on hand.

When inventory is acquired, the following transaction is recorded under the perpetual system:

Inventory	XX	
Accounts Payable		XX

If the business incurs a freight charge to acquire the goods, the cost of freight is also included in the debit to the Inventory account. When the business returns inventory to the vendor (called a purchase return and allowance), the entry is

Accounts Payable	XX	
Inventory		XX

Similarly, if the business earns a discount (called a purchase discount) when paying for the inventory, the entry is

Accounts Payable	XX (for the amount of the invoice)	
Inventory		XX (the amount of the discount)
Cash		XX (the amount of the cheque)

Combining the above entries means the Inventory account contains a balance representing the total net cost of the goods acquired for resale. If the Inventory account is to maintain a running balance of items on hand it must be updated when a sale is recorded. This requires two entries for each sale. The first entry records the sale, as follows:

Accounts Receivable	XXX	
Sales		XXX

The amounts of the debit and credit reflect the actual selling price of the items. The second entry updates the Inventory account, as follows:

Cost of Goods Sold	XXX	
Inventory		XXX

This entry is based on the cost of the items sold (using one of the costing methods discussed in Objective 2 below). Doing so updates the Inventory account so the balance in the account at any time represents the cost of the actual quantities on hand. Of course, the only way to verify the accuracy of the balance is to take a physical inventory. This is an important control feature because it will highlight any differences between what should be on hand and what is actually on hand.

Because inventory is the lifeblood of a merchandising business (and for many companies the largest current asset on the balance sheet), effective internal control procedures are as follows:

a. physical counts at least annually
b. efficient purchasing, receiving, and shipping policies
c. protection from theft and loss of value
d. limited access
e. other effective policies to properly manage inventory

Objective 2 – Analyze the various inventory methods

Inventories are initially recorded at historical cost. Inventory cost is what the business pays to acquire the inventory. Inventory cost includes the invoice cost of the goods, less purchase discounts, plus taxes, tariffs, transportation, and insurance while in transit.

Determining unit costs is easy when costs remain constant. But prices frequently change. GAAP allows four different methods of assigning costs to each inventory item that is sold: 1) **specific unit cost**, 2) **weighted-average cost**, 3) **first-in, first-out (FIFO)**, and 4) **last-in, first-out (LIFO)**.

Specific unit costing (also called the **specific identification method**) is used by businesses whose inventory items are expensive or have "one of a kind" characteristics—such as automobiles, jewelry, and real estate. Using specific unit cost to determine ending inventory is not practical for many businesses. When this is the case, the accountant has to make an assumption concerning the flow of costs through the inventory. Why is an assumption necessary? Because the actual (that is, specific) unit cost of each item cannot be determined.

The three cost flow assumptions are **weighted-average, FIFO,** and **LIFO**.

The **weighted-average cost** method is based on the average cost of all inventory items available for sale during the period. The weighted-average cost method requires the following computation:

$$\text{Average Unit Cost} = \frac{\text{Cost of Goods Available for Sale}}{\text{Number of Units Available for Sale}}$$

Cost of Goods Available for Sale = Beginning Inventory + Net Purchases
Ending Inventory = Number of Units Remaining × Average Unit Cost
Cost of Goods Sold = Cost of Goods Available for Sale - Ending Inventory

Under the **first-in, first-out (FIFO)** method, the first costs into inventory are the first costs out to cost of goods sold. Therefore, ending inventory reflects unit costs most recently incurred. If beginning inventory is 10 units at $4 each, 60 units were bought at $5 each, 80 more units were bought at $6 each, and there are 50 units left, the 50 remaining units would be assigned the $6 unit cost. Ending inventory would be $300.

Under the **last-in, first-out (LIFO)** method, the last costs into inventory are the first costs out to cost of goods sold. Ending inventory is based on the oldest inventory unit costs. If beginning inventory is again 10 units at $4 each, 60 units were bought at $5 each, 80 more units were bought at $6 each, and there are 50 units left, 10 of the remaining units would be assigned the $4 unit cost and 40 would be assigned the $5 unit cost. Ending inventory would be $240 [(10 × $4) + (40 × $5)]. (Helpful hint: review Exhibit 6-7 in your text.)

Objective 3 - Identify the income tax effects of the inventory methods

Review Exhibit 6-7 in your text to be sure that you understand the income effects of the FIFO, LIFO, and weighted-average cost inventory methods.

When inventory costs are increasing:

	FIFO	Weighted-Average Cost	LIFO
Ending Inventory	Highest	Middle	Lowest
Cost of Goods Sold	Lowest	Middle	Highest
Gross Margin	Highest	Middle	Lowest

When inventory costs are decreasing:

	FIFO	Weighted-Average Cost	LIFO
Ending Inventory	Lowest	Middle	Highest
Cost of Goods Sold	Highest	Middle	Lowest
Gross Margin	Lowest	Middle	Highest

In the United States, using LIFO to account for inventories has tax advantages when inventory costs are increasing. This is because using LIFO increases cost of goods sold, and thus decreases gross margin and operating income. If operating income is smaller, total tax payments will be smaller. LIFO matches the most recent inventory costs (last into inventory, first out to cost of goods sold) to revenue, but can result in absurd valuations of ending inventory on the balance sheet. The FIFO method presents an accurate ending inventory on the balance sheet, but does not match current costs of inventory to revenue since the current cost of inventory remains in ending inventory.

The Canadian *Income Tax Act* and its Regulations do not permit LIFO to be used for tax purposes. For this reason, almost no companies in Canada use LIFO for reporting purposes.

Different companies use different inventory methods to achieve a desired result. Notes to the financial statements disclose inventory accounting policies and may also report an alternative inventory amount. For example, if inventories are reported using LIFO in the financial statements, a firm may report inventories using FIFO in the notes to the financial statements. When this is done, substitute the FIFO amounts in place of the LIFO amounts for beginning and ending inventories to convert LIFO cost of goods sold to FIFO cost of goods sold. Note that net purchases will be the same for both methods.

LIFO vs. FIFO—some additional considerations:

a. Because LIFO results in the most recent costs reported on the income statement (as cost of goods sold), it presents the most recent cost/revenue relationship.

b. Because FIFO uses the most recent costs as ending inventory, it presents the most recent value for the asset on the balance sheet.
c. During periods of rising prices, FIFO results in inventory profits because the cost to replace a unit sold has risen.
d. Companies using LIFO can manage the income statement by timing inventory purchases at the end of the accounting period.
e. LIFO liquidation results when inventory quantities fall below the level of the previous period. If inventory costs are rising, the effect of LIFO liquidation is to shift lower cost units to cost of goods sold, resulting in higher net income.
f. FIFO and weighted-average are universally accepted, whereas many countries do not permit LIFO valuations.

Three accounting concepts or principles directly impact merchandise inventory. The **consistency principle** states that the cost flow assumption used should be followed over time. The **disclosure principle** requires companies to tell the readers of the financial statements all information that would assist in making knowledgeable decisions about the company. Finally, **conservatism** dictates that changes to historical cost as the basis for inventory values cannot be made when the value of the asset has risen. At the same time, a lower value can be used in certain circumstances.

The **lower-of-cost-or-market** rule (LCM) is a direct application of conservatism. Conservatism means that assets and income figures should not be overstated. Because the cost principle states that assets should be recorded at historical cost, the book value of assets is not reported at amounts higher than historical cost, even if the value of the asset has increased.

Conservatism also directs accountants to decrease the reported value of assets that appear overvalued. The LCM rule requires that assets be reported on the financial statements at the lower of (1) historical cost or (2) market value (replacement cost, net realizable value, or net realizable value less a normal profit margin). Thus, if inventory market value decreases below its historical cost, it should be written down to its market value. If ending inventory is written down, then cost of goods sold absorbs the impact of the write down. (Helpful hint: review Exhibit 6-9 in the text.)

Once the value of inventory is written down to market, it is not written back up even if the market value subsequently increases.

Study Tip: When LCM is applied, the effect will always reduce asset value (on the balance sheet) and net income (on the income statement).

Objective 4 – Use the gross profit percentage and inventory turnover to evaluate a business

A key measure of profitability for a merchandiser is the **gross margin percentage**.

$$\text{Gross Margin Percentage} = \frac{\text{Gross Margin}}{\text{Net Sales Revenues}}$$

Inventory turnover is a measure of the number of times a company sells its average level of inventory during a year.

$$\text{Inventory Turnover} = \frac{\text{Cost of Goods Sold}}{\text{Average Inventory}}$$

$$\text{Average inventory} = \frac{\text{Beginning Inventory} + \text{Ending Inventory}}{2}$$

Objective 5 - Estimate inventory by the gross margin method and the retail method

When a company wants an estimate of ending inventory, the **gross margin method** will calculate the amount quickly.

The gross margin (gross profit) method uses the historical gross margin rate to estimate cost of goods sold. Cost of goods sold is then subtracted from cost of goods available for sale to arrive at estimated ending inventory.

$$\text{Gross Margin Rate} = \frac{\text{Gross Margin}}{\text{Net Sales Revenue}}$$

To use the gross margin method, it is necessary to rearrange ending inventory and cost of goods sold in the cost of goods sold equation as follows:

> Beginning Inventory
> + Net Purchases
> = Cost of Goods Available for Sale
> - Cost of Goods Sold
> = Ending Inventory

Cost of goods sold will equal net sales minus the estimated gross margin (sales × gross margin rate) as illustrated in Exhibit 6-14 in your text.

Inventory transactions appear in the operating activities section of the cash flow statement. Inventory results in an inflow of cash when goods are sold and customers pay their bills. Cash outflows result when the business buys additional inventory and pays for the goods.

The **retail method** uses a two-step approach to estimate inventory:

(1) net sales are deducted from their retail value
(2) this estimated retail value is multiplied by the cost-to-retail ratio

Objective 6 - Show how inventory errors affect cost of goods sold and income

If the value of ending inventory is misstated, then cost of goods sold and net income will be misstated. Since the ending inventory for the current period becomes the beginning inventory for the next period, the errors will offset each other and total gross margin and net income for the two periods will be correct. Nevertheless, gross margin and net income for the individual periods will be misstated.

If ending inventory is overstated, then cost of goods sold is understated and net income is overstated. If ending inventory is understated, then cost of goods sold is overstated and net income is understated.

Study Exhibits 6-15 and 6-16 in your text carefully to familiarize yourself with the effect of inventory errors on 1) ending inventory, 2) cost of goods sold, and 3) net income.

APPENDIX TO CHAPTER 6

Accounting for Inventory in the Periodic System

Unlike the perpetual system, a periodic system does not keep a continuous record of inventory on hand. Therefore, the business takes a physical count of the inventory on hand at the end of the period and applies unit costs to the inventory to determine the cost of the ending inventory.

When inventory is acquired under the periodic system, the following entry is recorded:

Purchases	XX	
Accounts Payable		XX

Note that the Inventory account is not affected by this transaction. All additions of inventory are debited into the Purchases account. As a result, the Inventory account, containing the beginning inventory value, remains unchanged throughout the accounting period. At the end of the accounting period, the Inventory account needs to be updated to reflect the ending inventory value. This is accomplished with a dual adjusting entry, as follows:

Cost of Goods Sold	XX	
Inventory		XX
To transfer beginning inventory to Cost of Goods Sold		

Inventory	XX	
Cost of Goods Sold		XX
To establish the ending inventory		

In addition, the Purchases account will also be transferred to the Cost of Goods Sold account, as follows:

Cost of Goods Sold	XX	
Purchases		XX

After these entries have been recorded, the balance in the Cost of Goods Sold account will equal beginning inventory + purchases – ending inventory.

TEST YOURSELF

All the self-testing materials in this chapter focus on information and procedures that your instructor is likely to test in quizzes and examinations.

I. Matching *Match each numbered term with its lettered definition.*

_____ 1. purchase discount
_____ 2. inventory turnover
_____ 3. consistency principle
_____ 4. inventory cost
_____ 5. gross margin percentage
_____ 6. inventory
_____ 7. specific unit cost method
_____ 8. first-in, first-out (FIFO)
_____ 9. lower-of-cost-or-market rule
_____ 10. gross margin method

_____ 11. weighted-average cost method
_____ 12. last-in, first-out (LIFO)
_____ 13. periodic inventory system
_____ 14. perpetual inventory system
_____ 15. conservatism
_____ 16. purchase returns and allowances
_____ 17. net purchases
_____ 18. sales returns and allowances
_____ 19. disclosure principle
_____ 20. net sales

A. an inventory costing method in which the first costs into inventory are the first costs out to cost of goods sold
B. requires businesses to use the same accounting principles from period to period
C. a calculation indicating how quickly inventory is sold
D. a way to estimate inventory based on the cost of goods sold model: Beginning Inventory + Net Purchases = Cost of Goods Available for Sale. Cost of Goods Available for Sale - Cost of Goods Sold = Ending Inventory
E. the merchandise that a company holds with the intent to sell to customers
F. all costs incurred to make the goods ready for sale
G. requires that an asset be reported in the financial statements at the lower of its historical cost or its market value
H. an inventory system in which the business does not keep a continuous record of the inventory on hand
I. an inventory system in which the business keeps a continuous record for each inventory item to show the inventory on hand at all times
J. an inventory costing method based on the average cost of inventory during the period
K. a reduction in the cost of inventory that is offered by the seller as an incentive for the customers to pay promptly
L. an inventory costing method in which the last costs into inventory are the first costs out to cost of goods sold
M. an inventory costing method based on the cost of particular units of inventory
N. equals gross margin divided by net sales revenue
O. an accounting concept by which assets, revenues, and gains are not overstated and liabilities, expenses, and losses are not understated
P. sales less sales returns and allowances less sales discounts
Q. requires companies to inform others of the methods used to value inventory
R. a decrease in the seller's revenue because the buyer returned merchandise or the seller granted a reduction in the amount the customer owes
S. purchases less purchase discounts less purchase returns and allowances
T. a decrease in the cost of purchases because goods were sent back to the seller or the seller granted the buyer a reduction in the amount owed

II. Multiple Choice *Circle the best answer.*

1. To determine the inventory count, a business will count all merchandise that

   A. is physically present
   B. the business owns
   C. is physically present plus merchandise shipped to customers
   D. is physically present plus merchandise being shipped to the business

2. A diamond jeweler will value inventory using which method?

   A. weighted-average cost
   B. FIFO
   C. LIFO
   D. specific unit cost

3. When prices are increasing, which inventory method will produce the highest ending inventory cost?

   A. weighted-average cost
   B. FIFO
   C. LIFO
   D. cannot be determined

4. When prices are decreasing, which inventory method will produce the lowest cost of goods sold?

   A. weighted-average cost
   B. FIFO
   C. LIFO
   D. cannot be determined

5. Which inventory method reports ending inventory costs on the balance sheet at a value that reflects current cost?

   A. weighted-average cost
   B. FIFO
   C. LIFO
   D. cannot be determined

6. Which of the following can be used to estimate ending inventory?

   A. weighted-average cost
   B. FIFO
   C. LIFO
   D. gross margin

7. When a sale is made, cost of goods sold is debited directly using

   A. only the perpetual inventory system
   B. only the periodic inventory system
   C. only the serial inventory system
   D. both the periodic and perpetual inventory systems

8. Which of the following companies would not be considered a merchandising entity?

   A. a department store
   B. a car dealership
   C. an ice cream shop
   D. an airline

9. To which of the following does the lower-of-cost-or-market rule apply?

   A. disclosure
   B. materiality
   C. conservatism
   D. consistency

10. To calculate the weighted-average unit cost

    A. divide goods available for sale by ending inventory units
    B. divide goods available for sale by total units available for sale
    C. divide cost of goods sold by number of units sold
    D. divide cost of goods sold by number of units available for sale

11. A credit to purchase returns and allowances will

    A. increase inventory
    B. increase net purchases
    C. increase sales
    D. decrease net purchases

12. A company purchases 80 entertainment systems that sell for $250 each. There is a $500 freight charge on the invoice. Assuming the company uses the perpetual inventory system, the journal entry would

    A. debit Inventory $20,000
    B. credit Accounts Payable $20,000
    C. debit Inventory $20,500
    D. credit Cash $10,000

Use the following information for questions 13 and 14:

Beginning Inventory	10 units	@ $3	$30
Purchase	20 units	@ $5	$100
Sold	5 units	@ $12	$60
Purchase	10 units	@ $6	$60
Sold	10 units	@ $12	$120

13. Determine the ending inventory using LIFO and a periodic inventory system.

   A. $135
   B. $105
   C. $85
   D. $65

14. Determine the ending inventory using FIFO and a periodic inventory system.

   A. $85
   B. $105
   C. $65
   D. $135

15. Gross margin plus cost of goods sold equals

   A. net income
   B. cost of goods available for sale
   C. net sales
   D. operating income

III. Completion   *Complete each of the following statements.*

1. The largest current asset for most retailers is _____.

2. The largest single expense for most merchandisers is _____.

3. The inventory system that maintains continuous records of items in the inventory is called _____

   _____.

4. Which inventory system(s) require(s) a physical count of inventory? _____.

5. LIFO liquidation refers to _____.

6. The lower-of-cost-or-market rule for inventory is an example of the_____

   principle.

7. During periods of rising prices, _____results in the highest cost of goods sold.

8. The _____ensures that companies report enough information for outsiders to make

   informed and knowledgeable decisions about a business.

9. During periods of falling prices, _____results in the highest value for ending

   inventory.

10. The _____ and the _____ method can be used to estimate inventory.

11. A company debits the Purchases account when goods are acquired. It is using a _____ inventory system.

12. Sales minus cost of goods sold is called _____.

13. A company credits the Inventory account when merchandise is sold. It is using a _____ _____ inventory system.

14. The gross margin percentage is calculated as follows: _____

15. Inventory turnover is calculated by _____.

IV. True/False *For each of the following statements, circle* T *for true or* F *for false.*

1. T F The accounts Inventory and Cost of Goods Sold are used throughout the year in the periodic inventory system.
2. T F Cash discounts are used to delay payment to suppliers.
3. T F The calculation for cost of goods sold is beginning inventory plus net purchases less ending inventory.
4. T F The gross margin rate is determined by dividing gross profit by cost of goods sold.
5. T F The cash discount term "2/10, net 30" means the buyer has until the 10th day of the following month to earn the discount.
6. T F Inventory-related transactions appear in the investing activities section of the cash flow statement.
7. T F A high rate of inventory turnover is preferable to a low rate of inventory turnover.
8. T F An error in ending inventory will cause errors in both the current income statement and the next period's income statement.
9. T F When inventory costs are rising, LIFO results in the highest value for ending inventory.
10. T F LIFO liquidations occur when units on hand fall below the number of units in the beginning inventory.
11. T F LIFO reports the most realistic value for inventory on the balance sheet.
12. T F The specific cost method is an appropriate one for a large grocery store.
13. T F The conservatism principle is the basis for the lower-of-cost-or-market rule.
14. T F The retail method is used to estimate cost of goods sold without taking a physical inventory count.
15. T F The weighted-average method divides cost of goods available for sale by units of inventory available.

V. Exercises

1. The following information is given for Jane's Beach Shoes for the month of March. Jane uses a periodic inventory system.

		Pairs of shoes	Unit Cost
March 1	Inventory	900	$40
March 7	Purchase	1,000	44
March 13	Purchase	1,400	48
March 22	Purchase	1,400	50
March 29	Purchase	400	46

During the month, 3,500 pairs of shoes were sold.

A. How many shoes should be in inventory at the end of March?

B. Using the weighted-average cost method, what are the cost of ending inventory and cost of goods sold?

C. Using the FIFO method, what are the cost of ending inventory and cost of goods sold?

D. Using the LIFO method, what are the cost of ending inventory and cost of goods sold?

2. The Beckham Co.'s inventory was destroyed by a fire. The company's records show net sales of $1,420,000, beginning inventory of $160,000, net purchase of $800,000, and a gross margin rate of 50%. What is the estimated value of ending inventory?

3. Assume the following:

	2004	2005	2006
Beginning Inventory	$ 8,000	$15,000	$12,000
Net Purchases	45,000	50,000	55,000
Goods Available for Sale	53,000	65,000	67,000
Ending Inventory	15,000	12,000	8,000
Cost of Goods Sold	38,000	53,000	59,000

You discover the following errors:
   a. Ending inventory in 2004 was overstated by $6,000.
   b. Ending inventory in 2005 was understated by $4,000.

Considering these errors, recalculate cost of goods sold for all three years.

4. The following information is available for Lasky Co. for 2006:

Beginning Inventory	$ 4,000
Ending Inventory	2,400
Operating Expenses	3,150
Cost of Goods Sold	19,225
Sales Discounts	360
Sales	28,610
Sales Returns and Allowances	205

Required:

a. What is net sales for 2006?

b. What is gross margin for 2006?

c. What is net income for 2006?

d. What is the gross margin percentage?

e. What is the inventory turnover?

5. The following information is given for Will's Wraps for 2006:

Beginning Inventory	$ 12,250
Gross Margin	7,500
Operating Expenses	3,100
Purchase Returns and Allowances	600
Purchase Discounts	550
Purchases	39,250
Sales Discounts	500
Sales	51,500
Sales Returns and Allowances	1,700

Required

a. Compute net sales.

b. Compute net purchases.

c. Compute cost of goods sold.

d. Compute ending inventory.

e. Compute net income.

f. What is the inventory turnover?

g. What is the gross margin percentage?

VI. Critical Thinking

1. Re-examine the facts presented in Exercise 1. A physical count was taken, and ending inventory was determined to be 1,500 pairs. In re-checking the sales, you verify that 3,500 pairs were sold. How would you explain the 100 pair difference (1,600 pairs you expected to be on hand less the actual count of 1,500 pairs), and how would you "account" for it?

2. Do you think it is a problem for investors trying to interpret the financial statements of companies using different inventory methods?

DEMONSTRATION PROBLEMS

Demonstration Problem #1

Andrew's Appliances has the following records relating to its May 2006 inventory:

Date	Item	Quantity (units)	Unit Cost	Sale price
May 1	Beginning inventory	25	10	—
May 3	Purchase	40	11	—
May 9	Sale	45	—	18
May 11	Purchase	50	13	—
May 18	Sale	30	—	21
May 22	Purchase	20	14	—
May 28	Sale	30	—	25

Company accounting records indicate that the related operating expense for the month of May was $960.

Required:

1. Assume that Andrew's Appliances uses a periodic inventory system and a FIFO cost flow assumption. Record the May 3 through May 28 transactions (omit explanations).

2. Assume Andrew's Appliances uses a perpetual inventory system and a FIFO cost flow assumption. Record the May 3 through May 28 transactions (omit explanations).

Requirement 1 (Periodic Inventory System)

Date	Accounts and Explanation	PR	Debit	Credit

Requirement 2 (Perpetual Inventory System)

Date	Accounts and Explanation	PR	Debit	Credit

Demonstration Problem #2

1. Refer to the information in Demonstration Problem #1. Assuming Andrew's Appliances uses a periodic system, complete the income statement columns below. (Round income statement figures to whole dollar amounts.)

Andrew's Appliances

Income Statement

For the Month Ended May 31, 2006

	LIFO	FIFO	Weighted-Average
Sales revenue			
Cost of goods sold:			
Beginning inventory			
Net purchases			
Cost of goods available for sale			
Ending inventory			
Cost of goods sold			
Gross margin			
Operating expenses			
Operating income (loss)			

2. Refer to Demonstration Problem #1 and assume the same facts in the problem *except* the company uses the perpetual inventory system. Complete the income statement below, through operating income. (Round income statement figures to whole dollar amounts.)

Andrew's Appliances

Income Statement

For the Month Ended May 31, 2006

	LIFO	FIFO	Weighted-Average
Sales revenue			
Cost of goods sold			
Gross margin			
Operating expenses			
Operating income (loss)			

(Helpful hint: Before starting, think carefully about which income statement figures will change as a result of using the perpetual inventory system rather than the periodic inventory system. Those amounts that do not change can simply be transferred from your solution in Requirement #1.)

SOLUTIONS

A. TEST YOURSELF

I. Matching

1. K	5. N	9. G	13. H	17. S
2. C	6. E	10. D	14. I	18. R
3. B	7. M	11. J	15. O	19. Q
4. F	8. A	12. L	16. T	20. P

II. Multiple Choice

1. B   Answers A, C, and D do not include all of the inventory that the business owns.

2. D   Specific unit cost is appropriate for inventory items that can be identified individually, such as automobiles, jewels, and real estate.

3. B   To obtain the highest ending inventory when prices are increasing, it is necessary to have the most recent inventory costs on the balance sheet. The FIFO method accomplishes this.

4. C   To obtain the lowest cost of goods sold when prices are decreasing, it is necessary to have the newest inventory costs on the income statement. The LIFO method accomplishes this.

5. B   LIFO assigns the most recent inventory costs to the income statement and older inventory cost to the balance sheet. FIFO, on the other hand, assigns the most recent inventory costs to the balance sheet and older inventory costs to the income statement.

6. D   Of the items listed, only gross margin is an estimation technique. FIFO, LIFO, and weighted-average cost are techniques for establishing actual ending inventory levels, not estimates.

7. D   Under the periodic inventory system, there is a Cost of Goods Sold general ledger account. It is used at period end to close the opening inventory and total purchases for the period, and to enter the closing inventory. The net amount in the account is the Cost of Goods Sold for the period. Under the perpetual inventory system, Cost of Goods Sold is a general ledger account and the cost of the items sold is debited directly to it throughout the period.

8. D   An airline is a service business; the other three all sell products.

9. C   LCM is an extension of the application of conservatism because it reduces the ending inventory value and therefore net income.

10. B   The unit cost for the weighted-average method is calculated by dividing goods available for sale (beginning inventory + net purchases) by the total units available for sale.

11. D   Purchase Returns and Allowances is contra to the Purchases account. A credit to Purchase Returns and Allowances increases its balance. Since it is contra to Purchases, this will decrease net purchases.

12. C Freight charges are additions to the purchase price of the goods. Entries to record purchases are based on the total price of the merchandise, which includes all related costs.

13. B Ending inventory under FIFO periodic consists of 25 units = (10 @ $3 + 15 @ $5 = $105)

14. D Ending inventory under LIFO periodic consists of 25 units = (10 @ $6 + 15 @ $5 = $135)

15. C You are required to work backwards. Since Net Sales - Cost of Goods Sold = Gross Margin; therefore, Net Sales = Gross Margin + Cost of Goods Sold.

III. Completion

1. merchandise inventory
2. cost of goods sold
3. perpetual
4. Both systems require a physical count. In a perpetual inventory system, this verifies that the inventory listed in the accounting records actually exists.
5. the level of inventory falling below the level from the previous period
6. conservatism (The LCM rule ensures that a business reports its inventory at its replacement cost if that is lower than its original cost. This rule ensures that assets are not overstated and that declines in inventory value are reported on the income statement in the period of the decline.)
7. LIFO (The oldest and therefore lower prices are used to value ending inventory.)
8. disclosure principle
9. LIFO (The oldest and therefore higher prices are used to value ending inventory.)
10. retail method and gross margin method
11. periodic (In a periodic system, Purchases is debited and Cash (or Accounts Payable) is credited.)
12. gross margin or gross profit (The basic income statement formula for a merchandising company is:

       Sales
    - Cost of Goods Sold
    = Gross margin
    - Operating expenses
    = Net income (Net loss)
13. perpetual (Under the perpetual system, all merchandise is debited to the Inventory account when acquired and credited to the Inventory account when sold.)
14. gross margin divided by net sales
15. cost of goods sold divided by average inventory

IV. True/False

1. F Inventory and Cost of Goods Sold accounts are features of a perpetual inventory system, but they are posted to at the end of a period in a periodic inventory system.
2. F Cash discounts are used to ensure prompt payment.
3. T
4. F While gross margin and gross profit are synonymous terms, the denominator in the calculation for the gross margin rate is net sales revenue, not cost of goods sold.
5. F The term "2/10, net 30" means that a 2% discount is available if payment is made within 10 days of the invoice date; otherwise the net amount of the invoice is due in 30 days.
6. F Inventory transactions are operating activities, not investing activities.
7. T
8. T

9. F   With rising costs, FIFO results in the highest value for ending inventory because FIFO assigns the most recent costs (and therefore the highest costs) to ending inventory.
10. T
11. F   LIFO reports old cost amounts for ending inventory because it assigns the most recent costs to cost of goods sold.
12. F   It would be virtually impossible for a grocery store to trace each item on hand (a large grocery store will have thousands of items on hand) with its actual cost.
13. T
14. F   The retail method is used to estimate inventory.
15. T

V. Exercises

1. A.

	Beginning inventory	900
+	Purchases*	4,200
	Shoes available for sale	5,100
-	Shoes sold	3,500
=	Ending inventory	1,600

*Sum of purchases on March 7 (1,000), March 13 (1,400), March 22 (1,400), and March 29 (400).

B.

March 1	900	pairs at	$40	$ 36,000
March 7	1,000		44	44,000
March 13	1,400		48	67,200
March 22	1,400		50	70,000
March 29	400		46	18,400
Goods available	5,100			$235,600

Average unit cost – $235,600 ÷ 5,100 = $46.20 (rounded)
Ending inventory = 1,600 pairs × $46.20 = $73,920

Cost of goods available for sale	$235,600
- Ending inventory	73,920
= Cost of goods sold	$161,680

Note that this is slightly different from 3,500 pairs × $46.20 = $161,700 because of rounding in the average unit cost.

C. Ending inventory will be the last 1,600 pairs purchased.

March 29	400 pairs at $46	$18,400
March 22	1,200 pairs at $50	60,000
	Ending inventory	$78,400

Cost of goods available for sale	$ 235,600
- Ending inventory	78,400
Cost of goods sold	$ 157,200

D. Ending inventory will be the 1,600 pairs that have been in inventory the longest.

Beginning inventory	900 pairs at $40	$36,000
March 7	700 pairs at $44	30,800
Ending inventory		$66,800

Cost of goods available for sale	$235,600
- Ending inventory	- 66,800
Cost of goods sold	$168,800

2.

	Beginning inventory	$160,000
+	Purchases	800,000
	Cost of goods available for sale	960,000
-	Cost of goods sold [$960,000 × (1-0.50)]	480,000
=	Ending inventory	$480,000

3. For 2004, ending inventory decreases to $9,000, so cost of goods sold will increase to $44,000.

For 2005, beginning inventory decreases to $9,000, and ending inventory increases to $16,000, so:

	Beginning inventory	$ 9,000
+	Net purchases	50,000
	Goods available for sale	59,000
-	Ending inventory	16,000
=	Cost of goods sold	$43,000

For 2006, beginning inventory increases to $16,000, so cost of goods sold increases to $63,000.

4. a. Sales - Sales Returns and Allowances - Sales Discount = Net Sales
$28,610 - $205 - $360 = $28,045

b. Net Sales - Cost of Goods Sold = Gross Margin (or Gross Profit)
$28,045 - $19,225 = $8,820

c. Gross Margin - Operating Expenses = Net Income
$8,820 - $3,150 = $5,670

d. Gross Margin ÷ Net Sales
$8,820 ÷ $28,045 = 31.4%

e. Cost of Goods Sold ÷ Average Inventory
Average Inventory = ($4,000 + $2,400) ÷ 2 = $3,200
$19,225 ÷ $3,200 = 6 times

5. a. Sales - Sales Discounts - Sales Returns and Allowances = Net Sales
        $51,500 - $500 - $1,700 = $49,300

    b. Purchases - Purchase Discounts - Purchase Returns and Allowances = Net Purchases
        $39,250 - $550 - $600 = $38,100

    c. Net Sales - Cost of Goods Sold = Gross Margin
        Cost of Goods Sold = $49,300 - $7,500 = $41,800

    d. Beginning Inventory + Net Purchases - Ending Inventory = Cost of Goods Sold
        Therefore, Ending Inventory = Beginning Inventory + Net Purchase - Cost of Goods Sold
        Ending Inventory = $12,250 + $38,100 - $41,800 = $8,550

    e. Gross Margin - Operating Expenses = Net Income
        $7,500 - $3,100 = $4,400

    f. Inventory Turnover = Cost of Goods Sold ÷ Average Inventory
        Average Inventory = ($12,250 + $8,550) ÷ 2 = $10,400
        Inventory Turnover = $41,800 ÷ $10,400 = 4 times

    g. Gross Margin Percentage = Gross Margin ÷ Net sales
        Gross Margin Percentage = $7,500 ÷ $49,300 = 15.2%

VI. Critical Thinking

1. The 100-pair difference is called inventory shrinkage. Since the figure that appears on the balance sheet for ending inventory must represent the actual amount on hand (1,500 pairs), the shrinkage is accounted for by a larger cost of goods sold figure on the income statement. Possible explanations for the shrinkage are errors in the physical count, theft, or errors in recording purchases during the period. Internal control requires that the cause of the difference be investigated and appropriate corrective procedures be taken.

2. Investors must always consider differences in methods of companies, but as long as the companies maintain a consistent method of accounting for inventory, and an investor understands the implications to cost of goods sold and inventory when prices are rising/falling, they should be able to compare and analyze different companies.

DEMONSTRATION PROBLEMS

Demonstration Problem #1 Solved and Explained

Requirement 1 (Periodic Inventory System)

Date	Accounts and Explanation	PR	Debit	Credit
May 3	Purchases		440	
	Accounts Payable			440
May 9	Accounts Receivable		810	
	Sales			810
May 11	Purchases		650	
	Accounts Payable			650
May 18	Accounts Receivable		630	
	Sales			630
May 22	Purchases		280	
	Accounts Payable			280
May 28	Accounts Receivable		750	
	Sales			750

These six journal entries are straightforward. With a periodic system, the Purchases account is debited as merchandise for resale is acquired, but is not affected when goods are sold.

> **Study Tip**: In a periodic system, the cost flow assumption (in this case FIFO) is irrelevant as far as these transactions are concerned. It becomes important only when you need to determine the value of ending inventory.

Requirement 2 (Perpetual Inventory System)

Date	Accounts and Explanation	PR	Debit	Credit
May 3	Inventory		440	
	Accounts Payable			440
May 9	Accounts Receivable		810	
	Sales			810
	Cost of Goods Sold		470	
	Inventory			470
	$[(25 \times \$10) + (20 \times \$11)]$			
May 11	Inventory		650	
	Accounts Payable			650

Date	Accounts and Explanation	PR	Debit	Credit
May 18	Accounts Receivable		630	
	Sales			630
	Cost of Goods Sold		350	
	Inventory			350
	[(20 × $11) + (10 × $13)]			
May 22	Inventory		280	
	Accounts Payable			280
May 28	Accounts Receivable		750	
	Sales			750
	Cost of Goods Sold		390	
	Inventory			390
	(30 × $13)			

In a perpetual system, goods for resale are debited to the Inventory account. When a sale occurs, the entry is identical to those recorded in a periodic system. However, a second entry is required for each sale. This entry transfers the cost of the sale from the Inventory account to a Cost of Goods Sold account. The amount of the entry is determined by the cost flow assumption used. In this problem, FIFO is assumed. Therefore, the cost of each sale is assigned using the oldest costs in the inventory. For instance, the May 9 sale was 45 units. How much did these units cost the business? Assuming FIFO, 25 of the units cost $10 each (these are the units from the beginning inventory, that is, the first units (oldest) in the inventory), and the next 20 units (45–25) cost $11 each (the purchase on May 3). This same analysis applies to the May 18 and May 28 sales. The details for each entry are provided following each entry.

Demonstration Problem #2

Requirement 1

Andrew's Appliances
Income Statement
For the Month Ended May 31, 2006

	LIFO		FIFO		Weighted-Average	
Sales revenue		$2,190		$2,190		$2,190
Cost of goods sold:						
Beginning inventory	250		250		250	
Net purchases	1,370		1,370		1,370	
Cost of goods available for sale	1,620		1,620		1,620	
Ending inventory	305		410		360	
Cost of goods sold		1,315		1,210		1,260
Gross margin		875		980		930
Operating expenses		960		960		960
Operating income (loss)		$ (85)		$ 20		$ (30)

Computations:

Sales Revenue:

Sale Date	Quantity	Price	Total
May 9	45	$18	$ 810
May 18	30	21	630
May 28	30	25	750
	105		$2,190

Sales revenue is unaffected by the firm's method of accounting for inventory costs. Quantity × Price = Total.

Beginning inventory: May 1 quantity (25 units) × unit cost ($10) = $250

Purchase Date	Quantity	Price	Total
May 3	40	$11	$ 440
May 11	50	13	650
May 22	20	14	280
	110		$1,370

Computation for beginning inventory, purchases, and goods available for sale are identical under the three methods.

	Beginning inventory in units	25
+	Total May purchases in units	110
	Units available for sale	135
-	Units sold	105
=	Ending inventory in units	30

Valued at LIFO:

Purchase Date	Quantity	Price	Total
Beginning inventory	25	$10	$250
May 3	5	11	55
	30		$305

LIFO attains the best matching of current expense with current revenue. The most recently acquired costs (the last items in) are deemed sold first (the first ones out). Logically, ending inventory should consist of the oldest layers of cost.

Valued at FIFO:

Purchase Date	Quantity	Price	Total
May 22	20	$14	$280
May 11	10	13	130
	30		$410

FIFO reports the ending inventory at its most recent cost. The oldest costs are expensed as cost of goods sold. Note that net income under FIFO is larger than that reported under LIFO. In a period of rising prices, LIFO will generally produce a lower net income. The potential tax savings achieved under a LIFO valuation has made it an increasingly popular valuation method in recent years.

Valued at weighted-average cost:

Purchase Date	Quantity	Price	Total
Beginning inventory	25	$10	$ 250
Purchases in May	110	Various	1,370
	135		$1,620

$1,620 inventory cost / 135 units = $12 per unit

30 ending inventory units × $12 weighted-average cost per unit = $360

The weighted-average cost method reports ending inventory and produces operating income that falls between the results of FIFO and LIFO.

Requirement 2

Andrew's Appliances

Income Statement

For the Month Ended May 31, 2006

	LIFO	FIFO	Weighted-Average
Sales revenue	$2,190	$2,190	$2,190
Cost of goods sold	1,290	1,210	1,234
Gross margin	900	980	956
Operating expenses	960	960	960
Operating income (loss)	$ (60)	$ 20	$ (4)

Computations:

Sales—Same as Demonstration Problem #1.

Cost of Goods Sold—Remember, in a perpetual system cost of goods sold is an account balance, not a calculation. Therefore, to arrive at the correct amount, you have to trace through each purchase and sale to determine which cost figures have been transferred from Inventory to Cost of Goods Sold, as follows:

LIFO:

Date	Quantity	Price		Total
May 9 Sale	40	$11	$440	
	5	10	50	
				$ 490
May 18 Sale	30	13		390
May 28 Sale	20	14	280	
	10	13	130	
				410
		Cost of goods sold, LIFO		$1,290
	20	10	200	
	10	13	130	
		Ending inventory, LIFO		$ 330*

*Note that this amount is not the same as LIFO periodic.

FIFO:

Date	Quantity	Price		Total
May 9 Sale	25	$10	$250	
	20	11	220	
				470
May 18 Sale	20	11	220	
	10	13	130	
				350
May 28 Sale	30	13		390
		Cost of goods sold, FIFO		$1,210
	20	14	280	
	10	13	130	
		Ending inventory, FIFO		$410**

**Note that this is the same as FIFO periodic.

Weighted-average cost—This is even more complicated because it requires you to re-calculate a new average each time there is an addition to inventory (for this reason it is referred to as a moving weighted-average system).

May 9   Sale   25 units at $10 per unit = $250
                               40 units at $11 per unit = 440
                               65                         $690
           Average unit cost = $690 = $10.615 per unit, therefore
                               65
                                        45 units × $10.615 = $477.68

May 18   Sale   20 units at $10.615 per unit = $212.30   (from above)
                               50 units at $13 per unit =   650.00
                               70                              $862.30
           Average unit cost = $862.30 = $12.319 per unit, therefore
                               70
                                        30 units × $12.319 = $369.57

May 28   Sale   40 units at $12.319 per unit $492.76   (from above)
                                      20 units at $14 per unit   =   280.00
                                      60   772.76

          Average unit cost   = $772.76   = $12.879 per unit, therefore
                                        60

                                              30 units × $12.879 = $386.37

                                  Cost of goods sold, weighted-average cost $1,233.62

                                  Ending inventory = 30 units × $12.879 = $386.37***

***Note that this amount is not the same as weighted-average periodic.

CHAPTER 7—CAPITAL ASSETS, NATURAL RESOURCES, AND INTANGIBLE ASSETS

CHAPTER OVERVIEW

Beginning with Chapter 4, you have learned more detail about some assets, specifically cash, receivables, and inventory. In this chapter, we examine long-term assets, both fixed and intangible. The specific learning objectives for the chapter are to

1. **Determine** the cost of a capital asset
2. **Account** for amortization
3. **Select** the best amortization method
4. **Analyze** the effect of a capital asset disposal
5. **Account** for natural resources and amortization
6. **Account** for intangible assets and amortization
7. **Report** capital asset transactions on the cash flow statement

CHAPTER REVIEW

Objective 1 - Determine the cost of a capital asset

Business assets are classified as current or long-lived (long-term) assets. Current assets are considered to be useful for one year or less. Long-lived assets are expected to be useful for longer than a year. Capital assets are long-lived assets such as land and equipment. Capital assets are tangible; that is, they have physical form and are typically called property, plant, and equipment on the balance sheet. There is also a class of long-lived assets called intangible assets that do not have any physical form, but have a special right to current and expected future benefits, such as goodwill.

The cost of a capital asset is the purchase price plus any other amount paid to acquire it and all costs incurred to bring the asset to its intended use, sometimes referred to as the "ready for use" rule.

Recent changes in the *CICA Handbook* require non-monetary long-lived assets, such as property, plant, and equipment, intangible assets with finite useful lives, such as trademarks, and certain other assets to be written down to their fair value if the assets carrying value exceeds its fair value.

The **cost of land** includes the purchase price, brokerage commission, survey fees, legal fees, transfer taxes, back property taxes, costs to grade or clear the land, and costs to demolish or remove any unwanted buildings or other structures. The costs of fencing, paving, and lighting is separated as *land improvements* and are subject to amortization.

The same standard is used to determine the **cost of constructing a building**, namely all costs are included that are necessary to prepare the asset for its intended use. In addition to the actual construction costs, you also include professional fees, permits, and other necessary charges.

The **cost of an existing building** includes the purchase price, brokerage commission, taxes, and any expenditure to repair or renovate the building to make it ready for use.

The **cost of machinery and equipment** includes the purchase price less any discounts, plus transportation charges, transportation insurance, commissions, and installation costs.

When a company purchases a group of assets for one single amount (also known as a **lump-sum purchase** or a **basket purchase**), the total cost of the assets is allocated to individual assets by the relative-sales-value method. To use the **relative-sales-value method**, it is necessary to

1. Determine the market value of each asset by appraisal of the assets.
2. Add the individual asset market values to obtain the total market value of all assets that have been acquired.
3. Calculate a ratio of the market value of each individual asset to the total market value of all assets (item 1 divided by item 2).
4. Multiply the ratio for each asset (from item 3) by the total purchase price paid for the assets. The resulting amounts will be considered the cost of each of the assets in the basket purchase.

Capital expenditures are expenditures that significantly affect an asset by 1) increasing the asset's productive capacity, 2) increasing the asset's efficiency, or 3) extending the asset's useful life. Capital expenditures are debited to an asset account:

Asset	XX	
Cash		XX

Repairs are expenditures that maintain the existing condition of an asset or restore an asset to good working order. Repairs are debited to an expense account:

Expense Account	XX	
Cash		XX

Many of the expenditures related to capital assets are repairs to the assets. **Extraordinary repairs** are capital expenditures, while ordinary repairs are repairs expenses.

Amortization is the process of allocating a capital asset's cost to expense over the useful life of the asset. Note that amortization is based on an asset's cost, and that amortization is not in any way related to cash. A contra account called Accumulated Amortization is used to record the total amount of a capital asset's cost that has been recorded as amortization expense. The adjusting journal entry to record amortization is:

Amortization Expense	XX	
Accumulated Amortization		XX

To measure amortization, it is necessary to determine the capital asset's cost, estimated useful life, and estimated residual value (salvage value or scrap value).

Estimated useful life is the length of service a business expects from the capital asset. Useful life may be expressed as a length of time, units of output, or other measures. For example, a computer may be expected to be useful for four years, while a printing press might be expected to print one billion sheets of paper over its useful life. Note that the useful life of an asset is an estimate of the usefulness of an asset and is not necessarily related to the physical life. For example, an asset such as a computer may become obsolete (not economically useful) long before it physically deteriorates. Assets can be amortized also because of physical wear and tear.

Estimated residual value is the expected cash value of an asset at the end of its useful life. It is also called scrap or salvage value.

The **amortizable cost** of an asset is its cost minus residual value.

Objective 2 - Account for amortization

1. The **straight-line (SL) amortization method** allocates the amortizable cost of a capital asset to amortization expense in equal amounts per period over the life of the asset. The formula for straight-line amortization is:

$$\text{Amortization expense} = \frac{\text{Cost - Residual value}}{\text{Useful life}}$$

Recall that the adjusting entry to record amortization expense is:

```
Amortization Expense          XX
     Accumulated Amortization       XX
```

As accumulated amortization increases each year, the remaining **book value of the asset** (cost - accumulated amortization) declines. The final book value of an asset will be its residual value. (Helpful hint: see Exhibit 7-5 in the text.)

2. The **units-of-production (UOP) amortization method** allocates the cost of an asset to amortization expense based on the output that the asset is expected to produce. The formula for units-of-production amortization is:

$$\text{UOP amortization per unit of output} = \frac{\text{Cost - Residual value}}{\text{Useful life in units}}$$

With UOP, the total amortization expense in a period is:

Amortization expense = UOP amortization per unit of output × units of output in the period

While the straight-line method could be used for any capital asset, the UOP method is not appropriate for all assets. Rather, it is used for assets where the life is a function of use rather than time (for example, an airplane where flying hours is a more accurate measure of life compared to years). (Helpful hint: review Exhibit 7-6 in the text.)

3. The **double-declining-balance (DDB) method** is an accelerated amortization method. **Accelerated amortization** simply means that a larger portion of an asset's cost is allocated to amortization expense in the early years of an asset's life, and a smaller portion is allocated to amortization expense toward the end of the asset's useful life.

To compute double-declining-balance amortization:

a. Compute the straight-line amortization rate per year:

(1/Useful life in years) = X%

b. Multiply the straight-line amortization rate per year by 2 (double it) to obtain the double-declining-balance rate:

DDB rate = (1/Useful life in years) × 2

c. Multiply the asset's beginning book value for a period (remember that book value equals cost minus accumulated amortization) by the DDB rate. Book value will decrease each period, therefore amortization expense will decrease each period. Note that the residual value of the asset is ignored until the net book value of the asset approaches the asset's residual value.

Amortization expense = DDB rate × book value

d. When the net book value of the asset approaches the asset's residual value, adjust the year's amortization so that the remaining book value of the asset is equal to the residual value. The final year's amortization amount will be equal to:

Book value at the beginning of the year - Residual value

Amortization is no longer recorded after the book value of the asset is reduced to its residual value, even if the asset is still in use.

Study Exhibit 7-7 in your text to familiarize yourself with the double-declining-balance method.

Some important points to remember:

1. You never amortize below the estimated salvage value.
2. Units-of-production ignores time.
3. Double-declining-balance ignores salvage value initially.
4. Double-declining-balance uses book value, while the other methods use amortizable cost.

Study Tip: The method used does not determine the total amount of the asset's cost to recognize as amortization expense over the asset's life. Rather, the method determines the amount of the total to allocate each accounting period. Regardless of method, accumulated amortization will be the same when the asset is fully amortized.

Exhibit 7-8 summarizes the three methods of amortization patterns.

Objective 3 - Select the best amortization method

The Canada Revenue Agency (CRA) allows taxpayers to deduct Capital Cost Allowance (CCA), the term the CRA uses to describe amortization for tax purposes, from business income. The CCA rates published by the CRA are maximums allowed. The taxpayer may claim any amount from zero to the maximum capital cost allowance for the year. Taxpayers usually claim the maximum allowable, thus decreasing immediate tax payments. The cash available to the business increases because the tax payment is reduced.

Review Exhibit 7-10 in your text to see how accelerated amortization reduces taxes and increases the cash balance of a business.

If a capital asset is held for only part of the year, **partial year amortization** is computed by multiplying the full year's amortization by the fraction of the year that the asset is held.

If a company finds that a **change** is warranted in its estimate of a capital asset's useful life, it computes revised annual amortization as follows:

$$\frac{\text{Book value - Residual value}}{\text{Remaining life}}$$

If an asset becomes **fully amortized** (i.e., book value = residual value) but remains in use, both the asset and contra asset account should remain in the ledger until the business disposes of the asset, without further amortization.

Objective 4 - Analyze the effect of a capital asset disposal

With the possible exception of land, eventually a capital asset will no longer serve the needs of the business. The business will generally dispose of the asset by junking it, selling it, or exchanging it. The simplest accounting entry occurs when a company junks an asset. If the asset is fully amortized with no residual value, the entry to record its disposal is

Accumulated Amortization—Asset	XX	
Asset		XX

If the asset is not fully amortized, a loss is recorded for the remaining book value:

Accumulated Amortization —Asset	XX	
Loss on Disposal of Asset	XX	
Asset		XX

These entries have the effect of removing the asset from the books.

When an asset is sold, the first step is to update amortization for the partial year of service. Amortization is recorded from the beginning of the accounting period to the date of the sale:

Amortization Expense	XX	
Accumulated Amortization —Asset		XX

The second step is to compute the remaining book value:

Book Value = Cost - Accumulated Amortization

If the cash received is greater than the remaining book value, a gain is recorded:

Cash	XX	
Accumulated Amortization —Asset	XX	
Asset		XX
Gain on Sale of Asset		XX

If the cash received is less than the remaining book value, a loss is recorded:

Cash	XX	
Loss on Sale of Asset	XX	
Accumulated Amortization —Asset	XX	
Asset		XX

Note that gains will increase income and losses will decrease income. Therefore, both gains and losses are listed on the income statement.

When capital assets are **exchanged or traded in**, the balance for the old asset must be removed from the books and the replacement asset must be recorded. No gain or loss is recognized on an exchange.

New Asset	XX	
Accumulated Amortization (old)	XX	
Old Asset		XX
Cash		XX

Objective 5 - Account for natural resources and amortization

Amortization expense is that portion of the cost of **natural resources** used up (depleted) in a particular period. It is computed in the same way as UOP amortization (refer to Objective 2 for the UOP formula). The appropriate entry is

Amortization Expense	XX	
Accumulated Amortization		XX

Objective 6 - Account for intangible assets and amortization

Intangible assets are assets that have no physical substance. Examples include patents, copyrights, trademarks, franchises, leaseholds, and goodwill. The cost of intangible assets is expensed through **amortization** over the asset's useful life unless the asset is determined to have an indefinite life (for example, goodwill).

The acquisition cost of an intangible asset is recorded as follows:

Intangible Asset	XX	
Cash		XX

Amortization is usually computed on a straight-line basis. Amortization is recorded as follows:

Amortization Expense	XX	
Intangible Asset		XX

Note that the book value of the intangible asset is reduced directly. There is no Accumulated Amortization account. Additionally, the residual value of most intangible assets is zero. Finally, the useful life of many amortizable assets is much shorter than the legal life of such assets—for example, copyrights.

One important type of intangible asset is **goodwill**. Goodwill is recorded only when another company is acquired. The amount of goodwill, if any, is equal to the difference between the price paid for the acquired company and the market value of the acquired company's net assets (assets - liabilities):

Goodwill = Price Paid - Market Value of Net Assets

If the purchase price paid is less than the market value of the acquired company's net assets, there is no goodwill.

Some intangible assets have indefinite lives. Examples are trademarks, licenses, and goodwill. Because they have indefinite lives, they are not subject to amortization. However, the value of the intangible may decrease over time (impairment test) and therefore the loss in value needs to be recorded as follows:

Loss on Intangible Asset	XX	
Intangible Asset		XX

If the value of an intangible increases, no entry is recorded.

Objective 7 - Report capital asset transactions on the cash flow statement

The cash flow statement will reflect the acquisition of capital assets, the sale of capital assets, and amortization. The purchase or sale of capital assets is an investing activity, whereas amortization is listed in the operating activities section of the cash flow statement. Cash inflows result when capital assets are sold for cash while cash outflows result when capital assets are purchased for cash. Amortization is included in the operating activities section because the expense was listed on the income statement as a deduction to arrive at net income. However, amortization expense does not require a cash payment and therefore needs to be added back to net income to convert it from an accrual-based amount to cash flows from operating activities.

TEST YOURSELF

All the self-testing materials in this chapter focus on information and procedures that your instructor is likely to test in quizzes and examinations.

I. Matching   *Match each numbered term with its lettered definition.*

_____ 1. accelerated amortization
_____ 2. extraordinary repairs
_____ 3. double-declining-balance method
_____ 4. franchises and licenses
_____ 5. estimated residual value
_____ 6. straight-line amortization
_____ 7. amortizable cost
_____ 8. units-of-production method
_____ 9. amortization
_____ 10. copyright

_____ 11. estimated useful life
_____ 12. goodwill
_____ 13. leasehold improvements
_____ 14. capital asset
_____ 15. intangible asset
_____ 16. repairs expenses
_____ 17. patent
_____ 18. trademarks
_____ 19. CCA
_____ 20. capitalize

A. the exclusive right to reproduce and sell a book, musical composition, film, or other work of art
B. a method of amortization for income tax purposes
C. length of service that a business expects to get from an asset

D. an accelerated method of amortization that computes annual amortization by multiplying the asset's decreasing book value by a constant percentage, which is two times the straight-line rate
E. repair work that generates a capital expenditure
F. privileges granted by a private business or a government to sell a product or service in accordance with specified conditions
G. excess of the cost of an acquired company over the sum of the market value of its net assets
H. an asset with no physical form
I. a cost a renter incurs to improve rented facilities
J. costs incurred to maintain an asset
K. a grant from the federal government giving the holder the exclusive right to produce and sell an invention
L. expected cash value at the end of an asset's useful life
M. an amortization method that writes off a relatively large amount of an asset's cost nearer the start of its useful life than does the straight-line method
N. an allocation of cost that applies to tangible or intangible assets
O. long-lived assets that are tangible
P. an amortization method in which an equal amount of amortization expense is assigned to each year (or period) of the asset's use
Q. cost of a capital asset less estimated residual value
R. distinctive identifications of a product or service
S. an amortization method in which a fixed amount of amortization is assigned to each unit of output produced by the capital asset
T. to include a related cost as part of an asset's cost

II. Multiple Choice   *Circle the best answer.*

1. All of the following are intangible assets *except*

    A. computer
    B. patent
    C. leasehold
    D. trademark

2. Which of the following long-lived assets is not amortized?

    A. vehicles
    B. building
    C. machinery
    D. land

3. The cost of equipment includes all of the following *except*

    A. sales tax
    B. repairs that occur one year after installation
    C. freight charges
    D. installation costs

4. Amortization expense for an asset is the same every year. The amortization method is

   A. double-declining-balance
   B. CCA
   C. straight-line
   D. units-of-production

5. An amortization method that is not related to specific periods of time is

   A. double-declining-balance
   B. CCA
   C. straight-line
   D. units-of-production

6. Which of the following amortization methods would you use for amortizing a building?

   A. double-declining-balance
   B. CCA
   C. straight-line
   D. units-of-production

7. Which of the following methods is most closely associated with intangible assets?

   A. double-declining-balance
   B. units-of-production
   C. straight-line
   D. CCA

8. Which amortization method will usually result in the lowest income tax expense in the first year of an asset's life?

   A. double-declining-balance
   B. CCA
   C. straight-line
   D. units-of-production

9. The amortizable cost of an asset equals

   A. cost - sales tax
   B. cost - accumulated amortization
   C. cost - residual value
   D. cost - the current year's amortization expense

10. The book value of a capital asset is equal to

    A. cost - residual value
    B. cost - accumulated amortization
    C. cost - current year's amortization
    D. original cost

11. The cost of repairing a gear on a machine would probably be classified as a(n)

    A. capital expenditure
    B. extraordinary repair expense
    C. intangible asset
    D. repair

12. Which of the following costs should be capitalized?

    A. gas and oil for a delivery van
    B. repainting the interior of a sales office
    C. research and development costs for new products
    D. real estate commission paid to purchase property

Use the following information to answer questions 13 – 15.

Jackson Manufacturing purchased a car for $20,000 with a residual value estimated at $4,000. The car is expected to be used for the next five years and Jackson expects that it will be used to drive 100,000 km in total (25,000 in year 1, 20,000 in each of years 2–4, and 15,000 in year 5).

13. Using the straight-line amortization method, determine the amount of amortization in year 3.

    A. $4,000
    B. $3,200
    C. $4,800
    D. $800

14. Using the units-of-production method, determine the amount of amortization in year 2.

    A. $4,000
    B. $3,200
    C. $4,800
    D. $800

15. Using the double-declining-balance method, determine the amount of amortization in year 2.

    A. $4,000
    B. $3,200
    C. $4,800
    D. $800

III. Completion   *Complete each of the following statements.*

1. Two distinguishing characteristics of capital assets are that they are _____ and

    _____.

2. Amortization is defined as _____.

3. Amortization is a _____ expense.

4. A _____ expenditure increases an asset's capacity or efficiency or extends its useful life.

5. _____ is used for calculating amortization for tax purposes.

6. When two or more assets are purchased in a group, the total cost of the assets is allocated to individual assets by the _____ method.

7. To calculate amortization, you must know the following four items: 1)_____, 2)_____, 3)_____, and 4)_____.

8. Amortization is an example of the _____ principle.

9. The cost of a capital asset minus its estimated residual value is the_____.

10. _____ is an asset that has been fully amortized and reached the end of its useful life.

11. Proceeds from the sale of capital assets are listed in the _____ activities section of the cash flow statement.

12. The most widely used amortization method for financial statements is _____.

13. Amortization expense is listed in the _____ activities section of the cash flow statement.

14. Costs related to capital assets can be classified as either _____ expenditures or _____ expense.

15. _____ is the term used for the amortization of natural resources.

IV. True/False *For each of the following statements, circle* T *for true or* F *for false.*

1. T F Research and development costs are treated as a capital expenditure.
2. T F Accelerated amortization results in a higher book value when capital assets are newer.
3. T F The amount of amortization expense over the life of an asset will be greater if a company uses accelerated amortization.
4. T F Capital costs are debited to assets.
5. T F Repairs are debited to asset accounts.
6. T F Amortizable cost equals cost less accumulated amortization.
7. T F Using accelerated amortization results in increasing amounts of amortization expense as the asset ages.
8. T F Double-declining-balance amortization initially ignores residual value.
9. T F Straight-line amortization is calculated by dividing useful life into amortizable cost.
10. T F Leasehold improvements are amortized over the life of the lease.
11. T F Capital costs provide future benefit to the company.
12. T F Intangible assets are amortized over the lesser of the legal life or the economic life.
13. T F Cash expenditures for capital assets are reported as operating activities on the cash flow statement.
14. T F When calculating amortization based on a revised life estimate, the formula is book value divided by remaining life estimate.
15. T F Residual value, scrap value, and salvage value are synonymous terms.

V. Exercises

1. A company buys Machines 1, 2, and 3 for $150,000. The market values of the machines are $90,000, $36,000, and $66,000, respectively. What cost will be allocated to each machine?

2. Wendy's Weavings purchased equipment for $54,000 on January 4, 2005. The company expects the machine to produce 125,000 units over four years and then expects to sell the machine for $14,000. The company produced 30,000 units the first year and 45,000 units the second year. Compute the amortization expense for 2005 and 2006. Round your answer to the nearest dollar.

	2005	2006
Straight-line	_____	_____
Units-of-production	_____	_____
Double-declining-balance	_____	_____

3. On January 2, 2005, Lexington Landscape purchased used equipment for $48,000. The company expected the equipment to remain in service for five years. The company amortized the equipment on a straight-line basis with a $2,000 salvage value. On June 30, 2007, The company sold the equipment for $23,500. Record the amortization expense for the equipment for the six months ended June 30, 2007, and also record the sale of the equipment.

Date	Account and Explanation	PR	Debit	Credit

4. On August 20, 2006, May Lieu, owner of May's Manufacturing, purchased a new drill press for the business. The new equipment carried an invoice price of $9,700 plus 6% sales tax. In addition, the purchaser was responsible for $460 of freight charges. The sale was subject to 3/15, n/45 discount terms. Upon receipt of the new equipment, May paid $925 to have the press installed and connected. To finance this purchase, May borrowed $11,000 from the bank for 90 days at 10% interest. May paid the invoice within 15 days, earning the 3% discount.

   a. Classify each of the following costs as expenses or capital expenditures:

Cost	Classification
1) $9,700 (equipment)	
2) $582 (sales tax)	
3) $460 (freight)	
4) $291 (discount)	
5) $925 (installation)	
6) $275 (interest on loan)	

   b. Based on your answers from part a above, calculate the fully capitalized cost of the new equipment.

   c. Calculate the 2006 amortization using double-declining-balance, assuming a six-year life with estimated residual value of $1,000.

5. On October 1, 2006, Star Company purchased Wars Company for $10,400,000 cash. The market value of Wars's assets was $16,200,000, and Wars had liabilities of $9,000,000.

   a. Compute the cost of the goodwill purchased by Star Company.

   b. Record the purchase by Star Company.

Date	Account and Explanation	PR	Debit	Credit

6. On January 1, 2004, XYZ Co. purchased equipment for $23,000 with a residual value of $8,000. They expected to use the equipment for five years and use the straight-line method of amortization. On January 1, 2006, the company decided the equipment would be useful for an additional two years beyond the original estimation. They determined the new salvage value would be $4,000 at the end of the new period. Determine the amount of amortization that should be recorded in 2006.

VI. Critical Thinking

1. Evaluate the following statement: "I do not see any problems in paying for next year's budgeted capital expenditures. We have estimated we will need approximately $110,000 for new equipment, and we have more than three times that amount in our amortization reserves (accumulated amortization) at the moment."

2. When analyzing two airlines that each use straight-line amortization, but one amortizes planes over 25 years while the other uses 20 years, what differences and similarities would you encounter?

DEMONSTRATION PROBLEMS

Demonstration Problem #1

On January 1, 2006, Marilyn Pensada purchased three pieces of equipment. Details of the cost, economic life, residual value, and method of amortization are shown below:

Equipment	Cost	Useful Life	Residual Value	Amortization Method
X	$39,000	6 years	$3,000	straight-line
Y	16,000	40,000 units	800	units-of-production
Z	48,000	5 years	10,000	double-declining-balance

Required:

1. Prepare a schedule computing the amortization expense for each piece of equipment over its useful life.
2. Prepare the journal entry to record the disposal of Equipment X. Assume that it has been amortized over its useful life, and that it cannot be sold or exchanged (it is being scrapped).
3. Prepare the journal entry to record the sale of Equipment Y for $1,000. Assume that it has been amortized over its useful life.

Requirement 1 (Schedule of amortization)

	X	Y	Z
Asset cost			
Less: Residual value			
Amortizable cost			

Equipment X
Schedule of Amortization Expense
(Straight-Line Method)

Year	Amortizable Cost	Amortization Rate	Amortization Expense

Equipment Y
Schedule of Amortization Expense
(Units-of-Production Method)

Year	Amortizable Cost	Units Produced	Amortization Expense
		12,400	
		10,750	
		11,230	
		6,100	

Equipment Z
Schedule of Amortization Expense
(Double-Declining-Balance Method)

Year	Book Value × Rate	Amortization Expense	Book Value

Requirement 2 (Journal entry—Equipment X)

Date	Account and Explanation	PR	Debit	Credit

Requirement 3 (Journal entry—Equipment Y)

Date	Account and Explanation	PR	Debit	Credit

Demonstration Problem #2

On June 10, 2001, Clark Catering purchased new kitchen equipment costing $22,500 plus 6% sales tax. The equipment is expected to last eight years and retain an estimated $1,500 residual value. In addition, Clark paid transportation and insurance charges of $410. The equipment arrived on June 21 and required modification of the existing electrical system. An electrician was scheduled the following day and spent two days installing the new equipment. The electrician's charge was $65 per hour for two, eight-hour days, or $1,040 total. The equipment was placed in service on June 24, 2001.

On January 5, 2005, repairs costing $4,500 were made, which increased the life of the equipment two additional years. On August 18, 2006, some routine repairs were made costing $480.

On April 10, 2007, Clark decided the 80-hour work weeks were taking too heavy a toll on his personal life and closed the business. He sold the equipment for $4,200 cash.

The company closes its books on December 31 and uses the straight-line method.

Required:

Present journal entries to record the following:
1. the purchase of the equipment on June 10, 2001
2. payment of the transportation and insurance charges
3. payment of the electrician's charges
4. amortization for 2001
5. the repair on January 5, 2005
6. amortization for 2005
7. the repair on August 18, 2006
8. amortization for 2006

9. amortization up to date of sale
10. the equipment sale on April 10, 2007

Date	Account and Explanation	PR	Debit	Credit

SOLUTIONS

A. TEST YOURSELF

I. Matching

1. M	5. L	9. N	13. I	17. K
2. E	6. P	10. A	14. O	18. R
3. D	7. Q	11. C	15. H	19. B
4. F	8. S	12. G	16. J	20. T

II. Multiple Choice

1.   A   A computer is a tangible asset.

2.   D   Land is said to have infinite useful life and is not amortized.

3.   B   The cost of equipment includes all amounts paid to acquire the asset and to ready it for its intended use. Repairs to equipment indicate that it is in use and therefore should not be included as part of the equipment's cost.

4.   C   Straight-line amortization is the only method of amortization that results in the same amount of amortization every year. The other methods listed are accelerated (double-declining-balance) or can result in differing amounts of amortization each year (UOP and CCA).

5.   D   Units-of-production amortization is based on the number of units produced by the amortizable asset. The other methods listed all depend on time in the amortization calculation.

6.   C   A building is used equally from year to year.

7.   C   Straight-line is the method used to amortize an intangible asset.

8.   B   The amortization method that will result in the lowest income tax in the first year is the method that results in the largest amortization deduction. CCA is the maximum allowable deduction in the asset's first year.

9.   C   Item B equals the asset's book value. Items A and D have no significance.

10.   B   Book value is the cost minus accumulated amortization.

11.   D   Capital expenditures are those that increase capacity or efficiency of the asset or extend its useful life. Repairs merely maintain an asset in its existing condition or restore the asset to good working order.

12.   D   The cost of the commission should be capitalized because it was necessary to purchase the property. The other costs are expenses and should be debited to expense accounts.

13.   B   ($20,000 - $4,000) / 5 years = $3,200 per year

14.   B   Step 1: ($20,000 - $4,000) / 100,000 km = $0.16 / km

              Step 2: $0.16 / km × 20,000 km = $3,200

15.   C   Step 1: 100% / 5 years = 20% × 2 = 40%

              Step 2: Year 1 = $20,000 × 40% = $8,000

                        Year 2 = ($20,000 - $8,000) = $12,000 × 40% = $4,800

III. Completion

1. long-lived, tangible (The physical form (tangibility) of capital assets provides their usefulness.)
2. a systematic allocation of an asset's cost to expense (Amortization is not a method of asset valuation.)
3. noncash (Cash is expended either at the acquisition of a capital asset or over time as the asset is paid for. The debit to Amortization Expense is balanced by a credit to Accumulated Amortization, not Cash.)
4. capital (Ordinary repairs are an immediate expense.)
5. capital cost allowance (CCA)
6. relative-sales-value (The need to amortize each asset separately makes it necessary to allocate the purchase price by some reasonable manner.)
7. cost; estimated useful life; estimated residual value; amortization method (Order is not important.)
8. matching (Matching means to identify and measure all expenses incurred during the period and to match them against the revenue earned during that period.)
9. amortizable cost
10. Fully amortized
11. investing
12. straight-line
13. operating
14. capital; repairs
15. depletion

IV. True/False

1.   F   In Canada, development costs must be capitalized, while research costs must be expensed.
2.   F   Accelerated amortization records larger amounts of amortization expense when the asset is newer and lesser amounts as the asset ages. Therefore, book value (cost less accumulated amortization) will be lower when the asset is newer.
3.   F   The amount of total amortization is not affected by the method used. Instead, the method determines how the amortizable cost is spread.
4.   T
5.   F   Repairs are recorded as expenses.
6.   F   Amortizable cost equals cost less residual value.
7.   F   Accelerated amortization results in the opposite—decreasing amounts as the assets become older.
8.   T
9.   T
10.   T
11.   T
12.   T
13.   F   The acquisition of capital assets is an investing activity, not an operating activity.
14.   F   The formula is remaining amortizable value divided by remaining useful life.
15.   T

V. Exercises

1. Machine 1 = [$90,000 / ($90,000 + $36,000 + $66,000)] × $150,000 = $70,312.50
   Machine 2 = [$36,000 / ($90,000 + $36,000 + $66,000)] × $150,000 = $28,125.00
   Machine 3 = [$66,000 / ($90,000 + $36,000 + $66,000)] × $150,000 = $51,562.50
   (Proof: $70,312.50 + $28,125 + $51,562.50 = $150,000)

2.

	2005	2006
Straight-line	10,000	10,000
Units-of-production	9,600	14,400
Double-declining-balance	27,000	13,500

Straight-line = ($54,000 - $14,000) / 4 years = $10,000

Units-of-production = (54,000 - 14,000) / 125,000 units = $0.32 per unit
    2005 = 30,000 × $0.32 = $9,600
    2006 = 45,000 × $0.32 = $14,400

Double-declining-balance:
    DDB rate = (1/4) × 2 = 0.50
    2005 = 0.50 × $54,000 = $27,000
    Book value = $54,000 - $27,000 = $27,000
    2006 = 0.50 × $27,000 = $13,500

3.

Annual amortization = ($48,000 - $2,000) / 5 = $9,200
Accumulated amortization on Jan. 1, 2007 = 2 years @ $9,200 per year = $18,400

June 30	Amortization Expense	4,600	
	Accumulated Amortization		4,600
	Amort. for 6 months (6/12 × 9,200) = 4,600		

June 30	Cash	23,500	
	Loss on Sale of Asset	1,500	
	Accumulated Amortization	23,000	
	Equipment		48,000
	Loss = Cash + Accumulated. Amort. - Cost		

Because cash received ($23,500) is less than book value ($48,000 - $23,000 = $25,000), there is a loss of $1,500 ($25,000 - $23,500) on the sale.

4.
a. 1. capital expenditure
    2. capital expenditure
    3. capital expenditure
    4. (capital expenditure)
    5. capital expenditure
    6. expense

Study Tip: The discount is in parentheses because it represents a reduction in the cost of the equipment.

b. $11,376

Given the answers from part a, the calculation is $9,700 + 582 + 460 - 291 + 925. The accounts would appear as follows:

Drill Press		Interest Expense	
9,700	291	271	
582			
460			
925			
Bal. 11,376			

$([\$11,000 \times 0.10] \div [90 \times 365] = \$271.23)$

c. Double-declining-balance = Book value × Rate
Book value = $11,376
Rate = 33 1/3 %
$11,376 × 33 1/3% = $3,792
Amortization from 8/20/06 – 12/31/06 = 4 months
$3,792 × 4/12 = $1,264

Study Tip: Double-declining-balance is the only method that ignores residual value in the formula.

5.
a.

Purchase price for Wars		$10,400,000
Market value of Wars's assets	16,200,000	
Less: Wars's liabilities	9,000,000	
Market value of Wars's net assets		7,200,000
Goodwill		$3,200,000

b.

Date	Account and Explanation	PR	Debit	Credit
Oct. 1	Assets		16,200,000	
	Goodwill		3,200,000	
	Liabilities			9,000,000
	Cash			10,400,000

6. Amortization for years 2004 and 2005: ($23,000 - $8,000) / 5 = $3,000 per year × 2 = $6,000
New amortization = ($23,000 - $6,000) = $17,000 remaining book value
($17,000 - $4,000) / 5 years = $2,600

Amortization expense (2006)	$2,600	
Accumulated amortization		$2,600

VI. Critical Thinking

1. There is no such thing as an amortization reserve. What appears on the books is accumulated amortization. There is no cash involved in accounting for amortization; therefore, the balance in accumulated amortization does not represent any money available for future use. The balance in accumulated amortization represents the amount of the related asset's cost that has been recognized as an expense because of the asset's loss of usefulness to the business.

2. The differences would be a different level of net income and thus a different amount of total assets (planes – accumulated amortization) and equities (net income affected by different amortization expense). Despite these two companies having different balance sheets and income statements, they are not different. Since CCA is used for tax purposes, they would have the same cash flows.

DEMONSTRATION PROBLEMS

Demonstration Problem #1 Solved and Explained

Requirement 1 (Schedule of amortization)

	X	Y	Z
Asset cost	$39,000	$16,000	$18,000
Less: Residual value	3,000	800	3,000
Amortizable cost	$36,000	$15,200	$15,000

Study Tip: Under the double-declining-balance method, the residual value is not considered until the book value approaches residual value.

Equipment X
Schedule of Amortization Expense
(Straight-Line Method)

Year	Amortizable Cost	Amortizable Rate	Amortization Expense
2006	$39,000	1/6	$ 6,000
2007	39,000	1/6	6,000
2008	39,000	1/6	6,000
2009	39,000	1/6	6,000
2010	39,000	1/6	6,000
2011	39,000	1/6	6,000
		Total	$36,000

The book value of the equipment after 2011 is $3,000 (cost - accumulated amortization = $39,000 - $36,000 = $3,000).

Equipment Y
Schedule of Amortization Expense
(Units-of-Production Method)

Year	Amortizable Cost	Units Produced	Amortization Expense
2006	$15,200	12,400	$ 4,712*
2007	15,200	10,750	4,085
2008	15,200	11,230	4,267 (rounded)
2009	15,200	6,100	2,136 (rounded)**
		Total	$15,200

*The per-unit cost is $0.38 ($15,200 / 40,000 units = $0.38)
The book value after 2009 is $800 ($16,000 - $15,200 = $800).

**The original production estimate for the equipment was 40,000 units. The actual production over the life of the equipment was 40,480. Assuming the original estimates (for total production and residual value) are reasonable, the 2009 amortization should be based on 5,620 units, the number required to total 40,000 units.

> **Study Tip**: The amortizable cost is not affected by the method used. The method simply determines how the amortizable cost will be spread out over the asset's life.

Equipment Z
Schedule of Amortization Expense
(Double-Declining-Balance Method)

Year	Book Value × Rate	Amortization Expense	Book Value
2006	0.40 × 48,000	19,200	$28,800
2007	0.40 × 28,800	11,520	17,280
2008	0.40 × 17,280	6,912	10,368
2009	10,368 – 10,000	368	10,000
2010		0	10,000

The straight-line amortization rate for an asset with a useful life of five years is 1/5 per year, or 20%. Double the straight-line rate is 2/5, or 40%. This rate does not change from 2006 through 2010.

> **Study Tip**: The most frequent error made by students in applying double-declining-balance deals with the residual value. Unlike units-of-production, with DDB, the residual value is not taken into account until the final years (in this example, the fourth year) of the asset's life.

Amortization expense for Equipment Z in the fourth year is not $4,147.20 ($10,368 × 0.40) because this would bring the book value below the residual value. In the fourth year, amortization expense is the previous year's book value less the residual value ($10,368 - $10,000 = $368). As the asset is fully amortized at the end of the fourth year, there is no amortization recorded for the fifth year.

Requirement 2 (Journal entry—Equipment X)

Date	Account and Explanation	PR	Debit	Credit
	Accumulated Amortization —X		36,000	
	Loss on Disposal of Equipment		3,000	
	Equipment X			39,000

When fully amortized assets cannot be sold or exchanged, an entry removing them from the books is necessary upon disposal. The entry credits the asset account and debits its related Accumulated Amortization account. If the fully amortized asset has no residual value, no loss on the disposal occurs. In most cases, however, it will be necessary to record a debit to a Loss on Disposal account to write off the book value of a junked asset. There can never be a gain on the junking or scrapping of an asset.

Requirement 3 (Journal entry—Equipment Y)

Date	Account and Explanation	PR	Debit	Credit
	Cash		1,000	
	Accumulated amortization—Y		15,200	
	Equipment Y			16,000
	Gain on Sale of Equipment			200

A gain is recorded when an asset is sold for a price greater than its value. A loss is recorded when the sale price is less than book value. In this case, Equipment Y and its related Accumulated Amortization account are removed from the books in a manner similar to Equipment X. The gain of $200 is calculated by subtracting the book value of the asset sold ($800) from the cash received ($1,000). The Gain on the Sale of Equipment account is a revenue account and is closed to the Income Summary account at the end of the year.

Demonstration Problem #2 Solved and Explained

Date	Account and Explanation	PR	Debit	Credit
1.	Equipment		23,850	
	Cash			23,850
2.	Equipment		410	
	Cash			410
	Transportation and insurance cost.			
3.	Equipment		1,040	
	Cash			1,040
	Installation cost.			

The transportation, insurance and installation costs are debited to the Equipment account because they are necessary costs incurred to place the asset in service. Therefore, the total cost basis for the equipment is $25,300, not $22,500.

4.	Amortization Expense—Equipment		1,488	
	Accumulated Amortization			1,488

($25,300 - $1,500 (see above)) / 8 = 2,975 × 6/12 = $1,488)

Since the asset was acquired on June 10, but placed in service on June 24, the first year's amortization is June 12 of the company's financial period. Thereafter, annual amortization is $2,975.

| 5. | Equipment | 4,500 | |
| | Cash (or Accounts Payable) | | 4,500 |

This is clearly a capital expenditure because the equipment will last past its original life estimate. Therefore, the cost should be reflected in an asset account, not in an expense account.

| 6. | Amortization Expense—Equipment | 2,752 | |
| | Accumulated Amortization | | 2,752 |

Accumulated amortization through Dec. 31, 2004 is $10,413. For 2001, amortization is $1,488; 2002 to 2004 is equal to $2,975 per year × 3 = $8,925. $1,488 + $8,925 = $10,413.

Therefore, on Jan. 5, 2005, book value is $14,887 ($25,300 - $10,413). The $4,500 debit in entry (5) increases book value to $19,387, and now life is two years more than the original life estimate. As of Jan. 5, 2005, the equipment is three years, six months old. The revised life estimate is now ten years. Therefore, as of Jan. 5, 2005, the asset has six years, six months of life left (10 years - 3 years, 6 months). To calculate the new amortization amount, divide book value less residual value ($19,387 - $1,500) by remaining life (6.5 years) or $2,752 per year (rounded).

| 7. | Repair Expense | 480 | |
| | Cash | | 480 |

This is clearly a repair expense—one necessary to maintain the asset.

| 8. | Amortization Expense | 2,752 | |
| | Accumulated Amortization | | 2,752 |

See explanation for 6 above.

| 9. | Amortization Expense—Equipment | 688 | |
| | Accumulated Amortization | | 688 |

Study Tip: When an asset is disposed of during the fiscal period, first update the amortization.

Amortization from Dec. 31, 2006–April 10, 2007 = $2,752 × 3/12 = $688

10.	Cash	4,200	
	Accumulated Amortization	16,605	
	Loss on Sale	8,995	
	Equipment		29,800

The Equipment account and Accumulated Amortization account appear as follows:

Equipment			Accumulated Amortization	
(1)	23,850		1,488	Dec. 31, 2001
(2)	410		2,975	Dec. 31, 2002
(3)	1,040		2,975	Dec. 31, 2003
(5)	4,500		2,975	Dec. 31, 2004
Bal.	29,800		2,752	Dec. 31, 2005
			2,752	Dec. 31, 2006
			688	Apr. 10, 2007
			16,605	Bal.

Therefore, on date of disposal, book value is $13,195 ($29,800 - $16,605); comparing book value with sales price results in a loss of $8,995.

CHAPTER 8—CURRENT AND LONG-TERM LIABILITIES

CHAPTER OVERVIEW

In the last four chapters, we have concentrated on a detailed examination of assets—specifically cash (Chapter 4), receivables and short-term investments (Chapter 5), inventory (Chapter 6), and capital assets (Chapter 7). We now turn our attention to liabilities, both current and long term. Whereas assets relate to investing activities, liabilities relate to financing activities. The specific learning objectives for this chapter are to

1. **Account** for current liabilities and contingent liabilities
2. **Account** for bonds-payable transactions
3. **Measure** interest expense
4. **Understand** the advantages and disadvantages of borrowing
5. **Report** liabilities on the cash flow statement

CHAPTER REVIEW

Liabilities are obligations to transfer assets (for example, to make cash payments for purchases on account) or to provide services in the future (for example, to earn unearned revenue). Current liabilities are due within one year or within the company's operating cycle if it is longer than one year. Long-term liabilities are those not classified as current.

Objective 1 - Account for current liabilities and contingent liabilities

Current liabilities include liabilities of a known amount and liabilities that are estimated. Current liabilities of a known amount are: **accounts payable**—amounts owed to suppliers for goods or services purchased on account, and **short-term notes payable**—notes due within one year. Companies issue notes payable to borrow cash, to purchase inventory, or to purchase capital assets. Interest expense and interest payable must be accrued at the end of the accounting period.

Suppose a company acquires a capital asset and issues a note payable. The entry is

Capital Asset	XX	
Notes Payable, Short-Term		XX

Interest expense and interest payable are recorded at the end of the accounting period with this entry:

Interest Expense	XX	
Interest Payable		XX

Interest expense is based on Principle × Interest × Time (PIT).

When the note is paid off at maturity, the entry is

Notes Payable, Short-Term	XX	
Interest Payable	XX	
Interest Expense	XX	
Cash		XX

Other current liabilities include the following: **sales taxes payable**, the **current portion of long-term debt**, **accrued expenses**, **unearned revenues**, **payroll liabilities**, and **contingent liabilities**.

Most provinces tax retail sales. **Sales tax** is collected in addition to the price of an item. Retailers are actually collecting the tax for the government, and therefore Sales Tax Payable is a current liability.

Sales taxes may be accounted for in one of two ways:

1. Record the tax separately for daily sales:

Cash	XX	
Sales Revenue		XX
Sales Tax Payable		XX

2. Record sales including the taxes collected:

Cash	XX	
Sales Revenue		XX

    At the end of each month, an adjusting entry is made to correct the Sales Revenue and Sales Tax Payable accounts:

Sales Revenue	XX	
Sales Tax Payable		XX

The first method is preferable, since it removes the need for an adjusting entry at month end, which could be done improperly or forgotten altogether.

In either case, when the taxes are paid to the government, the entry is

Sales Tax Payable	XX	
Cash		XX

Some long-term liabilities, such as notes, bonds, or mortgages, are paid in installments. The **current installment of long-term debt** (also called current maturity) is the amount of that debt that is payable within one year. It is reported in the current liabilities section of the balance sheet. The remainder is reported in the long-term liabilities section of the balance sheet.

Accrued expenses (also called **accrued liabilities**) such as accrued salaries, interest payable, income tax payable, and payroll items are current liabilities. Payroll liabilities refer to both the amount of money owed to the employees (more commonly referred to as net pay) and amounts owed to others based on the salaries and wages earned by employees. Examples of the latter are income taxes (both federal and provincial) and other deductions withheld from employee paycheques, such as Canada Pension Plan and Employment Insurance. At the time these amounts are withheld, they become liabilities of the business. Exhibit 8-1 in your text illustrates a typical entry recorded for payroll.

Unearned revenues (also called **deferred revenues, revenues collected in advance, customer prepayments**) occur when a company receives cash from customers before earning the revenue. As goods are delivered or services are rendered, revenue is recorded. A magazine subscription is typically paid for upfront, representing unearned revenue (obligation for the firm). As the magazines are sent each month, the unearned revenue becomes earned revenue. Unearned revenue is recorded as

Cash	XX	
Unearned Revenue		XX

As the unearned revenue is earned, it is recorded as

Unearned Revenue	XX	
Revenue		XX

Estimated Current Liabilities

Current liabilities that are estimated include warranties payable and vacation pay liability. Recall that the matching principle requires that expenses be matched with revenues. A company can reasonably estimate, often as a percentage of sales, the amount of **warranty expense** that will be incurred as a result of defective products. Estimated Warranty Payable is a current liability, recorded as

Warranty Expense	XX	
Estimated Warranty Payable		XX

> **Study Tip:** When a repair or replacement occurs within the warranty period, the Estimated Warranty Payable (rather than Warranty Expense) is debited.

A **contingent liability** is a potential liability that depends on a future event that may occur as a result of a past transaction. Contingent liabilities may be difficult to estimate, as in lawsuits, where the amounts are determined by the courts. The disclosure principle requires companies to keep outsiders informed of relevant information about the company.

The Accounting Standards Board of the CICA provides these guidelines for the reporting of contingent losses:

1. An actual liability is to be recorded if the loss is likely to occur and the amount can be reasonably estimated.
2. Report the contingency in a note to the financial statements if
   a) it is likely that a loss (or expense) will occur but the amount cannot be reasonably estimated.
   b) it cannot be determined that the loss (or expense) is likely to occur.

If recorded, the contingency will appear as a liability on the balance sheet and as a loss on the income statement.

Long-Term Liabilities: Bonds

Corporations issue **bonds** (typically in $1,000 units) to raise large amounts of money from multiple lenders. Bonds are long-term liabilities. The **bond certificate** states the 1) principal amount, 2) interest rate, 3) maturity date, and 4) dates that interest payments are due (which are generally every six months over the life of the bond). (Helpful hint: review Exhibit 8-2 in the text.) Companies usually hire a securities firm to underwrite the bonds. The **underwriter** buys the bonds and resells them to clients.

Term bonds mature at the same time for a particular issue. **Serial bonds** mature in installments over a period of time. Unsecured bonds are called **debentures**. The owners of a secured bond have the right to take specified assets of the issuer in the event of default. Other things being equal, debentures will carry a higher interest rate than secured bonds.

Bonds are often traded on bonds markets. Bond prices are quoted at a percentage of their maturity value. For example, a $10,000 bond selling for 97 would sell for $9,700.

Study Tip: Stock prices are quoted in dollars; bond prices are quoted in percentages.

When a bond is issued at a price above the face (par) value, it is being issued at a premium. When the bond is issued at a price below the face (par) value, it is being issued at a discount.

A basic understanding of the concept of **present value** is necessary to understand bond prices. When companies borrow money, they have to pay interest on the debt. To the lender this represents the time value of money. Therefore, a lender would not be interested in giving up $500 today to receive only $500 five years from now. If the lender wants to receive $500 five years from now, the question is, how much would the lender be willing to give up today to do so? The answer to this question represents the present value of that future amount ($500). Present value is discussed in detail in Appendix D.

The present value of the bond is determined by three factors: 1) the amount of the future payment (or receipt); 2) the length of time from the investment date to the date when the future amount is to be paid (received); and 3) the interest rate during the period.

The price at which bonds are sold is determined by the **contract interest (stated) rate** and the **market (effective) interest rate**. The contract rate is the amount (expressed as a percent) listed on the bond certificate. The market rate is the amount that potential investors are currently demanding for their money. When the contract rate is less than the market rate, the bonds have to be sold at less than their face value (called a **discount**) to attract investors. Conversely, when the contract price is greater than the market rate, the bonds will sell at a **premium**. (Helpful hint: review Exhibit 8-4 in the text.)

Objective 2 - Account for bonds-payable transactions

The simplest transaction occurs when bonds are issued on an interest date and no difference exists between the stated rate and the market rate. Debit Cash and credit Bonds Payable. When interest is paid, debit Interest Expense and credit Cash. When the bonds mature and are paid off, debit Bonds Payable and credit Cash.

Issue bond:

Cash	XX	
Bond Payable		XX

Interest Expense:

```
Interest Expense          XX
    Cash                        XX
```

Maturity:

```
Bonds Payable             XX
    Cash                        XX
```

Issuing Bonds at a Discount

If the market interest rate is higher than the stated rate of a bond issue, then the issuer must **sell the bonds at a discount**, that is, at less than face value to attract buyers. The entry debits Cash, debits Discount on Bonds Payable, and credits Bonds Payable.

Discount on Bonds Payable is a contra account to Bonds Payable. On the balance sheet, the discount balance is subtracted from Bonds Payable to equal the book value or carrying amount of the bond issue. The issuer will have to repay the face value of the bonds when they mature. Therefore, a discount is an additional cost to the issuer.

Issue of Bond:

```
Cash                           XX
Discount on Bond Payable       XX
    Bond Payable                      XX
```

Objective 3 - Measure interest expense

The **effective-interest method** is used to amortize the bond discount over the life of the bond or note. The objective of the effective-interest method is to match interest expense as a constant percentage of the changing carrying value of the bonds rather than as a constant amount each period. The effective-interest rate is the market rate in effect when the bonds are sold. Three steps are followed when using the effective-interest method:

1. Interest expense is calculated by multiplying the effective-interest rate by the carrying value of the bonds. (This amount changes each period.)
2. The cash paid to bondholders is calculated by multiplying the stated interest rate by the principal amount of the bonds. (This amount is the same each period.)
3. The difference between the interest expense and the cash paid is the amount of discount amortized.

Remember that amortization of bond discount will change the carrying value of the bonds before the next calculations are made. When a discount is amortized, the carrying value will increase.

Study Exhibits 8-5, 8-6, and 8-7 in your text to understand the effective-interest method. Pay particular attention to the graphs in Exhibits 8-6 and 8-7.

Issuing Bonds at a Premium

If the market rate is lower than the stated rate of a bond issue, then the issuer can **sell the bonds at a premium**, that is, for more than face value. The entry debits Cash, credits Bonds Payable, and credits Premium on Bonds

Payable. **Premium on Bonds Payable** is added to Bonds Payable on the balance sheet to show the book value or carrying amount. The issuer will have to repay only the face value of the bonds when they mature. Therefore, a premium is treated as a reduction of the issuer's interest expense. The premium is allocated to reduce interest expense over the life of the bonds, in accordance with the matching principle. (Helpful hint: review Exhibits 8-8, 8-9, and 8-10 in the text.)

Straight-line amortization of the discount or premium is computed by dividing the discount or premium by the number of accounting periods during the life of the bonds. On each interest date, the entry to record interest expense debits Interest Expense, debits Premium on Bonds Payable, or credits Discount on Bonds Payable, and credits Cash. The straight-line method is not as accurate as the effective-interest method.

Sometimes corporations retire bonds prior to the maturity date. **Callable bonds** may be retired at the option of the issuer. **Noncallable bonds** may be bought back on the open market and retired. If interest rates have dropped, the issuer may compare the book value of the bonds to the market price to decide whether to retire the bonds. When bonds are retired and the bonds were initially sold at either a premium or discount, the entry to retire the bonds must also remove the unamortized premium or discount from the books. A **gain (or loss) on retirement** results when the carrying value of the bonds is greater (or lesser for a loss) than the cash paid for the bonds. Any gain or loss on the retirement of bonds payable is reported as other income (loss) on the income statement.

Bonds that can be converted into common shares are called **convertible bonds**. Investors will convert the bonds when the share price of the issuing company increases to the point that the shares have a higher market value than the bonds. The entry transfers the bond carrying amount into shareholders' equity:

Bonds Payable	XX	
Premium on Bonds Payable (if applicable)	XX	
Discount on Bonds Payable (if applicable)		XX
Common shares		XX

Study Tip: Note both Premium and Discount cannot appear in the same entry.

Also, there will never be a gain or loss recorded on the conversion of bonds.

Objective 4 – Understand the advantages and disadvantages of borrowing

To pay for assets, companies can either issue shares, issue debt (bonds), borrow, or rely on profits of the business. **Earnings per share (EPS)** is the most widely used measure to evaluate companies, as it measures the amount of a company's net income per share of its outstanding common stock.

Advantages of borrowing: **Trading on the equity** usually increases earnings per share. This means that the corporation earns a return on the borrowed funds that is greater than the cost of the borrowed funds.

Disadvantages of borrowing:

1. High interest rates
2. Interest on debt must be paid; dividends on shares are optional

In earlier chapters, you learned how to calculate the debt ratio (total liabilities divided by total assets). The debt ratio relates to a company's financial position. However, it does not address the issue of the cost of the debt, that is, the interest expense. A second ratio, times-interest-earned, is used to relate income to interest expense. The times-interest-earned ratio is calculated as follows:

$$\text{Times-interest-earned Ratio} = \frac{\text{Operating income}}{\text{Interest expense}}$$

The lower the result, the greater the difficulty the company will have in paying interest expense.

Review the Decision Guidelines—Financing with Debt or with Stock to become familiar with the issues involved in this decision.

Long-Term Liabilities: Leases and Pensions

A **lease** is a rental agreement in which the tenant (lessee) agrees to make rent payments to the property owner (lessor) in exchange for the use of some asset. **Operating leases** are usually short term or cancelable. To account for an operating lease, the lessee debits Rent Expense and credits Cash for the amount of the lease payment.

Capital leases are long term and noncancelable. Accounting for capital leases is similar to accounting for the purchase of an asset. Debit the asset leased, credit Cash for the initial payment, and credit Lease Liability for the present value of future lease payments. Because the leased asset is capitalized, it must be amortized. Leased assets are usually amortized over the term of the lease. Debit Amortization Expense and credit the asset's Accumulated Amortization account.

Section 3065 of the *CICA Handbook* provides guidelines for the classification of leases. If a lease meets any one of the following criteria, it must be classified as a capital lease:

1. The lessee is likely to obtain ownership of the leased asset at the end of the lease either because the lease transfers title of the leased asset to the lessee at the end of the lease term or the lease contains a bargain purchase option.
2. The lease term is 75% or more of the estimated useful life of the leased asset.
3. The present value of the lease payments is 90% or more of the market value of the leased asset.

Operating leases are defined by exception: that is, operating leases are only those that fail to meet any of these three criteria.

In the past, companies were attracted to operating leases because they were not required to list the lease as a liability on the balance sheet—in other words, the company had the use of an asset (or service) without the related debt showing (called **off-balance-sheet financing**). This practice has been curtailed.

Pensions and **postretirement benefits** are other types of liabilities found on balance sheets. **Pensions** are compensation paid to employees after retirement, usually based on a variety of factors, including length of service. Companies are required to report the present value of promised future pension payments to retirees. If the plan assets exceed this amount, the plan is overfunded. Conversely, the fund could be underfunded if assets are less. In addition to pensions, companies are required to report the present value of future payments to retirees for other benefits. At the end of each period, companies accrue the expense and the liability of **postretirement benefits** based on information about the current workforce.

Objective 5 - Report liabilities on the balance sheet

Liabilities affect the cash flow statement. The issuance of debt (and receipt of cash) is a financing activity, as is the payment of debt. However, interest payments are operating activities because, as an expense, interest appears on the income statement.

TEST YOURSELF

All the self-testing materials in this chapter focus on information and procedures that your instructor is likely to test in quizzes and examinations.

I. Matching

1. *Match each numbered term with its lettered definition.*

_____ 1. discount (on a bond)
_____ 2. premium (on a bond)
_____ 3. callable bonds
_____ 4. contract interest rate
_____ 5. debentures
_____ 6. lessee
_____ 7. stated interest rate
_____ 8. market interest rate
_____ 9. accrued expense
_____ 10. trading on the equity
_____ 11. off-balance-sheet financing
_____ 12. current potion of long-term debt

_____ 13. bonds payable
_____ 14. capital lease
_____ 15. convertible bonds
_____ 16. contingent liability
_____ 17. lessor
_____ 18. short-term note payable
_____ 19. operating lease
_____ 20. serial bonds
_____ 21. term bonds
_____ 22. underwriter
_____ 23. discounting a note payable

A. a potential liability that depends on a future event arising out of a past transaction
B. another name for the contract interest rate
C. acquisition of assets or services with debt that is not reported on the balance sheet
D. an expense incurred but not yet paid by the company; also called accrued liability
E. bonds that may be exchanged for the common shares of the issuing company at the option of the investor
F. bonds that mature in installments over a period of time
G. bonds that the issuer may pay off at a specified price whenever the issuer desires
H. bonds that all mature at the same time for a particular issue
I. a note payable due within one year
J. amount of debt that comes due within the next year
K. earning more income than the interest on the borrowed amount
L. excess of a bond's maturity (par) value over its issue price
M. excess of a bond's issue price over its maturity (par) value
N. groups of notes payable issued to multiple lenders, called bondholders
O. interest rate that investors demand in order to lend their money
P. a lease agreement that meets any one of three special criteria
Q. organizations that purchase bonds from an issuing company and resell them to clients, or sell the bonds for a commission and agree to buy all unsold bonds
R. the property owner in a lease agreement
S. the tenant in a lease agreement
T. the interest rate that determines the amount of cash interest the borrower pays

U. unsecured bonds backed only by the good faith of the borrower

V. usually a short-term or cancelable rental agreement

W. a borrowing arrangement in which the bank subtracts the interest amount from the face value of a note payable

2. *Match each numbered term with its lettered definition.*

_____ 1. earnings per share   _____ 5. leverage

_____ 2. accrued liability   _____ 6. times-interest-earned ratio

_____ 3. effective interest rate   _____ 7. pension

_____ 4. lease   _____ 8. present value

A. an expense incurred but not yet paid for

B. trading on equity

C. employee compensation that will be received during retirement

D. an interest method that uses a constant percentage of bond carrying value to determine interest expense.

E. current value of an amount to be received in the future

F. net income attributable to common shareholders

G. income from operations divided by interest expense

H. rental agreement in which a lessee agrees to make payments to the lessor

II. Multiple Choice   *Circle the best answer.*

1. A $500,000 bond quoted at 104.375 has a market price of

   A. $500,000
   B. $521,875
   C. $52,187,500
   D. $52,187.50

2. All of the following affect the market price of bonds *except*

   A. bondholder's credit rating
   B. bond issuer's credit rating
   C. market interest rate
   D. length of time to maturity

3. Which of the following is not a current liability?

   A. warranty payable
   B. pension liability
   C. unearned revenue
   D. vacation liability

4. The interest rate demanded by investors in order to lend their money is the

A. contract rate
B. issue rate
C. effective rate
D. stated rate

5. The premium on a bond payable

A. increases the interest expense only in the year the bonds are sold
B. increases the interest expense over the life of the bonds
C. reduces interest expense only in the year the bonds mature
D. is a liability account that is amortized (to expense) over the life of the bonds

6. The book value of Bonds Payable on the balance sheet equals

A. Bonds Payable + Discount on Bonds Payable or + Premium on Bonds Payable
B. Bonds Payable - Discount on Bonds Payable or - Premium on Bonds Payable
C. Bonds Payable + Discount on Bonds Payable or - Premium on Bonds Payable
D. Bonds Payable - Discount on Bonds Payable or + Premium on Bonds Payable

7. When bonds are issued at a premium, their carrying amount

A. decreases from issuance to maturity
B. increases from issuance to maturity
C. remains constant over the life of the bonds
D. decreases when the market interest rate increases

8. Gains and losses from early retirement of debt are reported

A. as operating gains and losses on the income statement
B. as increases or decreases to retained earnings on the statement of retained earnings
C. as other income on the income statement
D. in the footnotes to the financial statements

9. When a convertible bond is exchanged for common shares

A. shareholders' equity increases
B. liabilities increase
C. revenues increase
D. expenses increase

10. Which of the following is not reported on the balance sheet?

A. capital lease
B. pension liabilities
C. postretirement benefit liabilities
D. operating leases

11. Interest expense on a discounted note payable is recorded

   A. at maturity
   B. at the end of the accounting period
   C. in monthly payments
   D. when the note is discounted

12. Which of the following is probably a contingent liability?

   A. interest payable
   B. notes payable
   C. lawsuit claims
   D. income tax payable

13. A contingent liability should be recognized as a liability on the balance sheet when

   A. the loss is probable but cannot be reasonably estimated
   B. the loss is probable
   C. the loss is probable and can reasonably be estimated
   D. the loss can be reasonably estimated

14. Which of the following is not an estimated liability?

   A. warranties
   B. postretirement benefits
   C. vacation pay
   D. notes payable

15. Which of the following would be considered a capital lease?

   A. an automobile leased for three years with an estimated useful life of six years
   B. a building costing $5,000,000 that can be purchased at the end of the lease period for $2,000
   C. a piece of equipment that is cancelable by either party
   D. the present value of the lease payments is 75% of the market value of the asset

III. Completion   *Complete each of the following statements.*

1. When the market interest rate is _____ than the stated rate, bonds will sell at a premium.

2. When the premium on bonds payable is reduced, the book value of bonds payable_____.

3. Gains or losses on early retirement of debt are _____ and reported separately on the income statement.

4. The liability to make _____ lease payments is not reported on the balance sheet.

5. If a lease transfers ownership of assets at the end of the lease term, the lease is a(n) _____ lease.

6. The _____ method of interest amortization results in the same amount of discount/premium amortization for identical periods of time.

7. Accruing pension and postretirement benefit liabilities is an example of the _____ principle.

8. When the market interest rate is greater than the stated rate, the bonds will sell at a _____.

9. Convertible bonds give the _____ the right to convert the bonds to common shares.

10. When the effective-interest method of amortization is used, the interest expense over the life of the bonds is calculated using _____.

11. Indicate whether each of the following liabilities is a known amount (K) or an estimated amount (E).

_____	A. Accounts Payable		_____	G. Sales Tax Payable
_____	B. Short-term Notes Payable		_____	H. Liability for Vacation Pay
_____	C. Property Taxes Payable		_____	I. Postretirement Benefits
_____	D. Warranty Liability		_____	J. Interest Payable
_____	E. Salaries Expense		_____	K. Pension Premium Payable
_____	F. Income Taxes Payable			

12. _____ of long-term debt represents the amount due within the next year.

13. Employees receiving compensation during retirement are receiving a _____.

14. The _____ ratio is the most widely used ratio to measure and evaluate companies of different sizes and in different industries.

15. _____ are expenses incurred but not yet paid for.

IV. True/False *For each of the following statements, circle* T *for true or* F *for false.*

1. T F A bond listed as selling at 96 means it is selling for $96.
2. T F Discount on Bonds Payable is a contra liability account.
3. T F The current portion of long-term debt is listed in the current liability section of the balance sheet and includes both the principal and accrued interest.
4. T F Accrued lessee and accrued liabilities are synonymous terms.
5. T F Salaries Payable represents the amount employees have earned and for which they have not been paid.
6. T F Unearned revenue is reported on the income statement after operating income.
7. T F The disclosure principle requires businesses to estimate warranty expense.
8. T F A debenture is an unsecured bond.
9. T F The carrying amount of a bond will equal its face value if the bond was sold at face value.
10. T F When a bond is sold at a premium, the interest expense over the life of the bond is greater than the total interest paid to the bondholder over the life of the bond.
11. T F Amortizing a bond discount using the effective-interest method results in a greater amount of interest expense over the life of the bond compared with the straight-line method.
12. T F The carrying value of a bond sold at a premium increases over the life of the bond.
13. T F A callable bond allows the bondholder to convert the bond into common shares.
14. T F An example of a capital lease is the lease a tenant signs to rent an apartment.
15. T F Postretirement benefits are one example of an estimated liability.

V. Exercises

1. Myspace Inc. issued $9,000,000 in 10-year bonds with a stated interest rate of 6 3/4%. The bonds were issued at par on June 1, 2006. Interest is paid on December 1 and June 1.

   Give the journal entries for:

   A. Issuance of the bonds on June 1, 2006.
   B. Payment of interest on December 1, 2006.
   C. Maturity payment of bonds on June 1, 2016.

	Date	Account and Explanation	Debit	Credit
A.				
B.				
C.				

2. Record journal entries for the following transactions:

   A. A company borrows $25,000 on October 1, giving a 10%, one-year note payable.

GENERAL JOURNAL

Date	Accounts and Explanation	PR	Debit	Credit

   B. Record an adjusting entry on December 31 for the note payable in (A).

GENERAL JOURNAL

Date	Accounts and Explanation	PR	Debit	Credit

3. Pine Forest Corporation issued $500,000 in seven-year bonds with a stated interest rate of 8%. The bonds were sold on January 1, 2006, for $477,956 to yield 9%. Interest is paid July 1 and January 1. Pine Forest uses the straight-line method to amortize Discount on Bonds Payable. (Assume an October 31 year end.)

Record the journal entries for:

A. Issuance of bonds on January 1, 2006.
B. Payment of interest on July 1, 2006.
C. Accrual of interest and related amortization on October 31, 2006 (year end).
D. Payment of interest on January 1, 2007.
E. Maturity payment of bonds on January 1, 2013.

	Date	Account and Explanation	Debit	Credit
A.				
B.				
C.				
D.				
E.				

4. Young Corporation issued $500,000 in seven-year callable bonds with a stated interest rate of 8%. The bonds were sold on January 1, 2006, for $558,420 to yield 6%. Interest is paid July 1 and January 1. Young uses the effective-interest method to amortize Premium on Bonds Payable. (Assume a December 31 year end.)

Record the journal entries for:

A. Issuance of bonds on January 1, 2006.
B. Payment of interest on July 1, 2006.
C. Accrual of interest and related amortization on December 31, 2006 (year end).
D. Payment of interest on January 1, 2007.
E. Maturity payment of bonds on January 1, 2013.

	Date	Account and Explanation	Debit	Credit
A.				

B.

C.

D.

E.

5. Review the information in Exercise 4 and assume Young Corporation exercised its option to call the bonds on July 1, 2008, at 105. Record the July 1, 2008 journal entry for

a. the interest payment on July 1, 2008

Date	Accounts and Explanation	Debit	Credit

b. the cash payment to the bondholders

Date	Accounts and Explanation	Debit	Credit

VI. Critical Thinking

1. Review the information in Exercises 3 and 4 above and assume, in each case, that each $1,000 bond is convertible, at the option of the holder, into 31.25 of the corporation's common shares. Determine when an investor should seriously consider exercising the option to convert the bonds to shares.

2. What impact would there be for a bank manager considering a loan to a restaurant chain that only uses operating leases for their restaurants, relative to a company that purchases their own buildings?

DEMONSTRATION PROBLEMS

Demonstration Problem #1

The following events occurred in December:

1. On December 1, the company borrowed $75,000 from the bank, signing a nine-month note at 8% interest.
2. On December 10, the company accepted advance payments from two customers as follows:
   a) A $60,000 payment from Simex for 20 custom-made polishers. As of December 31, six polishers had been produced.
   b) A 10% down payment on a $100,000 contract for a piece of equipment to be delivered by May 1 of the following year. As of December 31, no work had been started on the equipment.
3. During December, a competitor filed a lawsuit against the company alleging violation of anti-trust regulations. If the company loses the suit, it is estimated damages will exceed $1 million.
4. The December payroll totaled $145,000, which will be paid on January 10. Employees accrue vacation benefits at the rate of 2% of monthly payroll. (Ignore payroll deductions and the employer's payroll tax expense.)
5. Sales for the month amounted to 1,200 units at $350 each, subject to a retail sales tax of 6%. Each unit carries a 90-day warranty requiring the company to repair or replace the unit if it becomes defective during the warranty period. The estimated cost to the company to honor the warranty is $55, and past experience has shown that approximately 3% of the units will be returned during the warranty period.

Required:

Record the external transactions and, where appropriate, the required adjusting entry at December 31.

Date	Accounts and Explanation	PR	Debit	Credit

Demonstration Problem #2

Mariposa Corporation has outstanding an issue of 10% callable bonds that mature in 2015. The bonds are dated January 1, 2005, and pay interest each July 1 and January 1. Additional bond data is as follows:

a. Fiscal year end for Mariposa Corporation: September 30.
b. Maturity value of the bonds: $5,000,000.
c. Contract interest rate: 10%.
d. Interest is paid 5% semiannually, $250,000 ($5,000,000 × 0.05).
e. Market interest rate at time of issue: 9% annually, 4.5% semiannually.
f. Issue price: 106.

Required:

1. Complete the effective-interest method amortization table through January 1, 2007. Round to the nearest dollar. Use the form below.

2. Using the amortization table that you have completed, record the following transactions:
    a. Issuance of bonds on January 1, 2005.
    b. Payment of interest and amortization of premium on July 1, 2005.
    c. Accrued interest and amortization of premium as of September 30, 2005.
    d. Payment of interest and amortization of premium on January 1, 2006.
    e. Retirement of the bonds on January 2, 2006. Callable price of bonds was 108.

Requirement 1

Semi-annual Interest Date	A Interest Payment (5% of Maturity Value)	B Interest Expense (4.5% of Preceding Bond Carrying Value)	C Premium Amortization (A - B)	D Premium Account Balance (D – C)	E Bond Carrying Value ($5,000,000 + D)
Jan 1, 2005				$300,000	$5,300,000
July 1, 2005					
Jan 1, 2006					
July 1, 2006					
Jan 1, 2007					

Requirement 2

	Date	Account and Explanation	Debit	Credit
a.				
b.				
c.				
d.				
e.				

SOLUTIONS

A. TEST YOURSELF

I. Matching

1.

1. L	5. U	9. D	13. N	17. R	21. H
2. M	6. S	10. K	14. P	18. I	22. Q
3. G	7. B	11. C	15. E	19. V	23. W
4. T	8. O	12. J	16. A	20. F	

2.

1. F	2. A	3. D	4. H
5. B	6. G	7. C	8. E

II. Multiple Choice

1.   B   The number 104.375 means 104.375% (or 1.04375) of the face value: $500,000 × 104.375% = $521,875.

2.   A   Since anyone may be a bondholder, it does not make sense that a bondholder's credit rating would affect the market price of the bond. All the other listed items do affect the market price of the bond.

3.   B   Of the items listed, all are liabilities that are due within one year except for pensions, which are long term.

4.   C   Effective rate of interest and market rate of interest are synonymous.

5.   D   Amortization of the premium on bonds payable serves to reduce the recorded amount of interest expense over the life of the bonds.

6.   D   The book value or carrying amount of a bond is equal to the face amount of the bond minus the unamortized discount or plus the unamortized premium.

7.   A   The carrying amount of a bond is the face amount of the bond plus (minus) unamortized premium (discount). Since the balance of the premium (discount) account is amortized over the life of the bond, it moves toward zero. Accordingly, the carrying amount of bonds issued at a premium (discount) decreases (increases) over time.

8.   C   GAAP identifies gains and losses on early retirement of debt as other income (loss).

9.   A   The conversion of a bond to common shares converts a liability to shareholders' equity, which increases shareholders' equity.

10.   D   Of the items listed, only "operating lease" is not reported on the balance sheet. Operating leases are generally short-term rental agreements that transfer none of the rights of ownership.

11.   D   The note payable is discounted (interest is taken out) when the loan is made. The bank subtracts the interest from the note's face amount and the borrower receives the net amount.

12.   C   A contingent liability is not an actual liability. It is a potential liability that depends on a future event arising out of a past transaction. Of the items listed, all except "lawsuit claims" are real liabilities.

13.   C   The *CICA Handbook* says to record an actual liability when 1) it is probable that the business has suffered a loss, and 2) its amount can be reasonably estimated.

14.   D   Notes payable is a known liability, all the others are estimated.

15.   B   A capital lease is one where the owner will likely take ownership based on a bargain purchase option, 75% of the estimated useful life, or 90% of the PV of the market value.

III. Completion

1. lower (when market rate > stated rate, then discount; when market rate < stated rate, then premium)
2. decreases (The book value or carrying value amount of a bond is equal to the face amount of the bond plus (minus) the unamortized premium (discount).)
3. other income (loss)
4. operating (Operating leases are normally short term and transfer none of the rights of ownership to the lessee. Accordingly, neither an asset nor a liability is recorded for such leases.)
5. capital (Capital leases require that the lessee record the leased property as an asset and the obligation to make future lease payments as a liability.)
6. straight-line (This method divides the amount of the discount/premium by the number of time periods resulting in the same figure each period.)
7. matching
8. discount (because the lender expects a greater return on the loan than the stated rate provides)
9. lender (not the borrower; convertibility make the bonds more attractive to prospective lenders because of the potential for greater returns)
10. a constant percentage (as compared with the straight-line method where the amount of discount/premium is constant. The effective rate is required by GAAP, although the straight-line method can be used if the difference between the two is not material.)
11.

K	A.	Accounts Payable	K	G.	Sales Tax Payable
K	B.	Short-term Notes Payable	E or K	H.	Liability for Vacation Pay
E or K	C.	Property Taxes Payable	E	I.	Postretirement Benefits
E	D.	Warranty Liability	K	J.	Interest Payable
K	E.	Salaries Expense	E or K	K.	Pension Premium Payable
E or K	F.	Income Taxes Payable			

12. Current portion
13. pension
14. earnings per share
15. Accrued expenses

IV. True/False

1.   F   96 refers to a percent, so it means that the bond is selling for 96% of its face value.

> **Study Tip**: Bond prices are always quoted in percentages, while stock prices are always quoted in dollars.

2.   T

3.   F   While it is true that the current portion is listed in the current liability section, it is not true it includes accrued interest. Accrued interest would be reported separately in the current liability section.

4.   F   Accrued expense and accrued liability are synonymous terms.

5.   T

6.   F   Unearned Revenue is a liability account and reported on the balance sheet.

7.   F   The matching principle, not the disclosure principle, requires that warranties expense be estimated and included on the current period's income statement.

8.   T

9.   T

10.   F   The expense will be less than the interest payments. Why? Because a part of each interest payment is simply the return to the bondholder of the premium paid when the bond was originally sold.

11.   F   The method used for amortizing a bond discount (or premium) does not determine how much interest is recognized over the life of the bond, it simply determines how the total amount of interest is recognized.

12.   F   The carrying value of a bond sold at a discount increases over the life of the bond.

13.   F   The callable feature refers to a right of the issuing corporation, not the bondholder.

14.   F   An apartment lease is an example of an operating lease.

15.   T

V. Exercises

1. A.

Cash	9,000,000	
Bonds Payable		9,000,000

   B.

Interest Expense ($9,000,000 × 0.0675 × 6/12)	303,750	
Cash		303,750

   C.

Bonds Payable	9,000,000	
Cash		9,000,000

2. A.

Cash	25,000	
Note Payable		25,000

   B. Adjusting entry on December 31:

Interest Expense	625	
Interest Payable		625
($25,000 × 0.10 × 3/12)		

3. A. Cash   477,956

3.	A.	Cash	477,956	
		Discount on Bonds Payable	22,044	
		Bonds Payable		500,000
	B.	Interest Expense (20,000 + 1,575)	21,575	
		Cash (500,000 × 0.08 × 6/12)		20,000
		Discount on Bonds Payable		1,575
		(22,044 / 14 interest payments)		
	C.	Interest Expense (13,333 + 1,050)	14,383	
		Interest Payable (500,000 × 0.08 × 4/12)		13,333
		Discount on Bonds Payable (22,044 / 14 × 4/6)		1,050

Note: In this exercise, the year end is October 31, not December 31.

	D.	Interest Expense [(20,000 - 13,333) + 525]	7,192	
		Interest Payable	13,333	
		Cash (500,000 × 0.08 × 6/12)		20,000
		Discount on Bonds Payable (22,044/14 × 2/6)		525
	E.	Bonds Payable	500,000	
		Cash		500,000
4.	A.	Cash	558,420	
		Bonds Payable		500,000
		Premium on Bonds Payable		58,420
	B.	Interest Expense (558,420 × 0.06 × 6/12)	16,753	
		Premium on Bonds Payable	3,247	
		Cash (500,000 × 0.08 × 6/12)		20,000

New carrying value of bonds = Bonds Payable + Premium on Bonds Payable
= 500,000 + (58,420 - 3,247) = 555,173

	C.	Interest Expense (555,173 × 0.06 × 6/12)	16,655	
		Premium on Bonds Payable	3,345	
		Interest Payable (500,000 × 0.08 × 6/12)		20,000

New carrying value of bonds = 500,000 + (55,173 − 3,345) = 551,828

	D.	Interest Payable	20,000	
		Cash		20,000
	E.	Bonds Payable	500,000	
		Cash		500,000

Note that after the last interest payment, the account Premium on Bonds Payable has a zero balance.

5. In order to record the July 1, 2008, interest payment, you need to update the amortization of the premium through July 1, 2008, as follows:

Carrying value of bonds on Jan. 1, 2007 is $551,828 (see solution to Exercise 4 above).

Carrying value of bonds on July 1, 2007 is $500,000 + ($51,828 - $3,445) = $548,383.

Carrying value of bonds on Jan. 1, 2008 is $500,000 + ($48,383 - $3,549) = $544,834.

July 1, 2008	Interest Expense ($544,834 × 0.06 × 6/12)	16,345	
	Premium on Bonds Payable	3,655	
	Cash ($500,000 × 0.08 × 6/12)		20,000

The carrying value of the bonds is now $500,000 + (44,834 - 3,655) = $541,179

July 1, 2008	Bonds Payable	500,000	
	Premium of Bonds Payable	41,179	
	Cash		525,000
	Gain on Retirement of Bonds		16,179

Study Tip: Gains (or losses) on retirement of bonds are reported as other income (loss) on the income statement.

VI. Critical Thinking

1. If each $1,000 bond can be converted into 31.25 common shares, then a quick calculation indicates an investor should seriously think about converting when the market price of the shares reaches $32 per share ($1,000 divided by 31.25 shares). However, this assumes the investor paid face value for the bonds. In Exercise 3, investors purchased the bonds at a discount of 95.59% of face value, or $955.90 for each $1,000 bond. Therefore, investors in Pine Forest's bonds could consider converting at a lower price of approximately $30.59 per share ($955.90 divided by 31.25). In Exercise 4, the investors paid a premium for the bonds because they were purchased at 111.68% of face value ($558,420 divided by $500,000). These investors would not be interested in converting until the price rose to $35.74 ($1,116.80 divided by 31.25 shares).

2. Since the restaurant chain must have space to run the businesses, these should be considered by a bank manager as being like a capital lease (without the lease, they could not operate). Thus, when compared to a company that purchases its buildings, the restaurant chain would not have the same amount of debt since it uses operating leases, thus its ratios would be different for debt/equity or times-interest-earned, making it appear to have better ratios. A bank manager must be aware of such "off-balance-sheet financing."

DEMONSTRATION PROBLEMS

Demonstration Problem #1 Solved and Explained

1.

Dec. 1	Cash	75,000	
	Notes Payable		75,000
Dec. 31	Interest Expense	500	
	Interest Payable		500

The company needs to accrue interest expense for December, calculated as follows: $75,000 \times 0.08 \times 1/12 = $500

2.

a.

Dec. 10	Cash	60,000	
	Unearned Revenues		60,000
Dec. 31	Unearned Revenues	18,000	
	Revenues Earned		18,000

b.

Dec. 10	Cash	10,000	
	Unearned Revenues		10,000
Dec. 31	No entry as no work has begun on the contract.		

3. No entry required. However, the footnotes to the balance sheet should contain information about this lawsuit. This is an example of a contingent liability.

4.

Dec. 31	Salary Expense	145,000	
	Salary Payable		145,000
	Vacation Pay Expense	2,900	
	Estimated Vacation Pay Liability		2,900

The matching principle requires that the additional expense of vacation pay be included with December's other expenses. The calculation is $145,000 \times 0.02 = $2,900. As employees claim their vacation pay, the entry is

Estimated Vacation Pay Liability	XX	
Cash		XX

(Of course, vacation pay is subject to taxes, just as salaries are.)

5.

Dec. 31	Accounts Receivable	445,200		
	Sales		420,000	
	Sales Tax Payable		25,200	
Dec. 31	Warranty Expense	1,980		
	Estimated Warranty Liability		1,980	

The warranty expense is based on the cost to the company of repairing or replacing each unit. Therefore, the estimate is calculated as follows:

Unit sales × estimate × cost to repair/replace = 1,200 × 0.03 × $55 = $1,980

Estimating warranty expense is another example of the matching principle.

Demonstration Problem #2 Solved and Explained

Requirement 1

Semi-annual Interest Date	A Interest Payment (5% of Maturity Value)	B Interest Expense (4.5% of Preceding Bond Carrying Value)	C Premium Amortiza-tion (A - B)	D Premium Account Balance (D - C)	E Bond Carrying Value ($5,000,000 + D)
Jan. 1, 2005				300,000	5,300,000
July 1, 2005	250,000	238,500	11,500	288,500	5,288,500
Jan. 1, 2006	250,000	237,983	12,017	276,483	5,276,483
July 1, 2006	250,000	237,442	12,558	263,925	5,263,925
Jan. 1, 2007	250,000	236,877	13,123	250,802	5,250,802

Study Tip: As the premium is amortized, the carrying amount moves toward the maturity value.

Requirement 2

a.	Jan. 1, 2005	Cash ($5,000,000 × 106/100)	5,300,000	
		Premium on Bonds Payable		300,000
		Bonds Payable		5,000,000
		To issue 10%, 10-year bonds at a premium.		

The bonds were sold at 106, indicating that investors were willing to pay a premium of $300,000 to earn 10% interest on $5,000,000 of principal over a 10-year period. This is to be expected because the bond is paying 10% annual interest at a time when the market rate of interest is only 9%.

b. July 1, 2005   Interest Expense ($250,000 - $11,500 amortization)   238,500

         Premium on Bonds Payable   11,500

            Cash   250,000

         To pay interest and amortize bond premium for six months.

Note that the amortization of the premium has the effect of reducing interest expense from the stated rate ($250,000) to the market rate ($238,500). If the bond is sold at a discount, the interest expense is increased from the stated rate to the market rate.

c. Sept. 30, 2005   Interest Expense ($125,000 - $6,009 amortization)   118,991

         Premium on Bonds Payable ($12,017 × 3/6)   6,009

            Interest Payable   125,000

         To accrue three months' interest and amortize three months' premium.

d. Jan. 1, 2006   Interest Expense ($125,000 - $6,009 amortization)   118,991

         Interest Payable   125,000

         Premium on Bonds Payable ($12,017 × 3/6)   6,009

            Cash   250,000

         To pay semiannual interest, part of which was accrued, and amortize three

         months' premium on bonds payable.

In this entry, six months of interest is actually paid to the bondholders on January 1. Note, however, only half (three months' worth) of the interest is current accounting period expense; the remaining amount represents the payment of the September 30 accrual of three months' interest. (Note that the premium is actually 6,008.50, rounded to 6,009.)

e. Jan. 2, 2006   Bonds Payable   5,000,000

         Premium on Bonds Payable   276,483

         Loss on Retirement on Bonds   123,517

            Cash ($5,000,000 × 108/100)   5,400,000

         To record the retirement of bonds payable at 108, retired before maturity.

This entry removes the Bonds Payable and related premium account from the corporate records and records the loss on retirement. The carrying value of the bonds ($5,276,483) is less than the cost to call the bonds ($5,400,000), resulting in the $123,517 loss. Had the price paid to call the bonds been less than the carrying value, the entry would have recorded a gain. Gains and losses on the retirement of bonds are reported as other income (loss) on the income statement.

Points to Remember

The interest rate stated on a debt instrument such as a corporate bond will typically differ from the actual market rate of interest when the bond is ultimately issued to the public. This occurs because of the lag in time that frequently occurs between the approval of the bond by the corporation (and regulatory agencies), its actual printings, and, finally, its issuance to the public. Rather than reprint the bond and potentially miss the rapidly changing market interest rate again, bonds are sold at a discount or premium. Occasionally, bonds are sold at face amount.

A bond is sold at a discount when the stated interest rate of the bond is below the current market rate. A premium is paid when the contract rate is higher than interest rates paid by comparable investments.

Premiums and discounts are, in effect, an adjustment to the interest rates. Thus, premiums and discounts should be amortized over the life of the bond.

Study Tip:

A good rule to remember is that bonds payable are always recorded at the face amount of the bond. Premiums and discounts are recorded in separate accounts.

The actual interest paid to the bondholders at the periodic payment dates (generally, semiannually) will always be the face value of the bond multiplied by the stated interest rate. A discount or premium will not affect these periodic cash payments.

The carrying amount (or book value) of a bond is conceptually similar to the book value of a fixed asset. Premiums are added to the face amount of bonds payable, and discounts are subtracted.

	Bonds Payable
+	Bond Premium or
-	Bond Discount
=	Carrying Value

Note that bonds sold at a premium will have a carrying amount greater than the face amount owed and discounted bonds will have a smaller value. In both cases, the carrying value will always move toward the face amount of the bond as the discount or premium is amortized. (Because of this, it is possible to quickly double-check your amortization entries—be sure the bond carrying value is moving in the right direction.)

CHAPTER 9—SHAREHOLDERS' EQUITY

CHAPTER OVERVIEW

Chapters 4 to 8 have provided a detailed examination of assets and liabilities, two of the three sections on the balance sheet. We now turn our attention to the third section, shareholders' equity. The term refers to one of the three legal forms of business organization—a corporation. The corporate form is more complex than proprietorships or partnerships. Although proprietorships are greater in number, corporations account for more revenues and total assets than the other forms. The specific learning objectives for this chapter are to

1. **Explain** the advantages and disadvantages of a corporation
2. **Measure** the effect of issuing shares on a company's financial position
3. **Describe** how share repurchase transactions affect a company
4. **Account** for dividends and measure their impact on a company
5. **Use** different share values in decision making
6. **Evaluate** a company's return on assets and return on shareholders' equity
7. **Report** shareholders' equity transactions on the cash flow statement

CHAPTER REVIEW

Objective 1 - Explain the advantages and disadvantages of a corporation

1. A corporation is a **separate legal entity** formed under federal or provincial law. The owners' equity of a corporation is held by shareholders as shares in the corporation.
2. A corporation has **continuous life and transferability of ownership**. A change in ownership of the shares does not affect the life of the corporation. Transfer of ownership does not affect the continuous life.
3. Shareholders have **limited liability**. That is, they have no personal obligation for the debts of the corporation.
4. **Ownership and management are separated**. Corporations are controlled by boards of directors who appoint officers to manage the business. Boards of directors are elected by shareholders. Thus, shareholders are not obligated to manage the business; ownership is separate from management.
5. **Corporations pay taxes**. Corporations are separate taxable entities. They pay a variety of taxes including federal and provincial income taxes. Corporations pay dividends to shareholders who then pay personal income taxes on their dividends. This is considered **double taxation** of corporate earnings, although Canada's tax laws attempt to minimize double taxation.
6. Corporations are subject to more **government regulation** than proprietorships or partnerships. Both federal and provincial governments monitor corporations closely and require them to disclose information to investors and creditors.

Corporations come into existence when the federal or provincial government approves the articles of incorporation submitted by the corporation. **Bylaws** are then adopted. The shareholders elect a **board of directors**, who appoint the officers of the corporation. (Helpful hint: review Exhibits 9-1 and 9-2 in the text.)

Shareholders have five basic **rights**:

1. to sell their shares
2. to participate in management by voting their shares
3. to receive a proportionate share of any dividends
4. to receive a proportionate share of the assets remaining after payment of liabilities in the event of liquidation
5. to maintain a proportionate ownership in the corporation (**preemptive right**) should new shares be issued.

Shareholders' equity is reported differently than owners' equity of a proprietorship or a partnership because corporations must report the sources of their capital. These sources are **contributed capital** (also called **capital stock**) from sale of shares, and **retained earnings**. Generally, contributed capital is not subject to withdrawal. Retained Earnings is the account that at any time is the sum of earnings accumulated since incorporation, minus any losses, and minus all dividends distributed to shareholders.

Owners receive **share certificates** for their investment. The basic unit of investment is a **share**. Shares in the hands of shareholders are said to be outstanding. (Helpful hint: review Exhibit 9-3 in the text.)

The corporate charter specifies the number of shares a corporation is **authorized** to issue. The corporation is not required to issue all the shares that have been authorized. The number of shares sold to investors is the amount **issued**, and the amount actually in the hands of shareholders is the amount **outstanding.**

Shares may be **common** or **preferred**. Different classes of common or preferred shares may be issued. Each class of common or preferred shares is recorded separately. Preferred shareholders receive their dividends before common shareholders and take priority over common shareholders in the receipt of assets if the corporation liquidates. (Helpful hint: review Exhibits 9-4 and 9-5 in the text.)

No par value shares are shares that do not have a value assigned to them by the articles of incorporation. When the board of directors assigns a value to the shares issued, it is known as the **stated value.**

The *Canada Business Corporations Act* now requires common and preferred shares to be issued without nominal or par value.

Objective 2 - Measure the effect of issuing shares on a company's financial position

If a corporation sells common shares for cash equal to the par value, the entry to record the transaction is

Cash	XX	
Common Shares		XX

Accounting for preferred shares follows the same pattern as accounting for common shares. The difference is that instead of the word "Common," the word "Preferred" will appear in the titles of the general ledger accounts.

When noncash assets are contributed to the corporation in exchange for shares, a potential conflict may arise. Investors may think these contributed assets are "worth" more, which means they would receive more shares. The corporation, however, may think the noncash assets are worth a lesser amount. This poses an ethical dilemma. How do you define (and, in this case, quantify) "current market value"? The ethical course of action is to rely on good-faith estimates from independent appraisers to determine fair market value at the time of the exchange.

Equipment	XX	
Common Shares		XX

Objective 3 - Describe how share repurchase transactions affect a company

Shares that a corporation issues and later reacquires are called **repurchased shares** Repurchased shares do not receive dividends and have no voting rights. Corporations may want repurchased shares for distribution within the company, to support the market price by reducing the supply of shares, or to avoid a takeover. The entry to record the repurchase of shares is

Common Shares	XX	
Cash		XX
(Shares × market price per share)		

The debit entry reduces total shareholders' equity.

Study Tip: Repurchased shares are *not* an asset, and the corporation *never* incurs a gain or loss by dealing in its own shares.

Shares that a corporation issues and later reacquires are no longer considered issued and outstanding. The repurchased shares may be canceled or held for reissue. Shares that are reissued are accounted for in exactly the same way as shares that are issued for the first time.

The entry to record the repurchase of shares at a cost greater than the issue price of the shares is

Common Shares	XX	
Retained Earnings	XX	
Cash		XX

The entry to record the repurchase of shares at a cost less than the issue price of the shares is

Common Shares	XX	
Contributed Surplus		XX
Cash		XX

Retained Earnings is the account that holds all of the corporation's net income less net losses and less dividends declared, accumulated over the life of the business. A deficit or debit balance means net losses have exceeded net income. Income Summary is closed to Retained Earnings at the end of each period. Retained Earnings is not a fund or reservoir of cash.

Objective 4 - Account for dividends and measure their impact on a company

A **dividend** is a distribution of cash (or shares) to the shareholders of a corporation. A corporation must have retained earnings and sufficient cash (or shares) to declare a dividend. A dividend must be declared by the board of directors before the corporation can pay it. Once a dividend has been declared, it is a legal liability of the corporation.

On the **date of declaration** the board also announces the **date of record** and the **payment date**. Those owning the shares on the date of record will receive the dividend. The payment date is the date the dividends are actually paid to the shareholders (by mail or direct payment into their bank accounts). The **ex dividend date** is the date after which shares are sold without the right to receive the current dividend. The **payment ratio** is the percentage of net income paid out in dividends to shareholders. The **cum dividend** is when a buyer of shares is entitled to receive a dividend that has been declared, but not paid.

When a dividend is declared, this entry is recorded:

Retained Earnings	XX	
Dividends Payable		XX

Dividends Payable is a current liability.

The date of record falls between the declaration date and the payment date and requires no journal entry. The dividend is usually paid several weeks after it is declared. When it is paid, this entry is recorded:

Dividends Payable	XX	
Cash		XX

Preferred shareholders have priority over common shareholders for the receipt of dividends. In other words, common shareholders do not receive dividends unless the total declared dividend is sufficient to pay the preferred shareholders first.

Preferred shares usually carry a stated dollar amount per share. Shareholders holding "$3 preferred" shares would receive a $3 annual cash dividend. The dividend to common shareholders will equal

Common dividend = Total dividend - Preferred dividend

A dividend is passed when a corporation fails to pay an annual dividend to preferred shareholders. Passed dividends are said to be in arrears. **Cumulative preferred shares** continue to accumulate annual dividends until the dividends are paid. Therefore, a corporation must pay all dividends in arrears to cumulative preferred shareholders before it can pay dividends to other shareholders.

Dividends in arrears are not liabilities, but are disclosed in the notes to the financial statements. Preferred shares are considered cumulative unless specifically labeled as noncumulative. Noncumulative preferred shares do not accumulate dividends in arrears. Some preferred shares have a **participation feature** where shareholders can receive additional dividends. Preferred shares have limited voting rights. Preferred shares may be **callable**, which may allow the company, at their discretion, to repurchase shares at a predetermined price and retire them.

Corporations declare **share dividends** instead of cash dividends when they want to conserve cash or reduce the market price per share. Unlike cash dividends, share dividends are not distributions of corporate assets. A share dividend is a proportional distribution of the corporation's shares to its shareholders. Thus, a share dividend affects only a corporation's shareholders' equity accounts; the result of a share dividend is a reduction in Retained Earnings, an increase in contributed capital, and total shareholders' equity stays the same.

The effect of declaring a share dividend is to transfer a portion of Retained Earnings to Common Shares.

Share dividends are accounted for at market value on the declaration date. The entry is

Retained Earnings	XX	
Common Shares Dividend Distributable		XX

The amount of the debit to Retained Earnings and the credit to Common Shares Dividend Distributable is equal to

Number of Shares Outstanding × Dividend % × Market Price per Share

On the date of distribution of a share dividend, the entry is

Common Shares Dividend Distributable	XX	
Common Shares		XX

A **share split** increases the number of outstanding shares. A share split affects only the number of shares outstanding. No account balances are affected. Both share splits and share dividends increase the number of shares outstanding and may decrease the market price per share.

On occasion, retained earnings have restrictions placed upon them that are disclosed in the notes to the financial statements, which may be legal, contractual, or voluntary.

Objective 5 - Use different share values in decision making

Market value (market price) is the price at which a person could buy or sell a share. Daily newspapers report the market price of many publicly traded shares.

Sometimes preferred shares can be redeemed by the corporation for a stated amount per share. This amount, which is set when the share is issued, is called **redemption value**.

Liquidation value is the amount a corporation must pay preferred shareholders if the company liquidates.

Book value is the amount of shareholders' equity per share. If only common shares are outstanding,

$$\text{Book value} = \frac{\text{Total shareholders' equity}}{\text{Number of common shares outstanding}}$$

If both preferred and common shares are outstanding, preferred shareholders' equity must be calculated first. The total preferred equity in the equation below equals the total redemption value (redemption value per share × number of preferred shares).

$$\text{Preferred book value} = \frac{\text{Total preferred equity + Dividends in arrears}}{\text{Number of preferred shares outstanding}}$$

$$\text{Common book value} = \frac{\text{Total equity - (Total preferred/redemption equity + Dividends in arrears)}}{\text{Number of common shares outstanding}}$$

Objective 6 - Evaluate a company's return on assets and return on shareholders' equity

1. $\text{Rate of return on total assets} = \dfrac{\text{Net income + Interest expense}}{\text{Average total assets}}$

The return on total assets (or return on assets) measures how successful the company was in using its (average) assets to earn a profit.

2. **Rate of return on common shareholders' equity** = $\dfrac{\text{Net income - Preferred dividends}}{\text{Average common shareholders' equity}}$

The denominator, average common shareholders' equity, is equal to total shareholders' equity minus preferred equity. The rate of return on common shareholders' equity also measures the profitability of the company. The return on equity should always be higher than the return on assets.

Objective 7 - Report shareholders' equity transactions on the cash flow statement

Transactions affecting shareholders' equity are reported on the cash flow statement as financing activities. These activities fall into three groups: issuing shares, paying dividends, and repurchasing shares. When a company receives cash in exchange for shares, the total amount received is reported as an inflow of cash. When cash dividends are paid (note paid, not declared), the total amount disbursed is reported as a cash outflow.

Study Tip: Share dividends are not reported on the cash flow statement because no cash is involved.

When a company repurchases its shares, the total amount paid is reported as a cash outflow.

TEST YOURSELF

All the self-testing materials in this chapter focus on information and procedures that your instructor is likely to test in quizzes and examinations.

I. Matching *Match each numbered term with its lettered definition.*

_____ 1. authorized shares
_____ 2. book value
_____ 3. chairperson of the board
_____ 4. convertible preferred shares
_____ 5. cumulative shares
_____ 6. shareholder
_____ 7. stated value
_____ 8. rate of return on total assets
_____ 9. market value
_____ 10. outstanding shares
_____ 11. share dividend
_____ 12. preferred shares
_____ 13. shareholders' equity
_____ 14. retained earnings
_____ 15. share split

_____ 16. board of directors
_____ 17. bylaws
_____ 18. charter
_____ 19. common shares
_____ 20. deficit
_____ 21. dividends
_____ 22. limited liability
_____ 23. contributed capital
_____ 24. repurchased shares
_____ 25. return on equity
_____ 26. preemptive right
_____ 27. date of record
_____ 28. declaration date
_____ 29. double taxation

A. an increase in the number of authorized, issued, and outstanding shares coupled with a proportionate reduction in the share's book value

B. the amount of shareholders' equity the company has earned through profitable operations and has not given back to the shareholders

C. the amount of shareholders' equity that shareholders have contributed to the corporation

D. a debit balance in the Retained Earnings account

E. a group elected by the shareholders to set policy for a corporation and to appoint its officers

F. the date on which the liability for a dividend is determined

G. an arbitrary amount assigned by a corporation to a share at the time of issue

H. a shareholder's right to maintain a proportionate ownership in a corporation

I. net income minus preferred dividends divided by average common shareholders' equity

J. an elected person on a corporation's board of directors who is usually the most powerful person in the corporation

K. a person who owns the shares in a corporation

L. distributions by a corporation to its shareholders

M. a term that means the most a shareholder can lose on his or her investment in a corporation is the cost of the investment

N. the shareholders' ownership interest in the assets of a corporation

O. a proportional distribution by a corporation of its own shares to its shareholders

P. preferred shares that may be exchanged by the shareholders, if they choose, for another class of shares in the corporation

Q. preferred shares whose owners must receive all dividends in arrears before the corporation pays dividends to the common shareholders

R. the process by which the company pays taxes on their profits and shareholders pay taxes on dividends

S. shares in the hands of shareholders

T. shares that give its owners certain advantages, such as the priority to receive dividends and the priority to receive assets if the corporation liquidates

U. the maximum number of shares a corporation may issue

V. the amount of owners' equity on the company's books for each of its shares

W. the sum of net income plus interest expense divided by average total assets

X. the constitution for governing a corporation

Y. a corporation's own shares that it has issued and later reacquired

Z. the document that gives the government's permission to form a corporation

AA. the date that determines who will receive a declared dividend

BB. the most basic form of capital share

CC. the price for which a person could buy or sell a share

II. Multiple Choice   *Circle the best answer.*

1. Advantages of the corporate form of business include all of the following *except*

   A. can raise more capital than a proprietorship or partnership
   B. continuous life
   C. ease of transferring ownership
   D. separation of ownership and management

2. A shareholder has no personal obligation for corporation liabilities. This is called

   A. mutual agency
   B. limited agency
   C. transferability of ownership
   D. limited liability

3. The correct order for pertinent dividend dates is

   A. declaration date, record date, payment date
   B. record date, declaration date, payment date
   C. declaration date, payment date, record date
   D. record date, payment date, declaration date

4. The date on which the next dividend payment is announced by a company's board of directors is called the

   A. declaration date
   B. date of record
   C. ex dividend date
   D. payment date

5. The ownership of shares entitles common shareholders to all of the following rights *except*

   A. the right to receive guaranteed dividends
   B. voting rights
   C. preemptive rights
   D. the right to receive a proportionate share of assets in a liquidation

6. When a corporation declares a cash dividend

   A. liabilities decrease, assets decrease
   B. assets decrease, retained earnings decreases
   C. assets decrease, retained earnings increases
   D. liabilities increase, retained earnings decreases

7. When a corporation pays a cash dividend

   A. liabilities decrease, assets increase
   B. assets decrease, retained earnings decreases
   C. liabilities decrease, assets decrease
   D. retained earnings decreases, liabilities increase

8. When a company issues shares in exchange for assets other than cash, the assets are recorded at

   A. market value
   B. original cost
   C. book value
   D. replacement cost

9. Dividends payable is a(n)

   A. expense
   B. current liability
   C. long-term liability
   D. shareholders' equity account

10. Dividends in arrears on preferred shares are reported

   A. on the balance sheet
   B. as a reduction of retained earnings
   C. on the income statement
   D. as a footnote to the financial statements

11. Stock dividends are recorded at

   A. stated value
   B. market value
   C. book value
   D. carrying value

12. The market price of Jaffer Corporation's common shares is $90. If Jaffer Corporation declares and issues a 50% share dividend, the market price will adjust to approximately

   A. $45
   B. $180
   C. $135
   D. $60

13. Before a stock dividend can be initiated, what must be available to management?

   A. cash and enough outstanding shares to distribute
   B. cash and unissued shares of the stock
   C. enough repurchased shares for the distribution
   D. unrestricted retained earnings and unissued shares of the stock

14. The arbitrary amount assigned to a share is called the

   A. face value
   B. stated value
   C. charter value
   D. legal capital

15. If only a single class of shares is issued by the corporation, and those shares carry voting rights, they are called

   A. preferred shares
   B. voting shares
   C. common shares
   D. contributed capital

16. If ABC has 600,000 shares outstanding with a stated value of $3 prior to a 3:2 share split, then after the share split, ABC will have

   A. 900,000 shares with a stated value of $3
   B. 400,000 shares with a stated value of $2
   C. 900,000 shares with a stated value of $2
   D. 400,000 shares with a stated value of $3

III. Completion   *Complete each of the following statements.*

1. Every corporation issues _____ shares.
2. _____ shares do not receive cash dividends.
3. Preferred shareholders have preference over common shareholders in _____ and _____.
4. Dividends are declared by _____.
5. A corporation may repurchase shares in order to _____ _____ _____.
6. Shareholders' equity minus preferred equity equals _____.
7. The date of _____ determines who receives the dividend.
8. The date of _____ establishes the liability to pay a dividend.
9. Shares in the hands of shareholders are called _____ shares.
10. Corporations come into existence when a _____ is approved by the _____ government.
11. _____ are the maximum number of shares a company is _____ to issue by the board of directors.
12. _____ is the percentage of net income paid out in dividends to shareholders.
13. The _____ is (net income + interest expense) / average total assets
14. The rate of return on shareholders' equity is (_____) / average common shareholders' equity
15. A 2:1 _____ does not require a journal entry, but does _____ the number of shares outstanding.

IV. True/False   *For each of the following statements, circle* T *for true or* F *for false.*

1. T F   Dividends paid are a cash outflow reported as an operating activity on the cash flow statement.
2. T F   To calculate the rate of return on total assets, net income is added to interest expense then divided by average total assets.
3. T F   Both preferred shares and common shares have stated liquidation values.
4. T F   A 50% share dividend is the same as a 3-for-2 share split.
5. T F   Stock dividends are recorded at market value as of the record date.
6. T F   Noncumulative preferred shares mean that a shareholder cannot participate in additional dividends declared.
7. T F   When a cash dividend is paid, assets and shareholders' equity decrease.
8. T F   When a corporation repurchases its shares at a cost greater than the issue price of the shares, retained earnings is reduced.
9. T F   When a corporation repurchases its shares at a cost less than the issue price of the shares, the difference is considered contributed surplus.

10.   T F   An advantage of the corporate form of organization is that the income earned by the business is subject to less taxation than that earned by partnerships or proprietorships.

11.   T F   Preferred shares are assumed to be cumulative unless they are specifically labeled as noncumulative.

12.   T F   Issued shares and outstanding shares refer to the same number of shares.

13.   T F   Double taxation refers to both preferred dividends and common dividends being taxed in the hands of shareholders.

14.   T F   The preemptive right refers to a shareholder receiving a proportionate share of assets upon liquidation.

15.   T F   When a corporation issues only one class of shares, those shares are called common shares.

V. Exercises

1. Getitnow.com declared a cash dividend of $1.10 per common share on November 10. The dividend was paid on December 20 to shareholders of record on December 1. Getitnow.com has 4,500,000 common shares outstanding.

   a. Prepare the journal entry on November 10.

Date	Accounts and Explanation	PR	Debit	Credit

   b. Prepare the journal entry on December 1.

Date	Accounts and Explanation	PR	Debit	Credit

   c. Prepare the journal entry on December 20.

Date	Accounts and Explanation	PR	Debit	Credit

2. The charter of Spinke-Garman Inc. authorizes the issuance of 1,000,000 preferred shares and 5,000,000 common shares. During the first month of operation, Spinke-Garman, Inc. completed the following share-issuance transactions:

February 1   Issued 300,000 common shares at $18 per share.
February 10   Issued 20,000 $2.50 preferred shares. The issue price was $40 per share.
February 28   Received inventory valued at $80,000 and equipment with a market value of $120,000 in exchange for 20,000 common shares.

Record the necessary journal entries for the above three transactions (omit explanations).

Date	Account	Debit	Credit

3. Using your answers from Exercise 2 above, prepare the shareholders' equity section of the Spinke-Garman Inc. balance sheet at the end of the first month. Assume Retained Earnings has a balance of $85,000.

Shareholders' Equity	

4. Sanders Corporation has 10,000 $5.00 preferred shares outstanding. There were no dividends in arrears at the end of 2002, and no dividends were paid in 2003 or 2004. Sanders Corporation also has 20,000 common shares outstanding.

a. If Sanders Corporation pays a total of $220,000 in dividends in 2005, how much will each class of shareholders receive?

b. If Sanders Corporation pays a total of $140,000 in dividends in 2005, how much will each class of shareholders receive?

5. Indicate the effect of each of the following transactions on Assets, Liabilities, Contributed Capital, and Retained Earnings. Use + for increase, - for decrease, and 0 for no effect.

	Assets	Liabilities	Contributed Capital	Retained Earnings
A. Declaration of a cash dividend	_____	_____	_____	_____
B. Payment of a cash dividend	_____	_____	_____	_____
C. Declaration of a share dividend	_____	_____	_____	_____
D. Issuance of a share dividend	_____	_____	_____	_____
E. A share split	_____	_____	_____	_____
F. Cash repurchase of shares at greater than issue price	_____	_____	_____	_____
G. Sale of previously repurchased shares	_____	_____	_____	_____

6. New Venture Corporation had 1,500,000 common shares outstanding on March 1. Prepare a journal entry for the following transaction:

March 15   Declared and issued a 5% share dividend. The market price was $52 per share.

Date	Account and Explanation	PR	Debit	Credit

7. Prepare journal entries for the following transactions:

Feb. 10   Repurchased 800 common shares for $24.00 per share. The shares were originally issued at $26.00 per share.

July 1   Repurchased 1,000 common shares for $27.00 per share. The shares were originally issued at $26.00.

Dec. 12   Reissued 1,500 of the repurchased shares for $30.00.

Date	Account and Explanation	PR	Debit	Credit

VI. Critical Thinking

1. Review the facts in Exercise 6 with the following changes:

Oct. 10 Declared a 5-for-2 share split. The market price was $60 per share.
Oct. 30 Issued the shares.

Present the journal entries for the above share split.

2. Why is dividends declared and paid considered a financing activity on the cash flow statement ? Do stock dividends appear as a financing activity?

DEMONSTRATION PROBLEMS

Demonstration Problem #1

On January 1, 2006, DVD.com was authorized to issue 5,000,000 $3.00 preferred shares and 5,000,000 common shares. During its start-up phase, the company completed the following selected transactions related to its shareholders' equity:

Jan. 10   Sold 400,000 common shares at $22 per share.

Jan. 11   Issued 50,000 preferred shares for cash of $55 per share.

Jan. 17   Issued 30,000 common shares in exchange for equipment valued at $600,000.

Jan. 24   An old building and small parcel of land were acquired by the corporation for a future office site that would employ 60 people. The site value was $1,000,000; the building was worthless. DVD.com issued 80,000 common shares for the site and building.

Jan. 31   Earned a small profit for January resulting in a $72,000 credit balance in the Retained Earnings account.

Required:

1. Record the transactions in the general journal. No entry is required on January 31.
2. Post the journal entries into the equity accounts provided.
3. Prepare the shareholders' equity section of DVD.com's balance sheet at January 31, 2006.
4. Compute the book value per share of the preferred shares and the common shares. The preferred shares have a liquidation value of $52.50 per share. No dividends are in arrears.

Requirement 1 (journal entries)

Date	Accounts and Explanation	PR	Debit	Credit

Requirement 2 (postings)

Preferred Shares

Common Shares

Retained Earnings

72,000

Requirements 3 (Shareholders' equity section)

DVD.com
Balance Sheet—Shareholders' Equity Section
January 31, 2006

Requirement 4 (Book value per share)

Demonstration Problem #2

Dynamic Pensions Inc. reported the following shareholders' equity:

Shareholders' Equity:	
Preferred shares, $2.00	
Authorized—1,000,000 shares	
Issued 150,000 shares	$ 3,750,000
Common shares	
Authorized—5,000,000 shares	
Issued—800,000 shares	6,800,000
Retained earnings	6,841,180
Total shareholders' equity	$17,391,180

Required:

1. What was the average issue price per common share?
2. What was the average issue price per preferred share?

3. Assume the board of directors declares dividends totaling $1,800,000 to the shareholders. The preferred shares are cumulative and no dividends were declared last year. Calculate the amount per share each class of shares will receive.
4. Journalize the issuance of 10,000 additional common shares at $22.50 per share. Use the same account titles as shown in the problem.
5. How many common shares are outstanding after the 10,000 additional shares have been sold?
6. How many common shares would be outstanding after the corporation split its common shares 2-for-l?
7. Journalize the declaration of a 10% share dividend on common shares when the market price of the share is $11.25. Assume the stock dividend is declared after the 2-for-1 split.
8. Journalize the following share repurchase transactions in the order given:
   a. Dynamic Pensions Inc. repurchases 2,500 common shares at $25 per share.
   b. One month later, the corporation sells 1,000 of the repurchased shares for $27 per share.

Requirement 1

Requirement 2

Requirement 3

Requirement 4

Date	Account and Explanation	PR	Debit	Credit

Requirement 5

Requirement 6

Requirement 7

Date	Account and Explanation	PR	Debit	Credit

Requirement 8

a.

Date	Account and Explanation	PR	Debit	Credit

b.

Date	Account and Explanation	PR	Debit	Credit

SOLUTIONS

A. TEST YOURSELF

I. Matching

1. U	5. Q	9. CC	13. N	17. X	21. L	25. I	29. R
2. V	6. K	10. S	14. B	18. Z	22. M	26. H	
3. J	7. G	11. O	15. A	19. BB	23. C	27. AA	
4. P	8. W	12. T	16. E	20. D	24. Y	28. F	

II. Multiple Choice

1.   D   Separation of ownership and management is considered a disadvantage of the corporate form of business organization.

2.   D   Mutual agency is a characteristic of partnerships not present in corporations. Transferability of ownership is a characteristic that the corporate form of organization simplifies. Limited agency has no meaning.

3.   A   The board of directors declares a dividend on the declaration date, to shareholders of record on the record date, and that is paid on the payment date.

4.   A   Declaration date is the date on which the next dividend payment is announced by the company's board of directors.

5.   A   Dividends represent the distribution of the earnings of the corporation and are not guaranteed.

6.   D   The declaration of a dividend reduces Retained Earnings and increases the liability account, Dividends Payable.

7.   C   The payment of a cash dividend results in cash being paid to shareholders to settle the liability created by the declaration of the dividend.

8.   A   When shares are issued in exchange for noncash assets, the transaction should be recorded at fair market value.

9.   B   The declaration of a dividend by the board of directors creates a current liability.

10.   D   Dividends in arrears is not a liability since a dividend must be declared to create a liability. However, dividends in arrears do impair the amount of capital available to common shareholders. Dividends in arrears are usually disclosed in a footnote.

11.   B   A small share dividend is accounted for at market value on the date of declaration.

12.   D   If the market price for one pre-dividend share is $90, then approximately the same market value will apply to the 1.5 post-dividend shares since the shareholder's percentage ownership in the corporation has not changed. $90 ÷ 1.5 shares = $60 per share.

13. D

14. B

15. C

16. C   Increase the number of shares and decrease the stated value. The total value of the shares is still $1,800,000 (900,000 × $2 or 600,000 × $3).

III. Completion

1. common (Corporations may also issue preferred shares, but that is optional.)
2. Repurchased (Repurchased shares also have no voting rights.)
3. receiving dividends and in event of a liquidation
4. the board of directors
5. avoid a takeover; distribute to employees; keep the market price high
6. common shareholders' equity
7. record
8. declaration
9. outstanding
10. charter; federal or provincial
11. Authorized shares, authorized
12. Payment payout ratio
13. rate of return on total assets
14. (net income – preferred dividends)
15. share split, increase

IV. True/False

1.   F   Dividends are considered a financing activity.
2.   T
3.   F   Only preferred shares will have a liquidation value—common shareholders simply receive a proportionate share of assets remaining after all creditors have been paid and the preferred shareholders have received their cash (liquidation value plus dividends in arrears).
4.   F   This is a very "tricky" statement. It is true that a 50% share dividend will result in the same numbers of shares as a 3-for-2 share split. However, a stock dividend results in the capitalization of Retained Earnings while a stock split does not.
5.   F   Stock dividends are recorded at market value as of the declaration date, the date when the liability is established.
6.   F   Noncumulative preferred shares do not accumulate dividends in arrears if dividends are not declared in a particular year.
7.   F   The payment of a cash dividend results in a decrease in assets and liabilities—shareholders' equity is only affected when the dividend is declared and the liability is set up.
8.   T
9.   T
10. F   Corporate earnings are often subject to double taxation.
11. T

12.   F   Outstanding shares refers to the number of shares held by shareholders. Issued shares refers to the total number of shares the corporation has ever sold, including those that have been repurchased.

13.   F   Double taxation refers to a corporation being taxed on their profits and shareholders taxed on dividends received.

14.   F   In the case of a new share issue, the preemptive right allows a current shareholder to purchase additional shares in proportion to the owner's current amount.

15.   T

V. Exercises

1.

	Date	Accounts and Explanation	Debit	Credit
a.	Nov. 10	Retained Earnings	4,950,000	
		Dividends Payable		4,950,000
		(4,500,000 shares × $1.10)		
b.	Dec. 1	No entry		
c.	Dec. 20	Dividends Payable	4,950,000	
		Cash		4,950,000

2.

Date	Account	Debit	Credit
Feb. 1	Cash	5,400,000	
	Common Shares (300,000 × $18.00)		5,400,000
Feb. 10	Cash	800,000	
	Preferred Shares (20,000 × $40)		800,000
Feb. 28	Merchandise Inventory	80,000	
	Equipment	120,000	
	Common Shares (80,000 + 120,000)		200,000

3.

Shareholders' Equity

Contributed capital:	
Preferred shares, $2.50, 1,000,000 shares authorized, 20,000 shares issued	$ 800,000
Common shares, 5,000,000 shares authorized, 320,000 shares issued	5,600,000
Total contributed capital	6,400,000
Retained earnings	85,000
Total shareholders' equity	$6,485,000

4.

a. Preferred: 3 years × 10,000 shares × $5.00 = $150,000 (or $15 per share)
Common: $220,000 - $150,000 = $70,000 (or $3.50 per share)

b. Preferred: 3 years × 10,000 shares × $5.00 = $150,000
Since $140,000 is less than the $150,000 preferred shareholders must receive in dividends before common shareholders receive anything, all $140,000 goes to the preferred shareholders. The common shareholders receive nothing, and the preferred shares now have $10,000 dividends in arrears.

5.

	Assets	Liabilities	Contributed Capital	Retained Earnings
A. Declaration of a cash dividend	0	+	0	-
B. Payment of a cash dividend	-	-	0	0
C. Declaration of a share dividend	0	0	+	-
D. Issuance of a share dividend	0	0	0	0
E. A share split	0	0	0	0
F. Cash repurchase of shares at greater than issue price	-	0	-	-
G. Sale of previously repurchased shares	+	0	+	0

6.

Date	Account and Explanation	Debit	Credit
March 15	Retained Earnings (1,500,000 × 0.05 × $52)	3,900,000	
	Common Shares (1,500,000 × 0.05 × $52)		3,900,000

7.

Date	Account and Explanation	Debit	Credit
Feb. 10	Common Shares (800 × $26)	20,800	
	Contributed Surplus—Share Repurchase (800 × ($26 – $24))		1,600
	Cash		19,200
July 1	Common Shares (1,000 × $26)	26,000	
	Retained Earnings (1,000 × ($27 – $26))	1,000	
	Cash (1000 × $27)		27,000
Dec. 12	Cash (1,500 × $30)	45,000	
	Common Shares		45,000

VI. Critical Thinking

1. No journal entries are required when a company declares a share split. The outstanding shares are returned to the company and replaced with new shares. The total contributed capital remains unchanged.

2. Dividends represent a distribution of earnings to the shareholders, and not regular operating income. As such, they do not generate revenues for the firm, meaning they do not qualify as operating income. Stock dividends do not represent a cash flow and therefore are not reported on the cash flow statement.

DEMONSTRATION PROBLEMS

Demonstration Problem #1 Solved and Explained

Requirement 1 (Journal entries)

Jan. 10	Cash	8,800,000	
	Common Shares (400,000 × $22)		8,800,000
	Issued common shares at $22 per share.		

The receipt of cash is recorded by debiting Cash and crediting Common Shares for the number of shares times the selling price.

Jan. 11	Cash	2,750,000	
	Preferred Shares (50,000 × $55)		2,750,000
	Issued preferred shares at $55 per share.		

Preferred Shares is credited for the shares times the selling price.

Jan. 17	Equipment	600,000	
	Common Shares		600,000
	Issued 30,000 common shares in exchange for equipment.		

When a corporation issues shares in exchange for an asset other than cash, it debits the asset received (in this case, Equipment) for its fair market value and credits the capital accounts as it would do if cash were the asset received.

Jan. 24	Land	1,000,000	
	Common Shares		1,000,000
	Issued 80,000 common shares in exchange for land.		

Requirement 2 (Posting)

Preferred Shares		
	Jan. 11	2,750,000
	Bal.	2,750,000

Common Shares		
	Jan. 10	8,800,000
	Jan. 17	600,000
	Jan. 24	1,000,000
	Bal.	10,400,000

	Retained Earnings	
		72,000

Requirement 3 (Shareholders' equity section)

DVD.com
Balance Sheet—Shareholders' Equity Section
January 31, 2006

Shareholders' equity:

Preferred shares, $3.00, 5,000,000 shares authorized,	
50,000 shares issued	$ 2,750,000
Common shares, 5,000,000 shares authorized,	
510,000 shares	10,400,000
Total contributed capital	13,150,000
Retained earnings	72,000
Total shareholders' equity	$13,222,000

Requirement 4 (Book value per share)

Preferred:

Liquidation value (50,000 shares × $52.50)	$ 2,625,000
Cumulative dividends in arrears	0
Shareholders' equity allocated to preferred	$ 2,625,000
Book value per share ($2,625,000 / 50,000 shares)	$ 52.50

Common:

Total shareholders' equity	$13,222,000
Less: Shareholders' equity allocated to preferred	2,750,000
Shareholders' equity allocated to common	$10,472,000
Book value per share ($10,472,000 / 510,000 shares)	$ 20.53

(rounded to nearest cent)

Calculated as follows:

Date	No. of Shares	Transactions
Jan. 10	400,000	Issued
Jan. 17	30,000	Issued
Jan. 24	80,000	Issued
	510,000 shares	

Demonstration Problem #2 Solved and Explained

1. Average issue price of the common shares was $8.50 per share:

Total received common shares	$6,800,000
÷ number of issued shares	÷ 800,000
Average issue price	$8.50

2. Average issue price of the preferred shares was $25 per share:

Total received preferred shares	3,750,000
÷ number of issued shares	÷150,000
Average issue price	$ 25.00

3. Preferred: $2 per share × 2 years = $4 per share
$4 per share × 150,000 shares = $600,000

   Common: $1,200,000 available ($1,800,000 less $600,000 to preferred)
$1,200,000 ÷ 800,000 shares = $1.50 per share

4. Cash (10,000 shares × $22.50 selling price)   225,000
       Common Shares   225,000
   To issue common shares at $22.50 per share.

5. Shares outstanding = 810,000
   * 800,000 shares issued, plus 10,000 shares from answer 4 above.

6. Shares outstanding after 2-for-1 split = 1,620,000: ($10,000 shares before split × 2/1)

7. Retained Earnings (1,620,000 outstanding shares ×
       10% × $11.25)   1,822,500
       Common Share Dividend Distributable   1,822,500
   To declare a 10% share dividend.

   When a *stock dividend* occurs, Retained Earnings should be capitalized for the *fair market* value of the shares to be distributed (in this case, 1,822,500). Note that 1,620,000 shares were outstanding after answer 6 above. The 10% distribution was for 162,000 shares (1,620,000 × 10% = 162,000).

8. a. Common Shares (2,500 × $4.34*)   10,850
       Retained Earnings   51,650
           Cash (2,500 × $25)   62,500
       To repurchase shares for $25 per share (average issue price was $4.34 per share).

*Total paid for common shares ($6,800,000 + 225,000) =	7,025,000
Divided by number of shares issued	1,620,000
Average price per share	$4.34

b. Cash (1,000 × $27)   27,000
      Common Shares   27,000
   To issue 1,000 shares at $27 per share.

CHAPTER 10—LONG-TERM INVESTMENTS AND INTERNATIONAL OPERATIONS

CHAPTER OVERVIEW

In Chapter 9, you learned about share capital from the perspective of the issuing corporation. In Chapter 8 we examined long-term liabilities and how corporations account for bonds payable and other obligations. Now we expand these topics, but change the perspective. Corporations frequently purchase shares and bonds as investments. In addition, you'll learn about parent and subsidiary relationships and foreign currency transactions. The specific learning objectives for this chapter are to

1. **Account** for portfolio investments
2. **Use** the equity method for investments
3. **Understand** consolidated financial statements
4. **Account** for long-term investments in bonds
5. **Account** for international operations
6. **Report** investing transactions on the cash flow statement

CHAPTER REVIEW

Shares are traded in markets. Prices are quoted in dollars and cents. The owner of a share is the investor. The corporation that issues the share is the investee.

Share investments are assets to the investor. **Temporary investments** (sometimes called **marketable securities**) are 1) liquid (readily convertible to cash) and 2) expected to be converted to cash within one year, defined as financial assets held for trading (CICA 3855). **Long-term investments** are expected to be held for longer than one year.

Long-term share investments are divided into three groups for accounting purposes depending on the level of ownership of the investee:

1. less than 20% ownership (no influence—called other investments or portfolio investment)
2. between 20% and 50% ownership (significant influence)
3. over 50% ownership (investment in subsidiary—controlling interest)

Objective 1 - Account for portfolio investments

When an investor holds less than 20% ownership (a portfolio investment), the cost method is used to account for the investment. The cost method follows the procedures outlined in Chapter 5. Purchases increase long-term investment accounts, dividends are recognized as dividend revenue, and the LCM rule is applied. Gains and losses are recognized at the time of disposal of the asset.

Objective 2 - Use the equity method for investments

The **equity method** is used when an investor holds between 20% and 50% of an investee's voting shares because the investor may exert significant influence on the investee's business decisions.

The investment is recorded at cost; debit Long-Term Investment and credit Cash.

The investor records its proportionate ownership of the investee's net income and dividends. If the investor owns 40% of the voting shares, the investor will record 40% of the net income as revenue and will receive 40% of the dividends. The share of income is recorded with a debit to the Long-Term Investment account and a credit to Equity-Method Investment Revenue. The receipt of cash dividends reduces the investment. Therefore, the dividend is recorded with a debit to Cash and a credit to the Long-Term Investment account. Equity-method investment revenue is reported as "other revenue" on the income statement.

When the equity method is used and an investment is sold, the gain (or loss) on the sale is the difference between the proceeds and the balance in the Long-Term Investment account.

Objective 3 – Understand consolidated financial statements

An investor who owns more than 50% of an investee's voting shares has a controlling (majority) interest. The investor is called the **parent company**, and the investee is called the **subsidiary**. See Exhibits 10-3, 10-4, and 10-5 in your text. Parent-subsidiary relationships are very common (see Exhibit 10-6).

Consolidation accounting combines the financial statements of two or more companies that are controlled by the same owners. The assets, liabilities, revenues, and expenses of the subsidiary are added to the parent's accounts.

A separate set of books for the consolidated entity does not exist. The consolidation is accomplished by the use of a work sheet, such as that shown in Exhibit 10-7 in your text. Transactions that affect both the parent and the subsidiary must be eliminated from the consolidation. These transactions are called **intercompany transactions** and include loans between parent and subsidiary, the parent's investment in the subsidiary, and the subsidiary's equity accounts. **Goodwill** is recorded during the consolidation process if the parent buys the subsidiary for a price above the market value of the subsidiary's net assets.

A **minority interest** will appear on the consolidated balance sheet when the parent company owns more than 50% but less than 100% of the subsidiary's shares. Minority interest is listed as a liability on the consolidated balance sheet. Minority interest represents the ownership of the remaining shareholders.

Consolidated income is equal to the net income of the parent plus the parent's proportionate interest in the subsidiary's net income.

Objective 4 - Account for long-term investments in bonds

Investors purchase bonds issued by corporations. The investor can purchase short-term (current asset) or long-term (long-term investment) bonds.

Short-term investments in bonds are rare. More commonly, companies purchase bonds as long-term investments. When acquired, these bonds are recorded at cost. Thereafter they are reported on the balance sheet at their **amortized cost,** which determines their carrying value. This means the balance in the Long-Term Investment account reflects both the initial cost of the bond plus or minus a portion of the discount (an addition to the account) or premium (a reduction to the account) on the bond. No discount or premium account is used. If the bonds were initially purchased at a discount, the balance in the Long-Term Investment account increases as the bonds approach maturity. If the bonds were initially purchased at a premium, the balance in the Long-Term Investment account decreases as the bonds approach maturity. The amortization of a bond discount would appear as follows:

Long-Term Investment in Bonds	XX	
Interest Revenue		XX

> **Study Tip**: From the buyer's perspective, a discount means additional interest revenue while a premium means less interest revenue. This effect is exactly the opposite from the perspective of the issuer.

Carefully review the Decision Guideline in your text. It presents an excellent summary of the rules governing share and bond investments.

Objective 5 - Account for international operations

International accounting deals with business activities that cross national boundaries. Each country uses its own national currency; therefore, a step has been added to the transaction—one currency must be converted into another.

The price of one nation's currency stated in terms of another country's currency is called the **foreign currency exchange rate**. The conversion of one currency into another currency is called **translation**. Exchange rates are determined by supply and demand. The main factors influencing the supply and demand for a particular country's currency are 1) the ratio of a country's imports to its exports and 2) the rate of return available in the country's capital markets.

The import/export ratio is the level of exports relative to imports. If exports exceed imports, the customers must buy the country's currency to pay for the goods, driving up the demand and hence price of the currency. A strong currency is rising relative to other nations' currencies, and a weak currency is falling relative to other currencies.

When Company A in Country A purchases goods from Company B in Country B, the transaction price may be stated in the currency of either country. Suppose the transaction is stated in Country A's currency. The transaction requires two steps:

1. The transaction price must be translated for recording in the accounting records of Company B.
2. When payment is made, Company B may experience a foreign-currency translation gain or loss. This gain or loss results when there is a change in the exchange rate between the date of the purchase on account and the date of the subsequent payment of cash.

Note that there will be no foreign-currency gain or loss for Company A because the transaction price was stated in the currency of Country A.

The net amount of foreign-currency transaction gains and losses is accumulated for each accounting period and reported on the income statement as other revenue and gains, or other expenses and losses.

Hedging is a means of protecting the company from foreign-currency transaction losses. A **futures contract** gives the company the right to receive a certain amount of foreign currency on a particular future date.

Canadian companies with foreign subsidiaries must consolidate the subsidiary financial statements into their own for external reporting. This can cause two problems:

1. GAAP may be different in the foreign country. (Helpful hint: review Exhibit 10-11 in the text.)
2. When the foreign subsidiary's financial statements are translated into Canadian dollars, there may be a translation adjustment. (Helpful hint: review Exhibit 10-10 in your text.)

A **foreign-currency translation adjustment** arises because of changes in exchange rates over time. Assets and liabilities are translated using exchange rates as of the balance sheet date. Shareholders' equity, including revenues and expenses, is translated using the exchange rates that were in effect when those transactions were executed (this results in shareholders' equity not equaling assets minus liabilities). The adjustment necessary to bring the subsidiary's balance sheet back into balance ("translation adjustment") is reported as part of shareholders' equity on the consolidated balance sheet. The translation adjustment will be positive when the book value of the investment in the foreign subsidiary has increased. A negative amount reflects a reduction.

Objective 6 - Report investing transactions on the cash flow statement

The purchase and sale of shares and bond investments are reported on the cash flow statement in the investing activities section. Revenues from dividends and interest revenue (from bonds) are operating activities because they are reported in the income statement. However, the actual purchase of investments is listed as a cash outflow in the investing activities section of the cash flow statement while the proceeds from the sale of investments will appear as a cash inflow. Carefully review the statement for Onex Corporation (Exhibit 10-12) in your text.

TEST YOURSELF

All the self-testing materials in this chapter focus on information and procedures that your instructor is likely to test in quizzes and examinations.

I. Matching   *Match each numbered term with its lettered definition.*

_____ 1.	consolidated statements	_____ 11.	minority interest
_____ 2.	marketable securities	_____ 12.	parent company
_____ 3.	controlling interest	_____ 13.	majority interest
_____ 4.	cost method	_____ 14.	strong currency
_____ 5.	equity method for investments	_____ 15.	subsidiary company
_____ 6.	foreign currency exchange rate	_____ 16.	foreign-currency translation adjustment
_____ 7.	temporary investment	_____ 17.	weak currency
_____ 8.	hedging	_____ 18.	amortized cost
_____ 9.	long-term investment		
_____ 10.	portfolio investments		

A. short-term investments
B. the balancing figure that brings the dollar amount of the total liabilities and shareholders' equity of a foreign subsidiary into agreement with the dollar amount of total assets
C. a long-term share investment where the purpose is similar to that of short-term investing and the investor holds less than 20% of the investee's voting shares
D. combining the balance sheets, income statements, and other financial statements of the parent with those of the subsidiaries into an overall set as if the separate entities were one
E. a currency whose exchange rate is rising relative to other nations' currencies
F. investee company in which a parent owns more than 50% of the voting shares
G. investor company that owns more than 50% of the voting shares of a subsidiary company
H. ownership of more than 50% of an investee company's voting shares, also called controlling interest
I. a method used to account for investments in which the investor can significantly influence the decisions of the investee

J. a method of accounting for long-term share investments under which the beginning accounting value is cost, dividends are treated as income, and gains and losses are recorded as sales

K. ownership of more than 50% of an investee company's voting shares

L. an investment that is readily convertible to cash and that the investor intends to convert to cash within one year or to use to pay a current liability

M. a separate asset category reported on the balance sheet between current assets and capital assets

N. a strategy to avoid foreign-currency transaction losses

O. a subsidiary company's equity that is held by shareholders other than the parent company

P. the price of one country's currency stated in terms of another country's monetary unit

Q. a currency whose exchange rate is decreasing relative to other nations' currencies

R. the original cost of an investment in bonds plus discount amortization or less premium amortization

II. Multiple Choice   *Circle the best answer.*

1. A share is listed in the *Globe and Mail* as having a High of $22.25, a Low of $21.00, a Close of $21.75, and a Net Change of +0.25. What was the previous day's closing price?

   A. $22.50
   B. $21.25
   C. $22.00
   D. $21.50

2. Assets listed as short-term investments on the balance sheet are

   A. only liquid
   B. listed on a national share exchange
   C. only intended to be converted to cash within one year
   D. liquid and intended to be converted to cash within one year

3. Portfolio investments are reported on the balance sheet at

   A. current cost
   B. historical cost
   C. lower of cost or market
   D. market value

4. Intercompany payables and receivables are eliminated in the consolidated entries so that

   A. assets will not be overstated
   B. liabilities will not be understated
   C. shareholders' equity will not be understated
   D. net income will not be overstated

5. All of the following accounts are eliminated in the consolidated work sheet entries *except*

   A. investment in subsidiary
   B. subsidiary's cash
   C. subsidiary's common shares
   D. subsidiary's retained earnings

6. The minority interest account is classified as a(n)

    A. revenue
    B. expense
    C. liability
    D. asset

7. The rate at which one unit of a currency can be converted into another currency is called the foreign currency

    A. market rate
    B. interest rate
    C. exchange rate
    D. conversion rate

8. A strong currency has an exchange rate that is

    A. inelastic with respect to other nations' currencies
    B. inelastic with respect to its balance of trade
    C. increasing relative to other nations' currencies
    D. decreasing relative to other nations' currencies

9. In accounting for an investment where the investor company owns less than 20% of the voting shares of the investee as a long-term investment

    A. the cost method should be used
    B. the equity method should be used
    C. there should be a consolidation
    D. the lower-of-cost-or-market method should be used

10. In accounting for an investment where the investor company owns more than 50% of the voting shares of the investee

    A. the cost method should be used
    B. the equity method should be used
    C. there should be a consolidation
    D. the lower-of-cost-or-market method should be used

11. The process of protecting oneself from losing money in one transaction by engaging in a counterbalancing transaction is called

    A. consolidating
    B. adjusting
    C. hedging
    D. portfolio investing

12. Foreign currency gains and losses are reported on

    A. the asset or liability side of the balance sheet, depending on whether it is a gain or a loss
    B. the income statement as other gains or losses
    C. the equity category of the balance sheet
    D. the cash flow statement under investing activities

13. Dividends received under the equity method

    A. are recorded with a debit to dividend income
    B. are recorded with a credit to dividend income
    C. are recorded with a debit to long-term investments
    D. are recorded with a credit to long-term investments

14. Gains or losses on the sale of investments are recorded

    A   only when using the equity method
    B. only when using the portfolio method
    C. only when using the amortized method
    D. both A and B

15. If Redmond Brewery had a portfolio investment of $400,000 in Jones Corp., and Jones Corp. had revenues of $60,000 for the year and declared dividends of $50,000, the year-end investment in Jones Corp. by Redmond would be

    A. $400,000
    B. $410,000
    C. $460,000
    D. $350,000

III. Completion   *Complete each of the following statements.*

1. The price at which shares are bought and sold is determined by the _____.

2. Two main factors that determine the supply and demand for a particular currency are the country's _____ and _____.

3. Investments in shares are initially recorded at _____.

4. The _____ method is used to account for investments when the investor can significantly influence the actions of the investee.

5. A(n) _____ is ownership of at least 50% of the voting shares of a company.

6. Goodwill is a(n) _____ asset.

7. A change in the currency exchange rates between the date of purchase and the date of payment will result in a(n) _____.

8. Cash used to purchase bonds is reported on the cash flow statement as a(n) _____ activity.

9. When a parent owns less than 100% of a subsidiary, the other owners are called the _____.

10. GAAP requires financial instruments such as bonds to be written down to their _____ _____ when their value is deemed to be impaired.

11. _____ are financial assets held for trading and must be liquid.

12. _____ is recorded as the credit entry when dividends are received by a company that has a portfolio investment.

13. _____ is recorded as the credit entry when dividends are received by a company with a 40% investment in the firm providing the dividend.

14. The investor is called the _____ company and the investee is called the _____ company.

15. A _____ is used by companies as an offsetting transaction to counterbalance the potential risk of losing money in another transaction.

IV. True/False   *For each of the following statements, circle* T *for true or* F *for false.*

1.   T F   The interest received on bonds held as a long-term investment is reported as an investing activity on the cash flow statement.
2.   T F   Foreign-currency transaction gains/losses are reported on the income statement as other revenues/expenses.
3.   T F   If the Canadian dollar strengthens relative to a foreign currency between the time a receivable is billed and payment is received, a foreign-currency transaction gain will result.
4.   T F   Foreign-currency translation adjustments are reported on the income statement as other revenues/expenses.
5.   T F   The presence of a minority interest on a corporation's balance sheet indicates the corporation owns less than 100% of another company.
6.   T F   When the equity method is used, the parent's investment account is adjusted at the end of the accounting period to reflect the investment's current market value.
7.   T F   When bonds are purchased at a discount and held as a long-term investment, the carrying value of the investment increases over time.
8.   T F   When bonds are purchased at a premium and held as a long-term investment, the difference between the face value of the bonds and the amount paid is reflected in a companion account called Premium on Investment.
9.   T F   Goodwill results when a business is purchased at a price in excess of the fair market value of the net liabilities acquired.
10.   T F   The total amount of shareholders' equity reported on a consolidated balance sheet equals the total parent's shareholders' equity plus the total subsidiary's shareholders' equity.
11.   T F   A gain on sale of investment is treated as an addition to shareholders' equity on the balance sheet.
12.   T F   When the equity method is used, it is assumed the investor has no significant influence over the investee.
13.   T F   A company can protect itself against foreign exchange losses by hedging.
14.   T F   The receipt of a share dividend on a portfolio investment results in a lower cost per share of the investment.
15.   T F   Foreign-currency translation adjustment is used to balance the total amount of liabilities and equities to the total amount of assets less minority interest.

V. Exercises

1. Tiger Company purchased 110,000 shares of Woods Corporation on January 1, 2006, for $600,000. Woods Corporation has 1,375,000 shares outstanding. Woods earned income of $300,000 and paid dividends of $100,000 during 2006. Woods Corporation shares were trading at $12.63 on December 31, 2006.

   a. What method should be used to account for the investment in Woods?

   b. How much revenue will be recorded by Tiger in 2006 from the investment in Woods?

   c. What is the balance in Tiger's Investment account at the end of 2006?

2. Franklin Company purchased 40% of Crane Corporation on January 1, 2006, for $30,000,000. Crane Corporation earned income of $12,600,000 and paid dividends of $2,300,000 during 2006.

   a. What method should be used to account for the investment in Franklin Corporation?

   b. How much revenue will be recorded by Franklin Co. in 2006 from the investment in Crane Corporation?

   c. What is the balance in Franklin's Investment account at the end of 2006?

3. Diablo Company invested in Valley Corporation on January 1, 2006, by purchasing 60% of the total shares of Valley Corporation for $675,000. Valley Corporation had common shares of $400,000 and retained earnings of $725,000.

   a. What amount of minority interest will appear on a consolidated balance sheet prepared on January 1, 2006?

b. If Diablo Company owes Valley Corporation $72,000 on a note payable, prepare the two elimination entries in general journal form.

Date	Account and Explanation	Debit	Credit

4. Ireland Company purchased 100% of the common shares of Costa Rican Corporation for $11,425,000. Costa Rican Corporation showed common shares of $6,500,000 and retained earnings of $3,510,000. Compute the amount of goodwill resulting from the purchase.

5. Prepare journal entries for the following portfolio investment:

June 10   Purchased 6,000 common shares of Integrity.com at $35.25 per share, plus a broker's commission of $200.

Oct. 2   Received a $0.90 per share cash dividend.

Nov. 15   Sold 1,000 shares at $40.25 per share, less a commission of $80.

Dec. 31   Integrity.com shares closed at $34.15.

Date	Account and Explanation	Debit	Credit

6. Prepare journal entries for the following foreign currency transactions:

Jan. 15   Purchased 5,000 cases of dry cider from a British wholesaler for 4.55 pounds sterling per case. Today's exchange rate is $1.51 = 1 pound sterling.

Jan. 20   Purchased 2,000 cases of red wine from a cooperative in Coustouge, France. The price was 24 euros per case. Today's exchange rate is $1.00 = 0.975 euros.

Feb. 10   Paid the British wholesaler. Today's exchange rate is $1.43 = 1 pound sterling.

March 20   Paid for the French wine. Today's exchange rate is $1.00 = 0.96 euros.

Date	Account and Explanation	Debit	Credit

VI. Critical Thinking

1. Review the information in Exercise 5 and change the Oct. 2 entry to the following:

   Oct. 2 Received a 15% share dividend. The share was trading at $38 per share.

   Prepare journal entries for June 10, Oct. 2, Nov. 15, and Dec. 31.

Date	Account and Explanation	Debit	Credit

2. How does a hedge protect a company entering into a contract to purchase goods in three months?

DEMONSTRATION PROBLEMS

Demonstration Problem #1

On Dec. 31, 2006, Mariposa Corporation paid $2,400,000 for 80% of the common shares of Gamma Corporation. Gamma owes Mariposa $125,000 on a note payable.

1.   Complete the following work sheet:

	Mariposa Company	Gamma Company	Eliminations Debit	Eliminations Credit	12/31/06 Consolidated Amounts
Assets:					
Cash	1,216,000	525,000			
Note receivable from Gamma	125,000	-			
Investment in Gamma	2,400,000	-			
Goodwill	-	-			
Plant & equipment, net	695,000	2,600,000			
Other assets	264,000	175,000			
Total	4,700,000	3,300,000			
Liabilities and Shareholders' Equity:					
Accounts payable	838,000	825,000			
Notes payable	312,000	220,000			
Minority interest					
Common shares	2,850,000	1,000,000			
Retained earnings	700,000	1,255,000			
Total	4,700,000	3,300,000			

2. Using the following form, present a consolidated balance sheet for Mariposa Corporation:

Mariposa Corporation
Consolidated Balance Sheet
December 31, 2006

Demonstration Problem #2

At December 31, 2004, Alpha Corporation had the following long-term investments in its portfolio:

	Cost	Market Value
Shares		
4,000 shares Ajax, Inc.	$25.13	$28.00
10,000 shares Dot.com	10.38	18.50
3,800 shares Handy Co.	48.00	37.75
2,500 shares TJCO	63.50	66.25
Bonds		
$100,000, 9% BioLabs, Inc., due October 1, 2010	$100,000	$100,000

1. In the space below, present the long-term investments as they would appear on Alpha Corporation's Dec. 31, 2005 balance sheet. None of the share investments are influential. The bonds pay interest semiannually on April 1 and October 1.

2. Record the following 2006 events related to Alpha Corporation's long-term investments:

Ajax, Inc.—these shares paid quarterly dividends of $0.15/share on Feb. 10 and May 10. The shares were sold on July 2 for $32/share, less a broker's commission of $185.

Dot.com—these shares pay no cash dividends; however, a 10% share dividend was received on August 10. The investment remained in the portfolio at the end of the year, at which time its market value was $24.25 per share.

Handy Co.—these shares continued to decline in value throughout January, and management decided to sell them on Feb. 8 for $31/share, less a commission of $205.

TJCO—these shares remained in the portfolio throughout the year. On Sept. 15 the share split 3-for-2. At year end, the shares were trading for $55/share.

BioLabs, Inc.—cheques for interest were received April 1 and October 1. The bonds remained in the portfolio and were trading at face value at year end.

On June 5, 2006, Alpha Corporation paid $9.50 a share for 300,000 shares of iTight.com. This ownership represents 30% of the iTight.com outstanding shares and is influential. iTight.com paid 2 cents per share dividends on Aug. 10 and Nov. 10 and reported an $850,000 net loss at year end. The share was trading at $9 on December 31, 2006.

On November 1, 2006, Alpha Corporation purchased a $250,000, 10-year, 6% bond from Wood, Inc. The bond pays semiannual interest on May 1 and Nov. 1 and was purchased at 97.

Date	Account and Explanation	Debit	Credit

3. Record the necessary Dec. 31, 2006, adjusting entries.

Date	Account and Explanation	Debit	Credit

4. Present the long-term investments as they would appear on Alpha Corporation's Dec. 31, 2006, balance sheet, taking into consideration the events described in Requirement 2 above.

SOLUTIONS

A. TEST YOURSELF

I. Matching

1. D	5. I	9. M	13. H	17. Q
2. A	6. P	10. C	14. E	18. R
3. K	7. L	11. O	15. F	
4. J	8. N	12. G	16. B	

II. Multiple Choice

1. D The High is the previous day's highest price, the Low is the lowest price of the previous day. The Close is the last price at which the share traded yesterday. Net Change is the increase (+) or decrease (-) in the Close compared to the previous day. The previous day's close is $21.75 - $0.25 = $21.50.

2. D Note that besides the determinable liquidity of the investment, the intent of management determines an investment's classification as a short-term investment.

3. C GAAP requires portfolio investments to be reported at the lower of cost or market.

4. A Failure to eliminate intercompany payables and receivables would result in the overstatement of both assets and liabilities of the consolidated entity. Accordingly, of the items listed, only A is correct.

5. B Elimination is not intended to remove the assets and liabilities of the subsidiary. The intent of elimination is to remove only those things that would be counted twice if not eliminated, such as intercompany payables and receivables and the investment in subsidiary and subsidiary shareholders' equity.

6. C The Minority Interest account represents the ownership interest of parties outside of the parent-subsidiary relationship. In actual practice, it is most often reported as part of the liability section on the balance sheet.

7. C The exchange rate is used to convert one currency into another.

8. C Strong currencies are those that increase relative to other currencies.

9. A The cost method should be used for portfolio investments.

10. C The *CICA Handbook* requires consolidation if more than 50% of the voting shares of the investee are owned by the investor.

11. C Hedging is used to protect oneself from losing money in one transaction by engaging in a counterbalancing transaction.

12. B   Foreign exchange gains and losses are reported on the income statement

13. D   Dividends are a credit to long-term investment.

14. D   Both A and B are correct.

15. A   Under the portfolio method, net income is not reported and dividends are declared as dividend income.

III. Completion

1. market (the market allows buyers and sellers with opposing interests to arrive at a price acceptable to both)
2. import/export ratio, rate of return available in its capital markets
3. cost
4. equity
5. controlling interest
6. intangible
7. foreign-currency transaction gain or loss
8. investing
9. minority interest
10. net realizable value
11. Temporary investment
12. Dividend revenue
13. Long-term investment
14. parent, subsidiary
15. hedge

IV. True/False

1. F   The interest is an operating activity. However, the purchase or sale of the bonds is an investing activity.
2. T
3. F   A foreign-currency transaction loss will result if the foreign currency has weakened relative to the Canadian dollar.
4. F   Translation adjustments are reported on the balance sheet (in the shareholders' equity section), not the income statement.

Study Tip: Remember—transactions on the income statement, translations on the balance sheet.

5. T
6. F   The equity method ignores market value. When the equity method is used, the Investment account balance equals the original cost plus the investor's proportionate share of profits less dividends (and less the proportionate share of any losses).
7. T
8. F   When bonds are purchased at either a premium or a discount and are held as a long-term investment, the bonds are reported at their amortized cost. No premium or discount account is used.
9. F   Goodwill is the excess of fair market value over the net assets of the acquired company.

10. F The subsidiary's shareholders' equity is eliminated against the parent's Investment account, not added to the parent's shareholders' equity.
11. F A gain on sale is a realized gain and therefore reported on the income statement.
12. F The equity method indicates the company has significant influence over the investee.
13. T
14. T
15. F Foreign-currency translation adjustment is used to balance the total amount of liabilities and equities to the total amount of assets.

V. Exercises

1. a. Cost method
   b. 110,000 ÷ 1.375,000 shares outstanding = 8%; 8% of $100,000 = $8,000 dividend revenue
   c. $600,000. The portfolio investment will be carried at cost unless its value is impaired.

2. a. Equity method
   b. 0.40 × $12,600,000 = $5,040,000
   c. $30,000,000 + $5,040,000 - (0.40 × $2,300,000) = $34,120,000

3. a. 0.40 × ($400,000 + $725,000) = $450,000
   b. (1) Note Payable to Valley   72,000
            Note Receivable from Diablo   72,000
        (2) Common shares (Valley)   400,000
           Retained Earnings (Valley)   725,000
            Investment in Valley   675,000
            Minority Interest   450,000
        (Note: Refer to Exhibit 10-7 in your text.)

4. $11,425,000 - ($6,500,000 + $3,510,000) = $1,415,000

5. June 10 Investment—Integrity.com   211,700
           Cash   211,700
           (6,000 shares × $35.25 plus $200)
           Actual cost/share is 211,700 / 6,000 = $35.283

   Oct. 2 Cash   5,400
           Dividend Revenue   5,400

   Nov. 15 Cash   40,170
           Investment—Integrity.com   35,283   (rounded)
           Gain on Sale of Investment   4,886
           The gain is the difference between the proceeds and the cost. The cost is 1,000 × $35,280 = $35,283.

   Dec. 31 Loss on Portfolio Investments   5,667
           Portfolio Investments   5,667
           Our cost basis was $176,417 ($211,700 - $35,283). The current market value is 5,000 × $34.15 = $170,750; therefore, the unrealized loss to be recognized is 5,667.

6.

Jan. 5	Inventory	34,352.50	
	Accounts Payable		34,352.50
	(5,000 cases × 4.55 pounds sterling × $1.51)		

Jan. 20	Inventory	49,230.77	
	Accounts Payable		49,230.77
	(2,000 cases × 24 euros / 0.975)		

2/10	Accounts Payable	34,352.50	
	Foreign-Currency Transaction Gain		1,820.00
	Cash		32,532.50
	(5,000 cases × 4.55 pounds sterling × $1.43)		

3/20	Accounts Payable	49,230.77	
	Foreign-Currency Transaction Loss	769.23	
	Cash		50,000.00
	(2,000 cases × 24 euros / 0.96)		

Because the dollar strengthened relative to the British pound (on Jan. 5 it took $1.51 to purchase 1 pound sterling—a month later the same pound would only cost $1.43), a foreign-currency transaction gain was realized when the bill was paid. Conversely, the dollar weakened relative to the euro, so there was a foreign-currency transaction loss. Foreign-currency transaction gains and losses are reported on the income statement as "other revenues and expenses."

VI. Critical Thinking

1. June 10	Investment – Integrity.com	211,700	
	Cash		211,700
	(6,000 shares × $35.25 plus $200)		

Oct. 2   No entry—however we need to note the receipt of the additional 900 shares. We now own 6,900 shares, which cost $211,700, or $30.68 (rounded) per share.

> **Study Tip:** The current trading value of the shares is irrelevant from our perspective. It is only relevant to Integrity.com. They used it to record the charge against Retained Earnings when the dividend was declared.

Nov. 15	Cash	40,170	
	Investment—Integrity.com		30,680
	Gain on Sale of Investment		9,490

Our cost per share was $30.68 (rounded)—see Oct. 2 details. We sold 1,000 shares at $40.25/share, less the $80 commission. The gain is the difference between our proceeds (1,000 shares × $40.25 less $80) and the cost basis of those shares, $30.68 × 1,000.

Dec. 31   No entry—The market value is above our cost.

2. A hedge protects a company entering a contract against a foreign currency exchange risk. If, for example, a company needed to pay for goods to be received in three months at the time of delivery, and the foreign currency had increased (strengthened) relative to the home currency, then it would cost the company more to purchase the goods. The hedge, such as a forward contract, prevents this by guaranteeing the amount that will be paid in the future.

DEMONSTRATION PROBLEMS

Demonstration Problem #1 Solved and Explained

	Mariposa Company	Gamma Company		Eliminations Debit		Eliminations Credit	Consolidated Amounts
Assets:							
Cash	1,216,000	525,000					1,741,000
Note receivable from Gamma	125,000	-			(a)	125,000	
Investment in Gamma	2,400,000	-			(b)	2,400,000	
Goodwill	-	-	(b)	596,000			596,000
Plant & equipment, net	695,000	2,600,000					3,295,000
Other assets	264,000	175,000					439,000
Total	4,700,000	3,300,000					6,071,000
Liabilities and Shareholders' Equity:							
Accounts payable	838,000	825,000					1,663,000
Notes payable	312,000	220,000	(a)	125,000			407,000
Minority interest						451,000	451,000
Common shares	2,850,000	1,000,000	(b)	1,000,000			2,850,000
Retained earnings	700,000	1,255,000	(b)	1,255,000			700,000
Total	4,700,000	3,300,000		2,976,000		2,976,000	6,071,000

Entry (a) eliminated Mariposa's $125,000 intercompany note receivable against the note payable owed by Gamma. Note that the consolidated total represents the amount owed to outside creditors ($312,000 owed by Mariposa + $220,000 owed by Gamma less $125,000 intercompany debt = $407,000).

Entry (b) eliminates Mariposa's $2,400,000 investment balance against the $2,255,000 in Gamma's equity. Mariposa acquired an 80% interest, so the minority interest is $451,000 (20% × $2,255,000). Goodwill is the difference between the investment ($2,400,000) and 80% of Gamma's common shares and retained earnings, or $596,000 ($2,400,000 – 80% × $2,255,000).

Requirement 2

Mariposa Corporation
Consolidated Balance Sheet
December 31, 2006

Assets:

Cash	$ 1,741,000
Plant and equipment (net)	3,295,000
Goodwill	596,000
Other assets	439,000
Total assets	$6,071,000

Liabilities and Shareholders' Equity

Liabilities

Accounts payable	$ 1,663,000	
Notes payable	407,000	
Minority interest	451,000	
Total liabilities and minority interest		2,521,000

Shareholders' Equity

Common shares	2,850,000	
Retained earnings	700,000	
Total shareholders' equity		3,550,000
Total Liabilities and Shareholders' Equity		$6,071,000

Demonstration Problem #2 Solved and Explained

Requirement 1

Long-term Investments (at lower-of-cost-or-market value)	$606,520

Investments at lower of cost or market:

4,000 shares Ajax, Inc.	4,000 × $25.13	=	100,520
10,000 shares Dot.com	10,000 × $10.38	=	103,800
3,800 shares Handy Co.	3,800 × $37.75	=	143,450
2,500 shares TJCO	2,500 × $63.50	=	158,750
BioLabs Bonds			100,000
Total			606,520

The cost of the combined long-term investments (both equity and debt) is $645,470. The market value of Handy Co. shares is below cost ($37.75 versus $48.00). On the assumption that the decline is not temporary, an adjusting entry would have been recorded as follows:

Loss on Portfolio Investments		38,950	
Portfolio Investments			38,950

Requirement 2

Ajax, Inc.

Feb. 10	Cash		600	
	Dividend Revenue			600

May 10	Cash		600	
	Dividend Revenue			600

July 2	Cash		127,815	
	Long-term Investment			100,520
	Gain on Sale of Investment			27,295

The gain is the difference between the proceeds (4,000 shares × $32/share less the $185 commission) and the cost (4,000 shares × $25.13).

Dot.com

Aug. 10	No entry—memo only reflecting 11,000 shares now in the portfolio at an average cost of $9.437 per share ($103,800 ÷ 11,000 shares)

Handy Co.

Feb. 8	Cash		117,595	
	Loss on Sale of Investment		25,855	
	Long-Term Investment			143,450

The loss is the difference between the adjusted cost at December 31, 2005 (3,800 × $37.75) and the proceeds (3,800 × $31 less the $205 commission).

TJCO

Sept. 15	No entry—memo only reflecting 3,750 shares now in the portfolio at an average cost of $42.333 per share ($158,750 ÷ 3,750 shares)

BioLabs

April 1	Cash		4,500	
	Interest Receivable			2,250
	Interest Revenue			2,250

Note that 2,250 interest receivable would have been accrued at Dec. 31, 2005.

Oct. 1	Cash		4, 500	
	Interest Revenue			4,500

iTight.com

June 5	Long-term Investment – iTight.com	2,850,000	
	Cash		2,850,000
Aug. 10	Cash	6,000	
	Long-term Investment – iTight.com		6,000
Nov. 10	Cash	6,000	
	Long-term Investment – iTight.com		6,000
Dec. 31	Unrealized Loss on Long-term Investment	255,000	
	Long-term Investment – iTight.com		255,000

Because the investment in iTight.com is influential, the equity method is used; therefore, dividends received reduce the Investment account balance. Because iTight.com reported a net loss for the year, Alpha's proportional "equity" in the loss is also charged against the Investment account. If iTight.com had reported net income, the Investment account would have been increased.

Wood, Inc.

Nov. 1	Long-term Investment	242,500	
	Cash		242,500

As the purchaser of the bonds, we do not record the $7,500 discount in a contra account.

Requirement 3 (adjusting entries)

Dec. 31	Interest Receivable	2,250	
	Interest Revenue		2,250
	To adjust accrued interest ($100,000 × 0.09 × 3/12) on BioLabs bonds		

Dec. 31	Interest Receivable	2,500	
	Long-term Investment	125	
	Interest Revenue		2,625
	To adjust for accrued interest ($250,000 × 0.06 × 2/12) and amortize the discount ($7,500/10 years × 2/12).		

Recall that long-term investments in bonds must be reported on the balance sheet at their fully amortized cost. When bonds are purchased at a discount, the amortized cost will increase over the life of the bonds. At maturity, the amortized cost will equal the bond's face value.

Requirement 4

Long-term Investments (at lower of cost or market)	$605,175
Long-term Investments (at equity)	$2,583,000

The balance in the Long-term Investments (at lower of cost or market) account consists of the following:

Shares	($262,550 cost)	$262,550
Bonds	BioLabs	100,000
	Wood, Inc. ($242,500 + $125)	242,625
Total		$605,175

The balance in the Long-term Investments (at equity) comes from the iTight.com account, as follows:

iTight.com

June 5	2,850,000	Aug. 10	6,000
		Nov. 10	6,000
		Dec. 31	255,000
Balance	2,583,000		

Interest receivable will be listed among the current assets and interest revenue under "other revenues" on the income statement.

CHAPTER 11—THE INCOME STATEMENT AND THE STATEMENT OF SHAREHOLDERS' EQUITY

CHAPTER OVERVIEW

Throughout the last four chapters we have examined a variety of topics related to the balance sheet. In Chapter 7, we looked at capital and intangible assets, in Chapter 8 current and long-term liabilities, in Chapter 9 shareholders' equity, and in Chapter 10, long-term investments and international operations. While each of these topics impacts the income statement, the primary focus was the balance sheet. We now turn our attention to an in-depth examination of the corporate income statement and the statement of shareholders' equity. The specific learning objectives for this chapter are to

1. **Analyze** a complex income statement
2. **Account** for a corporation's income tax
3. **Analyze** a statement of shareholders' equity
4. **Understand** managers' and auditors' responsibilities for the financial statements

CHAPTER REVIEW

Objective 1 - Analyze a complex income statement

Investors may want to examine the trend of a company's earnings and the makeup of its net income. Therefore, the corporation's income statement starts with income from continuing operations, follows with income or loss from discontinued operations and extraordinary gains and losses, and concludes with earnings per share of common share.

Continuing operations are expected to continue in the future. Income from continuing operations helps investors make predictions about future earnings. Income from continuing operations is shown both before and after income tax has been deducted.

One way potential investors evaluate income from continuing operations is to determine the present value of a company's future income, then compare this result with the company's market value. To determine present value, an assumption must be made about an appropriate interest rate (also called the **investment capitalization rate**). The higher the risk, the higher the rate, and vice versa. The estimated value of a share can be calculated as the estimated annual income in the future divided by the investment capitalization rate.

To determine **market value**, multiply the number of outstanding common shares times the share's current selling price. Comparing these two values helps investors evaluate the company. If the estimated value of the company (based on the present value of future earnings) is greater than the current market value of the company, an investor would be more likely to consider the company favourably. Rather than evaluating based on the total market value of the company, an investor could do a similar kind of analysis for a single share. Using the same investment capitalization rate, divide it into the estimated annual earnings per share. If the result is greater than the current market price for one share, the company is considered more favourably as an investment.

When a corporation sells one of its segments, the sale is reported in a section of the income statement called **discontinued operations**. Such sales are viewed as one-time transactions and are therefore not a future source of income. Discontinued operations is separated into an operating component and a disposal component. Each is shown net of its related tax effect.

Extraordinary gains and losses (also called **extraordinary items**) are both unusual and infrequent and are reported net of tax. Extraordinary items are those which are unusual and not likely to occur in the future. Examples are natural disasters and expropriations of business assets by foreign governments. Section 3840 of the *CICA Handbook* identifies extraordinary items as gains and losses that have all of the following characteristics: 1) they are not expected to occur frequently over several years, 2) they do not typify the normal business activities of the entity, and 3) the do not depend primarily on decisions or determinations made by management or owners.

On occasion, companies **change an accounting policy**. When this occurs, it is difficult for financial statement users to compare consecutive years' activity unless they are informed of changes. For this reason, companies are required to make changes retroactively, which means they must go back and restate their previous income statements as well as the opening balance of their retained earnings.

Earnings per share (EPS) of common shares is computed for each source of income or loss: continuing operations, discontinued operations, and extraordinary items.

When a change in accounting principles has resulted in the restatement of prior period income statements, the EPS of these periods must also be restated.

To compute EPS, divide net income less preferred dividends by the average number of common shares outstanding for the period.

When preferred dividends exist, they must be subtracted from income subtotals (income from continuing operations, income before extraordinary items, and net income) in the computation of EPS. Preferred dividends are not subtracted from discontinued operations or extraordinary items.

Dilution must be considered if preferred shares or bonds can be converted into common shares (see Chapter 9) because there is the potential for more common shares to be divided into net income. Corporations therefore provide **basic EPS** and **diluted EPS** information.

Pro forma earnings are forecasted earnings issued by companies during the year. These forecasted figures do not conform to any GAAP standard nor are they based on independently audited figures; therefore, informed investors realize the amounts reported are only estimates and can be biased.

> **Study Tip**: Review this discussion by comparing each topic with the complex income statement in your text (Exhibit 11-1).

The **Price/earnings (P/E) ratio** is the ratio of the company's share to its EPS. All else being equal, a lower P/E ratio indicates a more attractive investment. A high P/E ratio usually indicates investors expect future earnings to be high for a company.

Comprehensive income is the company's change in total shareholders' equity from all sources other than the owners. It includes net income plus 1) unrealized gains (losses) on available-for-sale investments and 2) foreign-currency translation adjustments. These items do not enter into the determination of net income or EPS until they are realized. (Helpful hint: review Exhibit 11-2 in the text.)

To obtain a better understanding of a company, one needs to analyze more than the income statement. For instance, cash flows (discussed in detail in Chapter 12) should be considered, along with the other financial statements.

Objective 2 - Account for a corporation's income tax

Because corporations have a distinct legal identity (they have the right to contract, to sue, and be sued—just as individuals have these rights), their income is taxed just like individuals. However, unlike individuals, the amount of tax actually paid will differ from the expense incurred for the period (for individuals, these amounts are generally the same). The difference results for a number of reasons.

Income tax expense is calculated by multiplying the applicable tax rate times the amount of pretax accounting income as reported on the income statement, while **income tax payable** is calculated by multiplying the applicable tax rate times the amount of taxable income as reported on the corporate tax return. Because these results will differ due to differences such as the use of straight-line amortization for financial statements and capital cost allowance (accelerated amortization) for tax purposes, a third account, **Future Income Tax Liability or Asset**, is used to reconcile the difference.

Prior-period adjustments usually occur as the result of correcting an error in a previous accounting period. Because of the matching principle, prior-period adjustments *never* affect revenue or expense accounts in the current period. (Helpful hint: review Exhibit 11-3 in the text.)

Prior-period adjustments net of related tax effect are reported on the statement of retained earnings:

Retained earnings, beginning, as originally reported	$XX
Prior-period adjustment (plus or minus)	XX
Retained earnings, beginning, as adjusted	XX
Net income for current year	XX
	XX
Dividends for current year	(XX)
Retained earnings, ending	$XX

Many corporations obtain financing through long-term loans. Creditors wish to ensure that funds will be available to repay these loans. Thus, loan agreements frequently **restrict** the amount of retained earnings that can be used to pay dividends and repurchase shares. These restrictions are usually reported in notes to the financial statements.

Objective 3 - Analyze a statement of shareholders' equity

You already know that the two major components of shareholders' equity are contributed capital and retained earnings. However, you have also learned that there are additional items affecting shareholders' equity, such as repurchased cash and stock dividends and cumulative translation adjustments. A **statement of shareholders' equity** presents all of these elements with details about the changes to each that occurred during the year.

Exhibit 11-4 in your text illustrates a typical format for this statement. The particular elements of shareholders' equity are listed across the top of the statement, with ending balances from the previous year. The sources of change within shareholders' equity are listed down the left-hand side of the statement. This matrix format provides the user with both the dollar amount of specific changes and the item within shareholders' equity affected by the change. For instance, net income increases retained earnings, while dividends decrease retained earnings.

After all the changes have been listed under the appropriate shareholders' equity element, each column is summarized, thereby providing an end-of-year amount. Adding these ending amounts together results in total year-end shareholders' equity.

Objective 4 - Understand managers' and auditors' responsibilities for the financial statements

A **statement of responsibility** from the top managers of the company is included with the financial statements. Within the statement, management states its responsibility for the preparation, integrity, and objectivity of the financial statements. In addition, they will confirm the statements' conformance with generally accepted accounting principles (GAAP). (Helpful hint: review Exhibit 11-6 in the text.)

The various federal and provincial incorporating acts, and in the case of listed companies, the provincial securities commission and the stock exchanges, require companies that issue their shares publicly to file **audited financial statements**. Therefore, in addition to the statement by management, every annual report will include a report from the **independent external auditors.** This means that a public accounting firm has examined the financial statements to determine if they comply with GAAP. The report will contain a reference to the standards used by the public accounting firm in auditing the financial statements and an opinion. The opinion will usually fall into one of the following four categories: (Helpful hint: review Exhibit 11-7 in the text)

1. **Unqualified (clean)**—the statements are reliable
2. **Qualified**—the statements are reliable, except for one or more items for which the opinion is said to be qualified
3. **Adverse**—the statements are unreliable
4. **Disclaimer**—the auditor was unable to reach a professional opinion

Audited financial statements result in many advantages to shareholders, potential investors, and the general public.

TEST YOURSELF

All the self-testing materials in this chapter focus on information and procedures that your instructor is likely to test in quizzes and examinations.

I. Matching   *Match each numbered term with its lettered definition.*

_____ 1. earnings per share
_____ 2. price/earnings ratio
_____ 3. segment of a business
_____ 4. investment capitalization rate
_____ 5. taxable income
_____ 6. qualified
_____ 7. denial

_____ 8. extraordinary item
_____ 9. comprehensive income
_____ 10. prior-period adjustment
_____ 11. statement of shareholders' equity
_____ 12. pretax accounting income
_____ 13. unqualified
_____ 14. adverse

A. an audit opinion stating that the auditor was unable to reach a professional opinion regarding the quality of the financial statements
B. an audit opinion stating that the financial statements are unreliable

C. an audit opinion stating that the financial statements are reliable, except for one or more items
D. an audit opinion stating that the financial statements are reliable
E. the basis for computing the amount of tax payable to the government
F. income before income tax on the income statement
G. an earnings rate used to estimate the value of an investment in the share capital of another company
H. reports the changes in all categories of shareholders' equity during the period
I. one of various separate divisions of a company
J. a correction to retained earnings for an error in an earlier period
K. represents the change in total shareholders' equity from all sources other than owners
L. a ratio relating the price of a company's share to its earnings per share
M. a gain or loss that is both unusual for the company and infrequent
N. the amount of a company's net income per outstanding common share

II. Multiple Choice   *Circle the best answer.*

1. When the market price of a common share rises, the P/E ratio will

   A. rise
   B. remain unchanged
   C. fall
   D. cannot be determined

2. The correct order for the following income statement items is

   A. income from continuing operations, income from discontinued operations, prior-period adjustments, net income
   B. income from continuing operations, income from discontinued operations, extraordinary items, net income
   C. income from continuing operations, extraordinary items, income from discontinued operations, net income
   D. income from continuing operations, income from discontinued items, extraordinary items, net income

3. If a company shows $80,000 income from discontinued operations and is subject to a 30% tax rate, the amount added to income from continuing operations will be

   A. $80,000
   B. $104,000
   C. $56,000
   D. cannot be determined

4. Which of the following would be considered a segment of a business?

   A. the human resources department
   B. the company's warehouse
   C. all the offices located in a particular province
   D. a catering business owned by an airline

5. Which of the following events is *not* considered an extraordinary item?

    A. losses resulting from a strike by the company's employees
    B. a loss resulting from a tornado
    C. a loss resulting from an earthquake
    D. assets seized by a foreign government

6. Which of the following would *not* be reported on the statement of shareholders' equity?

    A. net income
    B. cash dividends
    C. issuance of common shares
    D. interest earned on investments

7. All of the following result in an increase in total shareholders' equity *except*

    A. sale of common shares
    B. repurchase of shares
    C. net income
    D. sale of preferred shares

8. Prior-period adjustments are found on the

    A. cash flow statement
    B. statement of retained earnings
    C. statement of shareholders' equity
    D. income statement

9. An appropriation of retained earnings will

    A. decrease total retained earnings
    B. increase total retained earnings
    C. not affect total retained earnings
    D. reduce net income

10. Which of the following is an audit report category?

    A. unconditional
    B. acceptable
    C. accurate
    D. unqualified

11. Which of the following would *not* be included in comprehensive income?

    A. unrealized gain on available-for-sale investment
    B. sale of product or service
    C. investment by owner
    D. foreign-currency translation loss

12. Kingston Inc. has net income of $88,000 with 200,000 common shares outstanding. During the year, they paid preferred dividends of $16,000. The year-end price of the common shares was $6 per share. What was the price/earnings ratio for Kingston Inc.?

    A. 6:1
    B. 1:6
    C. 7.33:1
    D. 8.67:1

13. Canvat Inc. had revenues of $400,000 for the current year. They incurred expense of $160,000 and tax of $12,000. They had an unrealized gain of $15,000 and foreign-currency translation adjustments of $6,000. The owners invested an additional $20,000 in the business. What is Canvat's comprehensive income for the year?

    A. $228,000
    B. $243,000
    C. $257,000
    D. $237,000

14. Extraordinary items include which of the following characteristics?

    A. they are not expected to occur frequently over several years
    B. they do not typify normal business activities of the entity
    C. they do not depend primarily on decisions or determinations by management or owners
    D. all of the above are included in the definition for extraordinary items

15. What opinion would auditors provide if they believed the financial statements were unreliable because the statements did not conform to GAAP?

    A. denial of opinion
    B. adverse opinion
    C. non-GAAP opinion
    D. unqualified opinion

III. Completion   *Complete each of the following statements.*

1. Income tax expense is calculated by multiplying the applicable tax rate by _____.

2. Income tax payable is calculated by multiplying the applicable tax rate by _____.

3. The difference between income tax expense and income tax payable is called _____.

4. Extraordinary gains and losses are both _____ and _____.

5. To calculate earnings per share, divide _____ by _____.

6. Number the following income statement categories to show the order in which they should appear. Use * to indicate those categories that should be shown net of tax.

    _____ A. Discontinued operations

    _____ B. Extraordinary items

    _____ C. Continuing operations

7. P/E is an abbreviation for the _____.

8. The denominator for the P/E ratio is _____.

9. The correction of an error affecting net income in a previous accounting period is called a _____.

10. The four categories of audit reports are _____, _____, _____, and _____.

11. _____ represents the changes in shareholders' equity during a period from all sources, excluding those from the owners.

12. The _____ the P/E ratio, the more attractive the shares to investors, all else being equal.

13. A _____ is provided by an auditor when the financial statements are reliable, except for one or more items.

14. A _____ is provided by an auditor when they cannot reach a professional opinion about a set of financial statements.

15. The _____ is used to estimate the value of an investment in the share capital of another company.

IV. True/False   *For each of the following statements, circle* T *for true or* F *for false.*

1. T F Fully diluted earnings per share will always be higher than basic earnings per share.
2. T F Realized gains on the sale of assets are reported as extraordinary items.
3. T F A company's market value is determined by multiplying the earnings per share by the number of outstanding common shares.
4. T F To qualify as extraordinary, an item/event must be either unusual or infrequent.
5. T F To calculate EPS, net income is divided by the number of preferred shares outstanding at year end.
6. T F Future Income Tax Liability could be credited or debited when recording a corporation's income tax expense.
7. T F Prior-period adjustments are reported on the income statement as extraordinary gains or losses.
8. T F The statement of shareholders' equity will include amounts for net income, dividends, and the sale of investments.
9. T F Pro forma earnings and forecasted earnings are synonymous terms.
10. T F Financial information on business segments is found in the notes to the financial statements.
11. T F Comprehensive income includes all sources of changes to shareholders' equity including investments by owners.
12. T F Generally, interim statements are unaudited.
13. T F Independent auditors are employees of the corporation.
14. T F A "clean" auditor's opinion is the same as an unqualified opinion.
15. T F Management issues a statement of responsibility to accompany a set of financial statements.

V. Exercises

1. For the current year, Porsche Corporation reported after-tax net income of $3,520,000. During the year, $128,000 was paid to preferred shareholders and $702,000 was paid to common shareholders. At the beginning of the year, Porsche had 300,000 common shares outstanding. On April 1, an additional 120,000 shares were issued. On October 1, the corporation reacquired 60,000 shares. Calculate earnings per share for the current year. Average common shares outstanding were 375,000.

2. Trujillo Inc. reported retained earnings of $1,615,000 as of December 31, 2005. During 2006, the company declared and paid $20,000 in preferred dividends and $104,000 in common dividends. Net income for 2006 was $395,000. A prior-period adjustment was recorded, resulting in a charge against retained earnings of $117,000. An extraordinary loss of $186,000 (net of taxes) was also incurred. In the space below, present a statement of retained earnings for Trujillo Inc. for 2006.

Trujillo Inc.
Statement of Retained Earnings
For the Year Ended December 31, 2006

3. Fraser Valley Corporation reported pretax income of $835,000 on its income statement and $698,000 taxable income on its tax return. Assuming a corporate tax rate of 40%, present the journal entry to record Fraser Valley Corporation's taxes for the year.

Date	Account and Explanation	Debit	Credit

4. Whitfield Corporation reported the following income statement items for the year:

Extraordinary loss	($540,000)
Income from continuing operations	$410,000
Discontinued operations:	
Operating loss	($12,950)
Loss on sale	($263,000)

Whitfield is subject to a 40% combined income tax rate. Using the form below, show the correct presentation on the income statement for the above items.

5. Refer to your solution for Exercise 4. Assuming Whitfield Corporation has an average of 75,000 common shares outstanding, present the earnings per share information.

6. Jackson Ltd. had revenues of $1,450,000 and expenses of $885,000, excluding tax during the current year. The company had an unrealized loss on investment of $62,000. The foreign-currency translation adjustment gain was $9,000. Jackson has an average tax rate of 40%. Compute Jackson's comprehensive income for the year.

VI. Critical Thinking

1. Examine the information in Exercise 1 above. Assume the following additional facts: the company's preferred shares are convertible into 50,000 common shares and company executives hold options on 100,000 common shares. Calculate fully diluted earnings per share.

2. Comprehensive income (CI) includes all changes excluding owner investments. Why is unrealized gains/losses and foreign currency included in CI separately from net income?

DEMONSTRATION PROBLEMS

Demonstration Problem #1

The following amounts were reported for Taylormaid Corporation for the current year.

Administrative expenses	$220,750
Cost of goods sold	1,385,000
Discontinued operations:	
Gain on sale	22,910
Operating loss	(205,610)
Dividend revenues	31,000
Gain on sale of short-term investments	87,000
Interest expense	29,040
Loss from hurricane	91,000
Loss on sale of capital assets	101,600
Sales revenue	2,230,000
Selling expenses	362,500

Taylormaid Corporation is subject to a combined 40% income tax rate.

1. Present a properly classified income statement for Taylormaid Corporation for the current year.

Taylormaid Corporation		
Income Statement		
For the Current Year		

2. Present earnings per share information for Taylormaid Corporation for the current year, assuming an average of 100,000 shares outstanding throughout the year.

3. Assuming Taylormaid Corporation's shares were trading for $8.50 at year end, calculate the P/E ratio based on income from continuing operations and the P/E ratio based on net income.

P/E ratio, based on income from continuing operations

P/E ratio, based on net income

Demonstration Problem #2

At the end of 2005, Baxter Inc. had the following shareholders' equity:

Preferred shares ($3.00, 1,000,000 shares authorized, 150,000 issued)	$ 7,500,000
Common shares (5,000,000 shares authorized, 2,850,000 issued)	17,100,000
Total contributed capital	24,600,000
Retained earnings	65,195,000
Cumulative translation adjustment	(1,250,000)
Total sharcholders' equity	$88,545,000

1. Answer the following questions:

   a. What was the average price paid for the preferred shares?

   b. What was the average price paid for the common shares?

   c. At the end of 2005, the preferred shares were trading at $50.00 and the common shares were trading at $31.25. What was the market value of Baxter Inc.?

2. During 2006, the following events occurred:

   a. Preferred shareholders received their dividends, as follows:

Declaration Date	Record Date	Payment Date
February 10	March 10	March 30
May 10	June 10	June 30
August 10	September 10	September 30
November 10	December 10	December 30

   b. On April 20, a $0.90 per share dividend was declared on the common shares to shareholders of record on May 20. The dividend was paid on June 20.
   c. On May 29, the corporation paid $36.13 per share for 150,000 common shares.
   d. On June 5, the amortization expense for 2004 was recalculated. The amount reported for 2005 was overstated by $105,000.
   e. Certain key employees hold options to purchase 1,000,000 common shares at varying prices. On August 30, options to purchase 240,000 were exercised at $25 per share.
   f. On September 5, the board declared a 10% share dividend on the common shares to shareholders of record on October 5. On September 5, the shares were trading at $45.25. The additional shares were distributed on November 5.
   g. At the end of 2006, Baxter Inc. reported after-tax profits of $2,615,000.

   Journalize the required 2006 entries.

Date	Account and Explanation	Debit	Credit

3. Using the forms provided, present a statement of retained earnings and a statement of shareholders' equity for Baxter Inc. for 2006. At the end of 2006, the amount of the cumulative translation adjustment was ($1,004,500).

Baxter Inc.	
Statement of Retained Earnings	
For the Year Ended December 31, 2006	

Baxter Inc.
Statement of Shareholders' Equity
For the Year Ended 12/31/06

	Preferred Shares	Common Shares	Retained Earnings	Cumulative Translation Adjustment	Total Shareholders' Equity
Balance, Dec. 31, 2005	$7,500,000	$17,100,000	$65,195,000	($1,250,000)	$88,545,000
Cash dividends					
10% share dividends					
Prior-period adjustment					
Repurchase of shares					
Exercise of share options					
Net income					
Translation adjustment					
Balance, Dec. 31, 2006					

The Income Statement and the Statement of Shareholders' Equity

4. At the end of 2006, Baxter's preferred shares were trading at $50.00 and the common shares were trading at $51.13. Calculate Baxter's market value as of the end of 2006.

5. Calculate Baxter's basic earnings per share for 2006.

6. Calculate Baxter's diluted earning per share for 2006.

7. Calculate Baxter's price/earnings ratio as of December 31, 2006.

SOLUTIONS

A. TEST YOURSELF

I. Matching

1. N	5. E	9. K	13. D
2. L	6. C	10. J	14. B
3. I	7. A	11. H	
4. G	8. M	12. F	

II. Multiple Choice

1. A Since the earnings per share figure does not change, an increase in the market price (the numerator) will cause an increase in the P/E ratio.

2. B The correct order is income from continuing operations, income from discontinued operations, extraordinary items, changes in accounting principles, net income. Prior-period adjustments do not appear on the income statement.

3. C Income from discontinued operations is reported net of the effects of tax on the income statement; therefore, the $80,000 income amount is reduced by the $24,000 (30% × $80,000) tax expense.

4. D The other three choices are not considered segments from an accounting perspective.

5. A The other choices are all unusual and infrequent, whereas strikes by employees are considered normal business events.

6. D Interest earned on investments is reported on the income statement.

7. B The repurchase of shares reduces total shareholders' equity.

8. B Prior-period adjustments reflect errors in previous accounting periods. Since these errors affected net income, and net income was closed to retained earnings, a prior-period adjustment only appears on the retained earnings statement.

9. C When retained earning are appropriated, total retained earnings do not change. The appropriation simply restricts the use of part of the total retained earnings amount.

10. D The four categories of opinion are unqualified, qualified, adverse, and denial of opinion.

11. C Investments by owners are not included in comprehensive income.

12. A [($88,000 - $16,000) / 200,000 shares] / $6 = 6:1

13. D Comprehensive income = ($400,000 - $160,000 - $12,000 + $15,000 - $6,000 = $237,000)

14.　D　All are included in the definition of extraordinary items.

15.　B　Unreliable statements due to nonconformance to GAAP would result in an auditor giving an adverse opinion.

III.　Completion

1.　pretax accounting income
2.　taxable income
3.　future income tax liability or asset
4.　unusual and infrequent (order not important)
5.　net income less preferred dividends, average number of common shares outstanding
6.　A.　2*
　　B.　3*
　　C.　1 (income from continuing operations is reported both before and after income taxes)
7.　price/earnings ratio
8.　earnings per share
9.　prior-period adjustment
10. unqualified, qualified, adverse, denial (order not important)
11. Comprehensive income
12. lower
13. qualified opinion
14. denial of opinion
15. investment capitalization rate

IV.　True/False

1.　F　Fully diluted shares will always be lower.
2.　F　Realized gains from the sale of assets are reported separately after income from operations, but not as extraordinary items.
3.　F　Market value is the number of common shares outstanding times the current market price per share.
4.　F　Extraordinary items must be both unusual AND infrequent.
5.　F　EPS equals net income (less preferred dividends, if any) divided by the weighted average number of common shares outstanding.
6.　F　Future Income Tax Liability is only credited.
7.　F　Prior-period adjustments are reported on the retained earnings statement, not the income statement.
8.　F　When investments are sold, gains and losses appear on the income statement, not the statement of shareholders' equity.
9.　T
10.　T
11.　F　Comprehensive income excludes investments by owners.
12.　T
13.　F　Independent auditors are employees of the public accounting firm hired to conduct the audit.
14.　T
15.　T

V. Exercises

1. Earnings per share = net income less preferred dividends / average number of common shares outstanding

   Net income - preferred dividends   = $3,520,000 - $128,000

                                       = $3,392,000

   EPS = $3,392,000 / 375,000 = $9.05 (rounded)

> **Study Tip:** When calculating EPS, only preferred dividends are deducted.

2.

Trujillo Inc.
Statement of Retained Earnings
For the Year Ended December 31, 2006

Retained earnings, Dec. 31, 2005, as reported		$1,615,000
Less: Prior-period adjustment		117,000
Retained earnings, Dec. 31, 2005, adjusted		1,498,000
Add: Net income		395,000
		1,893,000
Less: Preferred dividends	20,000	
Common dividends	104,000	124,000
Retained earnings, Dec. 31, 2006		$1,769,000

> **Study Tip:** The extraordinary loss of $186,000 does not appear on the retained earnings statement. It was listed on the income statement, net of taxes.

3.

Income Tax Expense	334,000	
Future Income Tax Liability		54,800
Income Tax Payable		279,200

Expense = $835,000 × 0.40 = $334,000
Payable = $698,000 × 0.40 = $279,200

> **Study Tip:** The expense is based on the financial statement while the liability is based on the tax return. The entry is reconciled (balanced) with a credit to Future Income Tax Liability (in this case it is a liability).

4.

Income from continuing operations		$410,000
Less: Income tax expense (0.40 × $410,000)		164,000
		246,000
Discontinued operations:		
Operating loss (net of tax benefit)	($7,770)	
Loss on sale (net of tax benefit)	(157,800)	(165,570)
Net income before extraordinary items and		
cumulative effect of change in inventory valuation		80,430
Extraordinary loss (net of tax benefit)		(324,000)
Net loss		($243,570)

Study Tip: For all the items "below the line" (that is, after the income from continuing operations), calculate the tax and **deduct** it. Why? If it's a gain, the tax reduces the amount; if it's a loss, the amount of the loss is reduced because of the tax benefit.

5.

Income from continuing operations (after tax)		$3.28
Discontinued operations:		
Operating income	(0.10)	
Loss on sale	(2.10)	(2.20)
		1.08
Extraordinary loss		(4.32)
Net income		($3.24)

Note: Most of these amounts are rounded.

6.

Revenues	$1,450,000	
Expenses	885,000	
Pretax in .	$ 565,000	
Taxes (40%)	197,750	
Net income	$ 367,250	
Other Comprehensive Income:		
Unrealized Loss	($62,000)	
Tax savings (40%)	21,700	$(40,300)
Foreign exchange gain	$ 9,000	
Tax (40%)	3,150	$ 5,850
Comprehensive Income		$332,800

VI. Critical Thinking

1. Most of the information provided has the effect of diluting basic earnings per share. In other words, if the preferred shares are converted into common shares, the number of outstanding shares will increase, thereby lowering (diluting) the earnings per share. The same is true if the share options are exercised. To recalculate earnings per share, the denominator changes from 375,000 to 525,000 (375,000 + 50,000 + 100,000). Therefore, EPS (fully diluted) is $3,392,000 / 525,000 = $6.46 (rounded).

Study Tip: Fully diluted EPS will always be lower than basic EPS when the corporation has a complex capital structure.

2. Comprehensive income includes unrealized gains/losses and foreign-currency translation adjustments separately, as these items do impact on shareholders' equity. However they do not directly result from earnings of the business, and hence are not captured on the income statement. They will not show up on the income statement until they are realized.

DEMONSTRATION PROBLEMS

Demonstration Problem #1 Solved and Explained

Requirement 1 (Income Statement)

Taylormaid Corporation
Income Statement
For the Current Year

Sales revenue		$2,230, 000
Less: Cost of goods sold		1,385,000
Gross margin		845,000
Less: Operating expenses		
Selling expenses	$362,500	
Administrative expenses	220,750	583,250
		261,750
Other revenues (expenses):		
Dividend revenues	31,000	
Gain on sale of short-term investments	87,000	
Interest expense	(29,040)	
Loss on sale of capital assets	(101,600)	(12,640)
Income from continuing operations, before taxes		249,110
Less: Income tax expense ($249,110 × 40%)		99,644
Income from continuing operations		149,466
Discontinued operations:		
Operating income (loss), net of tax benefit	(123,366)	
Gain on sale, net of tax	13,746	(109,620)
Income before extraordinary items		39,846
Extraordinary items:		
Loss from hurricane, net of tax benefit		(54,600)
Net income (loss)		$ (14,754)

Notes: The items above income from continuing operations could be organized in a single-step format, with income tax expense either included with the other deductions or listed separately.

The items following income from continuing operations are *always* listed net of tax. In addition, the order of the items is always continuing operations, discontinued operations, extraordinary items.

Requirement 2 (Earnings per Share)

Income from continuing operations (after tax)	$1.49
Discontinued operations	(1.09)
Income before extraordinary items	0.40
Extraordinary item	(0.55)
Net income	($0.15)

The above amounts are rounded. Note, however, that they reconcile. By far, the most important figure is the EPS from continuing operations. While the corporation did experience a net loss for the year, the items following income from continuing operations should not occur in the future. Therefore, to properly evaluate the company, investors and shareholders will place more emphasis on the continuing operations figure than on the net income amount.

Requirement 3

P/E, based on income from continuing operations:

$8.50 / $1.49 = 5.7

P/E, based on net income:

This value cannot be calculated because the company experienced an overall net loss.

> **Study Tip:** The P/E ratio can only be a positive value. A negative P/E ratio has no meaning.

Demonstration Problem #2 Solved and Explained

Requirement 1

a. $7,500,000 / 150,000 shares = $50 per share
b. $17,100,000 / 2,850,000 shares = $6 per share
c. Preferred market value = 150,000 shares × $50 ea. = $7,500,000
   Common market value = 2,850,000˙ shares × $31.25 ea. = $89,062,500
   Total market value = $7,500,000 + $89,062,500 = $96,562,500

Requirement 2

Feb. 10	Retained Earnings	112,500	
	Dividends Payable		112,500
	(150,000 shares × $0.75 per share)		

> **Study Tip:** No entry is made on the date of record.

Mar. 30	Dividends Payable	112,500	
	Cash		112,500
May 10	Retained Earnings	112,500	
	Dividends Payable		112,500

| June 30 | Dividends Payable | 112,500 | |
| | Cash | | 112,500 |

| Aug. 10 | Retained Earnings | 112,500 | |
| | Dividends Payable | | 112,500 |

| Sept. 30 | Dividends Payable | 112,500 | |
| | Cash | | 112,500 |

| Nov. 10 | Retained Earnings | 112,500 | |
| | Dividends Payable | | 112,500 |

| Dec. 30 | Dividends Payable | 112,500 | |
| | Cash | | 112,500 |

Apr. 20	Retained Earnings	2,565,000	
	Dividends Payable		2,565,000
	(2,850,000 shares × $0.90 per share)		

May 29	Common Shares	900,000	
	Retained Earnings	4,519,500	
	Cash		5,419,500
	(150,000 shares × $36.13)		

| June 5 | Accumulated Amortization | 105,000 | |
| | Retained Earnings | | 105,000 |

| June 20 | Dividends Payable | 2,565,000 | |
| | Cash | | 2,565,000 |

| Aug. 30 | Cash | 6,000,000 | |
| | Common Shares | | 6,000,000 |

| Sept. 5 | Retained Earnings | 13,303,500 | |
| | Common Share Dividend Distributable | | 13,303,500 |

On the date of declaration of the stock dividend there were (2,850,000 – 150,000 + 240,000) 2,940,000 shares outstanding.

2,940,000 × 10% × $45.25 = $13,303,500

| Nov. 5 | Common Share Dividends Distributable | 13,303,500 | |
| | Common Shares | | 13,303,500 |

Requirement 3

Baxter Inc.
Statement of Retained Earnings
For the Year Ended December 31, 2006

Retained earnings, December 31, 2005		$65,195,000
Add: Prior-period adjustment		105,000
Retained earnings, December 31, 2005 adjusted		65,300,000
Net income		2,615,000
		67,915,000
2006 dividends*		
Preferred - cash dividends	$ 450,000	
Common - cash dividends	2,565,000	
Common - share dividends	13,303,500	16,318,500
Retained earnings, December 31, 2006		$51,596,500

* Preferred dividends = 150,000 shares × $0.75 × 4 = $450,000

Common dividends:
Cash: In April, there were 2,850,000 shares outstanding × $0.90/share = $2,565,000

Share: On September 5 there were 2,940,000 shares outstanding × 10% × $45.25/share = $13,303,500

There are now 3,234,000 shares outstanding (2,540,000 plus 10% × 2,940,000).

Baxter Inc.
Statement of Shareholders' Equity
For the Year Ended December 31, 2006

	Preferred Shares	Common Shares	Retained Earnings	Cumulative Translation Adjustment	Total Shareholders' Equity
Balance, Dec. 31, 2005	$7,500,000	$17,100,000	$65,195,000	($1,250,000)	$88,545,000
Preferred dividends			(450,000)		(450,000)
Cash dividends			(2,565,500)		(2,565,500)
10% share dividends		13,303,500	(13,303,500)		-0-
Prior-period adjustment			105,000		105,000
Repurchase of shares		(900,000)	(4,519,500)		(5,419,500)
Exercise of share options		6,000,000			6,000,000
Net income			2,615,000		2,615,000
Translation adjustment				245,500	245,500
Balance, Dec. 31, 2006	$7,500,000	$35,503,500	$47,077,000	($1,004,500)	$89,076,000

The Income Statement and the Statement of Shareholders' Equity

Requirement 4

Preferred market value = 150,000 shares × $50 per share = $7,500,000
Common market value = 3,234,500 shares × $51.13 per share = $165,379,985
Total market value = $7,500,000 + $165,354,420 = $172,879,985

Requirement 5

Basic earnings per share = net income less preferred dividends / average number of common shares outstanding
= ($2,615,000 - $450,000) / (2,850,000 × 3,234,000)
= $2,165,000 / 3,042,000
= $0.71 (rounded)

Requirement 6

Basic earnings per share (Requirement 5 above) uses average common shares outstanding as the denominator. Diluted earnings per share uses average common shares outstanding *plus* any additional shares that could become outstanding. Remember that 760,000 options could still be exercised (1,000,000 less the 240,000 that were exercised in August). If those additional options are exercised, the total number of outstanding shares increases to 3,802,000 (3,042,000 + 760,000).

Therefore, diluted earnings per share becomes

($2,615,000 – $450,000) / $3,802,000 = $2,165,000 / 3,802,000 = $0.57 (rounded)

Additional items which could "dilute" earnings per share are convertible preferred shares and bonds that have a conversion feature attached to them.

Requirement 7

P/E ratio = market price per share / earnings per share
= $51.13 / $0.71 (from Requirement 5)
= 72 (rounded)

CHAPTER 12—THE CASH FLOW STATEMENT

CHAPTER OVERVIEW

In each of the preceding chapters, references have been made to the cash flow statement and the cash flow effects of selected transactions. Many people think the cash flow statement is more important than the income statement and the balance sheet. It is certainly the most complex of the published financial statements. The specific learning objectives for this chapter are to

1. **Identify** the purposes of the cash flow statement
2. **Distinguish** between operating, investing, and financing cash flows
3. **Prepare** a cash flow statement by the indirect method
4. **Prepare** a cash flow statement by the direct method

CHAPTER REVIEW

Objective 1 - Identify the purposes of the cash flow statement

Cash flows are cash receipts and cash payments. The **cash flow statement** reports all these receipts and disbursements under three categories—operating, investing, and financing—and shows the reasons for changes in the cash balance. The statement is used to

1. Predict future cash flows
2. Evaluate management decisions
3. Determine the company's ability to pay dividends to shareholders and interest and principal to creditors
4. Show the relationship of net income to the business's cash flows

The term cash includes **cash equivalents,** which are highly liquid short-term investments (such as T-bills and money market accounts).

Objective 2 - Distinguish among operating, investing, and financing cash flows

Operating activities create revenues, expenses, gains, and losses in the entity's major lines of business. Therefore, operating activities are related to the transactions that make up net income. This requires analysis of current assets and current liabilities.

Operating activities are always listed first because they are the most important source of cash for a business. If a firm cannot generate sufficient cash flows from operating activities, they will not be successful in the long run.

Investing activities increase and decrease the assets with which the business works. Investing activities require analysis of the long-term asset accounts.

Investing activities are critical because they help determine the future course of the business.

Financing activities obtain the funds from investors and creditors needed to launch and sustain the business. Financing activities require analysis of the long-term liability accounts and the shareholders' equity accounts.

Review Exhibit 12-2 in your text and become familiar with the relationships between cash flows and balance sheet accounts.

There are two ways to format the cash flow statement—the **direct method** and the **indirect method**. Both formats arrive at the same result; however, the manner in which they do so differs in the operating activities section of the statement. The other two sections (investing activities and financing activities) are the same regardless of the format used. The CICA recommends, but does not require, the direct method because it is easier for the user to understand.

Objective 3 - Prepare a cash flow statement by the indirect method

Study Tip: Carefully review Exhibit 12-3 in the text to understand the indirect method.

The **indirect method** reconciles net income to cash flows and affects only the operating activities section of the cash flow statement. The investing activities and financing activities sections are identical to the sections prepared using the direct method.

To prepare the operating activities section using the indirect method, we must add and subtract items that affect net income and cash flows differently. Begin with net income from the income statement.

1. Amortization is a noncash expense that reduces net income. Therefore, we add it back to net income as part of our effort to arrive at cash flow from operations.
2. Gains and losses from the sale of capital assets are reported as part of net income, and the proceeds are reported in the investing activities section. To avoid counting gains and losses twice, we must remove their effect from net income. Therefore, gains are subtracted from net income and losses are added to net income.
3. Changes in current assets and current liabilities are treated as follows:
   a. Increases in current assets, other than cash, are subtracted from net income.
   b. Decreases in current assets, other than cash, are added to net income.
   c. Decreases in current liabilities, other than dividends payable, are subtracted from net income.
   d. Increases in current liabilities are added to net income.

Study Tip: Under the indirect method, only changes in current assets and current liabilities are used.

Cash flows from investing activities include

1. cash payments for capital assets, investments, and loans to other companies
2. cash receipts from the sale of capital assets, investments, and the collection of loans

(Helpful hint: review Exhibit 12-8 in the text.)

Cash flows from financing activities include

1. cash receipts from issuing shares and debt
2. cash payments for debt and share repurchases
3. payments for cash dividends

(Helpful hint: review Exhibit 12-9 in your text.)

Review Exhibits 12-6 and 12-7. These are examples of the indirect method.

Noncash investing and financing activities are investments that do not require cash. As such, they are not reported on the cash flow statement, but are reported separately in a schedule accompanying the cash flow statement. (Helpful hint: review Exhibit 12-10 in the text.)

Objective 4 - Prepare a cash flow statement by the direct method

The cash flow statement reports cash flows from operating activities, investing activities, and financing activities, calculates the net increase or decrease in cash over the year, and adds that to the previous year's cash balance to arrive at the current year's cash balance. It shows where cash came from and how it was spent.

Preparing the cash flow statement by the direct method requires the following steps:

1. identify items that affect cash
2. classify the items as operating, investing, or financing activities
3. determine the increase or decrease in cash for each item

Cash flows from operating activities include

1. cash collections from customers
2. cash receipts of interest and dividends
3. payments to suppliers
4. payments to employees
5. payments for interest and income taxes

Although amortization expense is listed on the income statement and, therefore, affects operating income, it is not listed on the cash flow statement because no cash is involved.

> **Study Tip:** While principal payments on notes and bonds payable are a financing activity, the interest payments are classified as an operating activity.

Accounts may be analyzed for the cash effects of various transactions using the income statement amounts in conjunction with changes in the balance sheet amounts.

To determine cash flow amounts from operating activities, keep the following in mind:

Revenue/expense from the income statement $\longrightarrow$ Adjust for the change in related balance sheet accounts $\longrightarrow$ Amount for the cash flow statement

> **Study Tip:** Study Exhibit 12-11 in the text thoroughly and be familiar with these relationships.

Cash collections from customers can be computed using sales revenue from the income statement and the changes in accounts receivable from the balance sheet:

$$
\begin{array}{ccc}
\text{COLLECTIONS} & & \text{+ DECREASES IN ACCOUNTS RECEIVABLE} \\
\text{FROM} \quad = & \text{SALES REVENUE} & \text{or} \\
\text{CUSTOMERS} & & \text{- INCREASES IN ACCOUNTS RECEIVABLE}
\end{array}
$$

Payments to suppliers are computed as follows:

$$
\begin{array}{c}
\text{PAYMENTS} \\
\text{FOR} \\
\text{INVENTORY}
\end{array}
=
\begin{array}{c}
\text{COST OF} \\
\text{GOODS} \\
\text{SOLD}
\end{array}
\left[
\begin{array}{c}
\text{+ INCREASE IN} \\
\text{INVENTORY} \\
\text{or} \\
\text{- DECREASE IN} \\
\text{INVENTORY}
\end{array}
\right]
\text{and}
\left[
\begin{array}{c}
\text{+ DECREASE IN} \\
\text{ACCOUNTS PAYABLE} \\
\text{or} \\
\text{- INCREASE IN} \\
\text{ACCOUNTS PAYABLE}
\end{array}
\right]
$$

Payments for operating expenses are computed as follows:

$$
\begin{array}{c}
\text{PAYMENTS} \\
\text{FOR} \\
\text{OPERATING} \\
\text{EXPENSES}
\end{array}
=
\begin{array}{c}
\text{OPERATING} \\
\text{EXPENSES OTHER} \\
\text{THAN SALARIES,} \\
\text{WAGES, AND} \\
\text{AMORTIZATION}
\end{array}
\left[
\begin{array}{c}
\text{+ INCREASE IN} \\
\text{PREPAID} \\
\text{EXPENSES} \\
\text{or} \\
\text{- DECREASE IN} \\
\text{PREPAID} \\
\text{EXPENSES}
\end{array}
\right]
\text{and}
\left[
\begin{array}{c}
\text{+ DECREASE IN} \\
\text{ACCRUED} \\
\text{LIABILITIES} \\
\text{or} \\
\text{- INCREASE IN} \\
\text{ACCRUED} \\
\text{LIABILITIES}
\end{array}
\right]
$$

Remember that amortization is not included in operating expenses because amortization is a noncash expense.

Payments to employees are computed as follows:

$$
\begin{array}{c}
\text{PAYMENTS} \\
\text{TO} \\
\text{EMPLOYEES}
\end{array}
=
\begin{array}{c}
\text{SALARIES} \\
\text{AND WAGES} \\
\text{EXPENSE}
\end{array}
\left[
\begin{array}{c}
\text{+ DECREASES IN SALARIES AND WAGES PAYABLE} \\
\text{or} \\
\text{- INCREASES IN SALARIES AND WAGES PAYABLE}
\end{array}
\right]
$$

Payments of interest and taxes follow the pattern for payments to employees. Exhibit 12-15 in the text summarizes this discussion.

For investing activities we look to the asset accounts (Capital Assets, Investments, Notes Receivable).

Capital asset transactions can be analyzed by first determining book value:

$$
\begin{array}{c}
\text{BEGINNING} \\
\text{CAPITAL ASSET} \\
\text{BALANCE (NET)}
\end{array}
+
\text{ACQUISITIONS}
-
\text{AMORTIZATION}
-
\begin{array}{c}
\text{BOOK VALUE} \\
\text{OF CAPITAL} \\
\text{ASSETS SOLD}
\end{array}
=
\begin{array}{c}
\text{ENDING} \\
\text{CAPITAL} \\
\text{ASSET} \\
\text{BALANCE} \\
\text{(NET)}
\end{array}
$$

Sale proceeds are computed as follows:

$$\text{SALE PROCEEDS} = \text{BOOK VALUE SOLD} + \text{GAIN} - \text{LOSS}$$

Acquisitions will decrease cash, while sale proceeds will increase cash.

Investments and loans and notes receivable are analyzed in a manner similar to capital assets; however, there is no amortization to account for.

Financing activities affect liability and shareholders' equity accounts.

Long-term debt can be analyzed with this equation:

$$\begin{array}{c} \text{BEGINNING} \\ \text{LONG-TERM} \\ \text{DEBT} \\ \text{BALANCE} \end{array} + \begin{array}{c} \text{ISSUANCE} \\ \text{OF} \\ \text{NEW DEBT} \end{array} - \text{PAYMENTS} = \begin{array}{c} \text{ENDING} \\ \text{LONG-TERM} \\ \text{DEBT} \\ \text{BALANCE} \end{array}$$

Share transactions can be analyzed using this equation:

$$\begin{array}{c} \text{BEGINNING} \\ \text{SHARE} \\ \text{BALANCE} \end{array} + \begin{array}{c} \text{ISSUANCE} \\ \text{OF} \\ \text{NEW SHARES} \end{array} - \text{RETIREMENTS} = \begin{array}{c} \text{ENDING} \\ \text{SHARE} \\ \text{BALANCE} \end{array}$$

Issuances increase cash, while retirements decrease cash.

Dividend payments can be computed by analyzing Retained Earnings:

$$\begin{array}{c} \text{BEGINNING} \\ \text{RETAINED} \\ \text{EARNINGS} \\ \text{BALANCE} \end{array} + \begin{array}{c} \text{NET} \\ \text{INCOME} \end{array} - \begin{array}{c} \text{DIVIDENDS} \\ \text{DECLARATIONS} \end{array} = \begin{array}{c} \text{ENDING} \\ \text{RETAINED} \\ \text{EARNINGS} \\ \text{BALANCE} \end{array}$$

Remember that share dividends must be separated from cash dividends. Also, a change in the Dividends Payable account will affect the actual cash dividends paid.

Noncash investing and financing activities

Some investing and financing activities are noncash. Some typical noncash investing and financing activities include

1. Acquisition of assets by issuing shares
2. Acquisition of assets by issuing debt
3. Payment of long-term debt by transferring investment assets to the creditor

Noncash activities can be reported in a separate schedule that accompanies the cash flow statement. (Helpful hint: review Exhibit 12-10 in your text.)

Cash flows are only one source of information creditors and investors use to evaluate a company. The Decision Guidelines in your text provide an excellent summary of questions, factors to consider, and financial statement predictors from both a creditor's and an investor's perspective.

Free cash flow refers to the amount of cash flow that a company could access quickly should a need/opportunity arise. **Free cash flow** is defined as the amount of cash available from operations after paying for planned investments in plant, equipment, and other long-term assets. When net cash flows from operations exceed the amount of cash required for investments in long-term assets, the excess is available for additional investments. Obviously, a positive free cash flow is preferable to a negative amount. Free cash flow is yet another tool to be used in evaluating a company's performance.

TEST YOURSELF

All the self-testing materials in this chapter focus on information and procedures that your instructor is likely to test in quizzes and examinations.

I. Matching   *Match each numbered term with its lettered definition.*

_____ 1.   cash equivalents
_____ 2.   direct method
_____ 3.   indirect method
_____ 4.   operating activity
_____ 5.   cash flows

_____ 6.   financing activity
_____ 7.   investing activity
_____ 8.   cash flow statement
_____ 9.   free cash flow

A.   a report of cash receipts and cash disbursements classified according to the entity's major activities: operating, investing, and financing
B.   an activity that creates revenue or expense in the entity's major lines of business
C.   an activity that increases or decreases the assets that the business has to work with
D.   an activity that obtains the funds needed to launch and sustain the business or repays such funds
E.   cash receipts and cash disbursements
F.   the format of the operating activities section of the cash flow statement that lists the major categories of operating cash receipts and cash disbursements
G.   the format of the operating activities section of the cash flow statement that starts with net income and shows the reconciliation from net income to operating cash flows
H.   highly liquid short-term investments that can be converted into cash with little delay
I.   the amount of cash available from operations after paying for planned investments in plant, equipment, and other long-term assets

II. Multiple Choice   *Circle the best answer.*

1.   All of the following are uses of the cash flow statement *except*

   A.   evaluating employee performance
   B.   evaluating management decisions
   C.   predicting future cash flows
   D.   relating net income to changes in cash

2.   Activities that increase or decrease business assets such as machinery are called

   A.   financing activities
   B.   investing activities
   C.   operating activities
   D.   reporting activities

3. Transactions involving shareholders' equity or debt activities are called

   A. financing activities
   B. investing activities
   C. operating activities
   D. reporting activities

4. Which of the following is considered a cash equivalent?

   A. accounts receivable
   B. inventory
   C. supplies
   D. treasury bills

5. The receipt of cash dividend revenues would be reported on the

   A. balance sheet
   B. income statement
   C. cash flow statement
   D. both the income statement and the cash flow statement

6. All of the following are examples of operating activities *except*

   A. purchases from suppliers
   B. sales to customers
   C. sales of equipment
   D. recording rent expense

7. All of the following are examples of investing activities *except*

   A. sale of building
   B. payment of dividends
   C. purchase of equipment
   D. receipt of cash from sale of Government of Canada Bonds

8. All of the following are financing activities *except*

   A. issuing shares
   B. paying dividends
   C. selling equipment
   D. long-term borrowing

9. Cash collections from customers are computed by

   A. Sales Revenue + Increase in Accounts Receivable
   B. Sales Revenue - Increase in Accounts Receivable
   C. Sales Revenues + Decrease in Accounts Receivable
   D. Either B or C

10. All of the following are included in the free cash flow calculation *except*

   A. cash from operating activities
   B. cash payments for bond retirements
   C. cash payments for plant and equipment
   D. cash from the sale of shares

11. Highly liquid short-term investments that can be converted into cash readily are called

   A. cash flows
   B. cash gains
   C. cash equivalents
   D. cash parallels

12. The gain portion of a gain on the sale of machinery would be shown on the cash flow statement as

   A. an increase to operating activities
   B. a decrease to operating activities
   C. an increase to investing activities
   D. a decrease to investing activities

13. A long-term loan to another company would be listed as

   A. a cash outflow from operating activities
   B. a cash inflow from operating activities
   C. a cash outflow from investing activities
   D. a cash inflow from investing activities

14. The purchase of a building by the issuance of bonds would be recorded as

   A. an increase to investing activities only
   B. an increase to financing activities only
   C. an increase to investing and an increase to financing activities
   D. it would be listed in the separate schedule for noncash transactions

15. During the current year, the beginning inventory for ABC Corp. was $430,000. The ending inventory was $390,000 and cost of goods sold totaled $750,000. The company also had beginning accounts payable of $55,000 and ending balance of accounts payable of $90,000. ABC Corp. had a payment for inventory of

   A. $710,000
   B. $1,140,000
   C. $675,000
   D. $765,000

III. Completion *Complete each of the following statements.*

1. The _____ is the only financial statement that is dated as of the end of the period.

2. The largest cash inflow from operations is _____.

3. Both the _____ method and the _____ method of preparing the cash flow statement are permitted by the CICA.

4. Payments of dividends is a(n) _____ activity on the cash flow statement.

5. Making loans is a(n) _____ activity on the cash flow statement.

6. Amortization is included in the _____ activities section on the cash flow statement when using the indirect method.

7. The purchase of equipment is a(n) _____ activity on the cash flow statement.

8. While permitting both methods, CICA recommends the _____ method for preparing the cash flow statement.

9. The _____ method begins with net income.

10. The difference between the direct and indirect method is found in the _____ activities section of the cash flow statement.

11. Using the indirect method, a gain is _____ from net income in the operating activities section.

12. Free cash flow is calculated by subtracting cash outflows earmarked for _____ from net cash flows from operating activities.

13. Proceeds from cash dividends received from investments in other companies are listed in the _____ activities section of the cash flow statement.

14. The proper order for the cash flow statement is _____ activities, followed by _____ activities and _____ activities.

15. The issuance of bonds for the purchase of equipment would be listed as a(n) _____ activity on the cash flow statement.

IV. True/False *For each of the following statements, circle T for true or F for false.*

1. T F Free cash flow compares cash flows from operations with cash flows from financing activities.

2. T F The indirect approach reconciles net income to cash flows from operating activities.

3. T F An increase in accounts receivable indicates cash receipts from customers are more than net sales reported on the income statement.

4. T F When using the indirect method, increases in current liabilities are deducted from net income.

5. T F When using the indirect method, decreases in current assets are deducted from net income.

6. T F Differences between the direct method and indirect method are found in two of the three sections in the cash flow statement.

7. T F Short-term investments are cash equivalents.

8.   T F   Interest received on money market investments is reported as investing activities on the cash flow statement.

9.   T F   The receipt of dividends and the payment of dividends are reconciled to a net amount and reported as a cash flow from financing activities on the cash flow statement.

10. T F   Investing activities focus on the company's long-term assets.

11. T F   Gains on the sale of capital assets are reported as cash flows from operating activities on the cash flow statement.

12. T F   The repurchase of shares is reported as a financing activity on the cash flow statement.

13. T F   To determine cash paid for interest, begin with interest expense and add any decrease in interest payable.

14. T F   An increase in prepaid expenses results in a decrease in cash paid for operating expenses.

15. T F   The purchase of supplies on account is an example of a noncash investing and financing activity.

V. Exercises

1.   Classify each of the following as an operating, investing, or financing activity.

Item	Classification
a) payment to employees	
b) lending money	
c) receiving dividends on investments	
d) issuing shares	
e) raising funds by selling bonds	
f) receiving cash from customers	
g) paying taxes	
h) purchasing equipment by paying cash	
i) purchasing equipment and signing a note payable	
j) purchasing inventory on account	
k) receiving interest revenue	
l) paying dividends to shareholders	
m) selling short-term investments	
n) repurchasing common shares	

2.   Fox Company had interest expense of $54,000 in 2006. The balance in Interest Payable was $2,100 at the beginning of the year and $3,600 at the end of the year. How much cash was paid for interest during 2006?

3.   Batista Company had cost of goods sold of $920,000, an increase in inventory of $75,000, and an increase in accounts payable of $32,000 in 2006. How much cash was paid to suppliers?

4. Hound Company had sales of $2,100,000 in 2006. Ninety percent of sales were on credit. During the year, Accounts Receivable increased from $40,000 to $95,000. How much cash was received from customers during 2006?

5. Chow Company purchased equipment for $319,000, lent $75,000 to a customer, borrowed $120,000, and sold securities that were not cash equivalents for $27,000. What was the net cash flow from investing activities?

6. From the following list of cash receipts and payments, present the cash flows from the operating activities section of the cash flow statement using the direct method.

Cash receipts from interest revenues	$ 1,820
Cash paid for taxes	43,110
Cash payments to suppliers	328,590
Cash receipts from customers	615,200
Cash paid for dividends	12,700
Cash payments to employees	103,200
Cash receipts from dividend revenues	780
Cash payments for interest	4,965

VI. Critical Thinking

1. Review the information in Exercises 2 and 4 above. Calculate the same answer using a different approach.

2. ABC Corp. has beginning assets of $40,000 and accumulated amortization of $19,000. During the period, $70,000 worth of assets were purchased, and the year-end balance of assets was $90,000. Amortization expense for the period was $7,000, and the year-end balance of accumulated amortization was $12,000. If only one asset was sold during the year, and a $3,000 gain was recognized on the sale, reconstruct the journal entry to recognize the sale, and determine the amount of cash received on the sale.

DEMONSTRATION PROBLEMS

Demonstration Problem #1

The income statement, schedule of current account changes, and additional data for Value Village Books follows:

Value Village Books
Income Statement
For the Year Ended December 31, 2006

Revenues:		
Net sales revenue	$3,512,500	
Dividend revenue	67,500	$3,580,000
Expenses:		
Cost of goods sold	2,702,500	
Salary expense	322,500	
Other operating expense	77,500	
Amortization expense	137,500	
Interest expense	162,500	
Amortization expense—patents	12,500	3,415,000
Net income		$165,000

Additional data:

a. Collections exceeded sales by $27,500.
b. Dividend revenue equaled cash amounts received, $67,500.
c. Payments to suppliers were $45,000 less than cost of goods sold. Payments for other operating expense and interest expense were the same as 'Other operating expense' and 'Interest expense.'
d. Payments to employees were less than salary expense by $10,000.
e. Acquisition of capital assets totaled $325,000. Of this amount, $50,000 was paid in cash and the balance was financed by signing a note payable.
f. Proceeds from the sale of land were $212,500.
g. Proceeds from the issuance of common shares were $125,000.
h. Full payment was made on a long-term note payable, $100,000.
i. Dividends were paid in the amount of $40,000.
j. A small parcel of land located in an industrial park was purchased for $185,000.
k. Current asset and liability activity changes were as follows:

	December 31	
	2006	2005
Cash and cash equivalents	590,000	230,000
Accounts receivable	590,000	607,500
Inventory	945,000	960,000
Prepaid expense	30,000	30,000
Accounts payable	535,000	505,000
Salary payable	27,500	17,500
Income tax payable	8,000	8,000

Required

1. Using the direct method, prepare the December 31, 2006, cash flow statement and accompanying schedule of noncash investing and financing activities for Value Village Books.
2. Calculate the corporation's free cash flow.

Requirement 1 (Cash flow statement—direct method)

Value Village Books		
Cash Flow Statement		
For the Year Ended December 31, 2006		

Requirement 2 (Free cash flow)

Demonstration Problem #2

Using the information in Problem 1, prepare a cash flow statement and accompanying schedule of noncash investing and financing activities using the indirect method.

Indirect Method

Value Village Books
Cash Flow Statement
For the Year Ended December 31, 2006

SOLUTIONS

A. TEST YOURSELF

I. Matching

1. H	3. G	5. E	7. C	9. I
2. F	4. B	6. D	8. A	

II. Multiple Choice

1. A Replace A with "to determine ability to pay dividends and interest" and you have a list of all the purposes for the cash flow statement.

2. B Changes in capital assets are investing activities.

3. A Changes in capital and debt are financing activities.

4. D Cash and cash equivalents are highly liquid short-term investments that can be converted into cash with little delay and include money market investments and investments in T-bills.

5. D Recall that the receipt of a dividend from an investment accounted for under the cost method is treated as income and accordingly will be included on the income statement. For cash flow statement purposes, the receipt of dividends is considered an operating activity and will be reflected in that portion of the statement.

6. C Operating activities create revenues and expenses in the entity's major line of business. Equipment sales are assumed not to be this entity's major line of business.

7. B Investing activities increase and decrease the assets the business has to work with. Payment of a dividend is a financing activity. Note that while the receipt of interest on a bond is an operating activity, buying and selling bonds is an investing activity.

8. C Financing activities include transactions with investors and creditors needed to obtain funds to launch and sustain the business. Of the items listed, only C, an investing activity, does not fit that definition.

9. E Sales revenue is recorded on the accrual basis. To convert this to a cash flow, the net change in accounts receivable must be considered. A decrease in accounts receivable indicates that customers have paid for more than they purchased and should be added to sales. An increase in accounts receivable indicates that customers have purchased more than they paid for and should be subtracted from sales.

10. B Free cash flow refers to net cash flow from operating activities and investing activities.

11. C A highly liquid investment is a cash equivalent.

12.   B   The gain is decreased from operating activities as it would have been increased on the income statement and needs to be adjusted to avoid double counting.

13.   C   A long-term loan is an outflow from investing activities.

14.   D   Since no cash is exchanged, the purchase of a building for bonds is a noncash item and is shown in a separate schedule.

15.   C $430,000 + X - \$390,000 = \$750,000$, thus X = purchases = \$710,000
               $55,000 + \$710,000 - Y = \$90,000$, thus Y = payments = \$675,000

III. Completion

1. balance sheet (The income statement, statement of retained earnings, and cash flow statement all cover a period of time. Only the balance sheet is as of a particular date.)
2. collections of cash from customers
3. direct, indirect (order not important)
4. financing
5. investing
6. operating (Recall from our previous discussion that amortization is a noncash expense.)
7. investing
8. direct
9. indirect
10. operating activities
11. deducted
12. investment in plant, equipment, and other capital assets
13. investing
14. operating, investing, financing
15. a separate schedule of noncash items

IV. True/False

1.   F   Free cash flow begins with cash flows from operating activities then deducts cash flows from investing activities.
2.   T   The indirect approach begins with net income. The direct approach ignores net income.
3.   F   An increase in accounts receivable indicates that cash receipts are less than net sales
4.   F   Increases in current liabilities are added, not deducted.
5.   F   Using the indirect method, a decrease in current assets is added to net income
6.   F   The differences in presentation between the two approaches are only found in the operating activities section of the cash flow statement.

> **Study Tip**: Remember, either approach results in the same basic information on cash flows for the period.

7.   F   Short-term investments includes equity securities held for the short run which are not cash equivalents.
8.   F   Interest revenue is an operating activity.
9.   F   Dividend revenue is an operating activity, while dividends paid is a financing activity.
10.   T
11.   F   The cash received from the sale of capital assets is reported, not the gain (or loss).
12.   T

13.   T
14.   T
15.   F   Changes in both supplies and accounts payable affect the amounts reported in the operating activities section of the cash flow statement.

V. Exercises

1.
   a) operating activity
   b) investing activity
   c) operating activity
   d) financing activity
   e) financing activity
   f) operating activity
   g) operating activity
   h) investing activity
   i) none (this is a noncash investing activity)
   j) operating activity
   k) operating activity
   l) financing activity
   m) investing activity
   n) financing activity

Study Tip: Remember, operating activities relate to the income statement, investing activities to long-term assets, and financing activities to long-term liabilities and shareholders' equity.

2. Note that this exercise and the next ones may be solved using what you learned in earlier chapters.

	Interest Payable (beginning)	$2,100
+	Interest Expense	54,000
=	Subtotal	56,100
-	Cash Payments	?
=	Interest Payable (ending)	$3,600

$2,100 + $54,000 - x = $3,600
x = $52,500

3.

	Cost of Goods Sold	$920,000
+	Increase in Inventory	75,000
=	Subtotal	995,000
-	Increase in Accounts Payable	32,000
=	Cash paid to suppliers	$963,000

4. Cash received from credit sales:

	Accounts Receivable (beginning)	$40,000
+	Credit Sales (90% × 2,100,000)	1,890,000
=	Subtotal	1,930,000
-	Cash Collected from Customers	?
=	Accounts Receivable (ending)	$95,000

Cash received from credit sales ($1,930,000 - $95,000)	$1,835,000
Cash collected from cash sales (10% × 2,100,000)	210,000
= Total cash collected from customers	$2,045,000

5.

Purchase of equipment	$(319,000)
Loan made to customer	(75,000)
Sale of securities	27,000
Net cash flow from investing activities	$(367,000)

Borrowing $120,000 is not an investing activity. It is a financing activity.

6.

Cash flows from operating activities:

Cash receipts from customers	615,200
Cash receipts from dividends	780
Cash receipts from interest	1,820
Cash payments to suppliers	(328,590)
Cash payments to employees	(103,200)
Cash paid for taxes	(43,110)
Cash payments for interest	(4,965)
Net cash inflow from operating	$137,935

The cash paid for dividends is not an operating activity. Dividends paid to shareholders relate to shareholders' equity on the balance sheet and are, therefore, a financing activity.

VI. Critical Thinking

1. Exercise 2

Interest Expense	$54,000
Less increase in Interest Payable*	(1,500)
Payments for interest	$52,500

*The increase in the related liability is deducted because it represents an expense that has not been paid. Similarly, a decrease in the related liability would be added. Remember, we are concerned with *cash payments*.

Exercise 4

Sales	$2,100,000
Less increase in Accounts Receivable**	(55,000)
Cash received from customers	$2,045,000

**The increase in Accounts Receivable is deducted because it represents credit sales that have not been collected. Similarly, a decrease in Accounts Receivable would be added because it represents additional credit sales collected. Remember we are concerned with *cash receipts*.

2. Determine the asset sold $40,000 + $70,000 − X = $90,000$, the asset sold (X) was $20,000
    Accumulated amortization $19,000 + $7,000 − Y = $12,000$, accumulated amortization (Y) = $14,000

Cash	Z	
Accumulated amortization	$14,000	
Gain on sale		$3,000
Asset sold		$20,000

The cash received was $9,000 = $20,000 + $3,000 - $14,000

DEMONSTRATION PROBLEM S

Demonstration Problem #1 Solved and Explained

Requirement 1 (direct method)

Value Village Books
Cash Flow Statement
For the Year Ended December 31, 2006

Cash flows from operating activities:		
Receipts:		
Collections from customers	$3,540,000 (A)	
Dividends received on investments in shares	67,500 (B)	
Total cash receipts		$3,607,500
Payments:		
To suppliers	2,735,000 (C)	
To employees	312,500 (D)	
For interest	162,500 (C)	
Total cash payments		3,210,000
Net cash inflow from operating activities		397,500
Cash flows from investing activities:		
Acquisition of capital assets	(50,000) (E)	
Proceeds from sale of land	212,500 (F)	
Acquisition of industrial park land	(185,000) (J)	
Net cash outflow from investing activities		(22,500)
Cash flows from financing activities:		
Proceeds from issuance of common shares	125,000 (G)	
Payment of long-term note payable	(100,000) (H)	
Dividends	(40,000) (I)	
Net cash outflow from financing activities		(15,000)
Net increase in cash		360,000
Cash balance beginning of year		230,000
Cash balance end of year		$590,000
Noncash investing and financing activities:		
Acquisition of capital assets by issuing note payable		$275,000 (E)

Computations and Explanations

(A) The largest cash inflow from operations will almost always be the collection of cash from customers. Cash sales obviously will bring in cash immediately. Since sales on account increase Accounts Receivable (not Cash), companies need to know the actual collections from customers. Item (a) of the additional data indicates that collections from customers were more than sales by $27,500. Thus, collections must have been $3,540,000 ($3,512,500 sales plus $27,500).

(B) Dividends do not accrue with the passage of time, but rather are recorded when received. Item (b) of the additional data states that $67,500 was received, the identical amount shown in the income statement. Thus, no adjustment is necessary. Note that dividends received result in a cash inflow reported as an operating activity. Although the origin of the dividend was from an investment activity, in accordance with the CICA, dividends received were accounted for as part of operating activities because they have a direct impact on net income.

(C) Payments to suppliers is a broad category that includes all cash payments for inventory and all operating expenses except disbursements for:

1. employee compensation expense
2. interest expense
3. income tax expense

A review of Item (c) indicates that payments to suppliers were $2,735,000 ($2,657,500 + $77,500) as follows:

Cost of goods sold	$2,702,500
Less: Additional amounts owed to suppliers	(45,000)
Payments for inventory	$2,657,500
Payments for other operating expenses	$77,500

Payments to suppliers include all payments (except those listed above as exceptions) to those who supply the business with its inventory and essential services. Note that interest payment equals interest expense, an item that is separately disclosed in the cash flow statement.

(D) Payments to employees include all forms of employee compensation. The income statement reports the expense (including accrued amounts), whereas the cash flow statement reports only the payments. Item (d) indicates that actual payments were $312,500, which is $10,000 less than the $322,500 reported in the income statement as salary expense.

(E) The purchase of $325,000 in capital assets used $50,000 in cash. The balance was financed with a $275,000 promissory note. Because the note is not an outflow of cash, it is separately disclosed as a noncash investing activity at the bottom of the cash flow statement.

The $185,000 industrial park land (Item j) used $185,000 cash and is shown as a cash outflow or "use." A firm's investment in income-producing assets often signals to investors the direction that the firm is taking.

(F) The receipt of $212,500 from the land sale (Item f) is essentially the opposite of the acquisition of a capital asset, and should be reported as a cash inflow from an investment transaction.

(G) Investors and other financial statement users want to know how an entity obtains its financing. The financing activities section of the cash flow statement for Value Village Books discloses the effect of the sale of common shares (inflow of $125,000, Item g), payment of a long-term note (outflow of $100,000, Item h), and payment of cash dividends (outflow of $40,000, Item i).

Requirement 2 (Free cash flow)

$375,000

Free cash flow is the difference between cash flows from operating activities and cash flows from investing activities. A review of the cash flow statement shows cash inflows from operating activities of $397,500 and net cash outflows from investing activities of $22,500. Therefore, free cash flows are $397,500 - $22,500 = $375,000.

Demonstration Problem #2 Solved and Explained

Indirect Method

Value Village Books
Cash Flow Statement
For the Year Ended December 31, 2006

Cash flows from operating activities:		
Net income (from income statement)		$165,000
Add (subtract) items that affect net income and		
cash flow differently:		
Amortization	150,000	
Decrease in accounts receivable	27,500	
Decrease in inventory	15,000	
Increase in accounts payable	30,000	
Increase in salary payable	10,000	232,500
Net cash inflow from operating activities		397,500
Cash flows from investing activities:		
Acquisition of capital assets	(50,000)	
Proceeds from sale of land	212,500	
Acquisition of industrial park land	(185,000)	
Net cash outflow from investing activities		(22,500)
Cash flows from financing activities:		
Proceeds from issuance of common shares	125,000	
Payment of long-term note payable	(100,000)	
Dividends	(40,000)	
Net cash outflow from financing activities		(15,000)
Net increase in cash		$360,000
Cash balance beginning of year		230,000
Cash balance end of year		$590,000
Noncash investing and financing activities:		
Acquisition of capital assets by issuing note payable		$275,000

As emphasized many times in this chapter, the difference between the direct method and the indirect method appears only in the presentation of the cash flows from operating activities section of the statement. The indirect method begins with net income, then 'adjusts' the net income figure to convert it to a cash-based value. Regardless of method, the presentation of cash flows from investing activities and financing activities is the same. The CICA permits either method, but recommends the direct method because it is thought to be more "user friendly."

CHAPTER 13—FINANCIAL STATEMENT ANALYSIS

CHAPTER OVERVIEW

Financial statements are the primary means an outsider uses to evaluate a particular company. Once completed, the results can be compared with those of other companies. There are a variety of tools used to evaluate performance. In this chapter you are introduced to some of these techniques. The specific learning objectives for the chapter are to

1. **Perform** a horizontal analysis of comparative financial statements
2. **Perform** a vertical analysis of financial statements
3. **Prepare** and use common-size financial statements
4. **Use** the cash flow statement for decisions
5. **Compute** the standard financial ratios
6. **Use** ratios in decision making
7. **Measure** the economic value added by operations

CHAPTER REVIEW

Financial statement analysis is based on information taken from the annual report, articles in the business press, and so on. The objective of financial statement analysis is to provide information to creditors and investors to help them 1) predict future returns and 2) assess the risk of those returns. Past performance is often a good indicator of future performance. Four categories of financial statement analysis are horizontal, vertical, common size, and ratio analysis.

Objective 1 - Perform a horizontal analysis of comparative financial statements

The study of percentage changes in comparative statements is called **horizontal analysis**. Horizontal analysis highlights changes over time. Computing a percentage change in comparative statements requires two steps: 1) compute the dollar amount of the change from the base (earlier) period to the later period, and 2) compute the percentage change by dividing the dollar amount of the change by the base period amount.

The **base period** for horizontal analysis is the year prior to the year being considered. Suppose there are three years of data. The change from Year 1 to Year 2 is:

$$\frac{\$ \text{ YEAR 2} - \$ \text{ YEAR 1}}{\$ \text{ YEAR 1}}$$

and the change from Year 2 to Year 3 is:

$$\frac{\$ \text{ YEAR 3} - \$ \text{ YEAR 2}}{\$ \text{ YEAR 2}}$$

No percentage changes are computed if the base-year amount is zero or negative. Exhibits 13-2 and 13-3 illustrate horizontal analysis on an income statement and balance sheet.

Trend percentages are a form of horizontal analysis. They indicate the direction of business activities by comparing numbers over a span of several years. Trend percentages are computed by selecting a base year and expressing the amount of each item for each of the following years as a percentage of the base year's amount for that item. The base year is set at 100%.

$$\text{Trend \%} = \frac{\text{Any year \$}}{\text{Base year \$}}$$

Objective 2 - Perform a vertical analysis of financial statements

Vertical analysis of a financial statement reveals the percentage of the total that each statement item represents. Percentages on the comparative income statement are computed by dividing all amounts by net sales. Percentages on the comparative balance sheet are shown as either 1) a percentage of total assets or 2) a percentage of total liabilities and shareholders' equity.

Vertical analysis of the income statement highlights changes in such items as the gross margin percentage and net income.

$$\text{Vertical analysis \%} = \frac{\text{Each income statement (balance sheet) item}}{\text{Net sales or total assets (balance sheet)}}$$

Vertical analysis of the balance sheet shows the composition of balance sheet items. Trend analysis can be used to highlight year-to-year percentage changes. (Helpful hint: review Exhibits 13-4 and 13-5 in your text.)

Objective 3 - Prepare and use common-size financial statements

Common-size statements report amounts in percentages only. The common-size statement is a form of vertical analysis. On a common-size income statement, each item is expressed as a percentage of the net sales amount. In the balance sheet, the common size is the total on each side of the accounting equation. Note that common-size percentages are the same percentages shown on financial statements using vertical analysis. (Helpful hint: review Exhibit 13-6 in your text.)

Benchmarking is the practice of comparing a company's data to a standard set by other companies. Benchmarking is used to compare a company's results with the average for its industry. In addition, common-size statements can be compared with those of specific competitors within the industry. Exhibit 13-7 in your text illustrates these two uses of benchmarking.

Common-size percentages can be used to compare financial statements of different companies or to compare one company's financial statements to industry averages.

Objective 4 - Use the cash flow statement for decisions

The cash flow statement presents the cash flows from operating, investing, and financing activities. This is a document that can be used to see what the management team is doing with the cash available. (Helpful hint: review Exhibit 13-8.)

Questions to consider might include:

1. Does the company generate the majority of its cash from operations, from selling capital assets, or from borrowing? Is the company selling off assets?
2. Does the company retain enough income to finance future operations?

> **Study Tip:** Remember back to Chapter 12 and free cash flow

Objective 5 - Compute the standard financial ratios

There are many, many different ratios used in financial analysis. Sometimes a ratio is used alone, but more frequently a group of ratios are calculated and used to analyze a particular issue. Ratios by themselves are useless; they must be considered in relation or comparison to another ratio (previous year – trend, or competitor). The ratios discussed in this section are grouped as follows:

1. Ratios that measure ability to pay current liabilities
2. Ratios that measure ability to sell inventory and collect receivables
3. Ratios that measure ability to pay long-term debt
4. Ratios that measure profitability
5. Ratios used to analyze shares as an investment

1. **Ratios that measure ability to pay current liabilities**

    Working capital is used to measure a business's ability to meet its short-term obligations with its current assets.

    WORKING CAPITAL = CURRENT ASSETS - CURRENT LIABILITIES

    The **current ratio** is used to measure the availability of sufficient liquid assets to maintain normal business operations.

$$\text{CURRENT RATIO} \quad = \quad \frac{\text{CURRENT ASSETS}}{\text{CURRENT LIABILITIES}}$$

    The **acid-test (quick) ratio** measures the ability of a business to pay all of its current liabilities if they came due immediately.

$$\text{ACID-TEST RATIO} \quad = \quad \frac{\text{CASH + SHORT-TERM INVESTMENTS} \quad + \quad \text{NET CURRENT RECEIVABLES}}{\text{CURRENT LIABILITIES}}$$

> **Study Tip:** Inventory and prepaid expenses are not used to compute the acid-test ratio.

2. **Ratios that measure ability to sell inventory and collect receivables**

    Inventory turnover is a measure of the number of times a company sells an average level of inventory during a year.

$$\text{INVENTORY TURNOVER} = \frac{\text{COST OF GOODS SOLD}}{\text{AVERAGE INVENTORY}}$$

$$\text{AVERAGE INVENTORY} = \frac{\text{BEGINNING INVENTORY} + \text{ENDING INVENTORY}}{2}$$

Accounts receivable turnover measures the ability of a company to collect cash from its credit customers.

$$\text{ACCOUNTS RECEIVABLE TURNOVER} = \frac{\text{NET CREDIT SALES}}{\text{AVERAGE NET ACCOUNTS RECEIVABLE}}$$

$$\text{AVERAGE NET ACCOUNTS RECEIVABLE} = \frac{\text{BEGINNING ACCOUNTS RECEIVABLE} + \text{ENDING ACCOUNTS RECEIVABLE}}{2}$$

Days' sales in receivables measures in sales days the value of accounts receivable; it tells how many days' sales remain uncollected (in accounts receivable).

$$\text{ONE DAY'S SALES} = \frac{\text{NET SALES}}{365}$$

$$\text{DAYS' SALES IN AVERAGE ACCOUNTS RECEIVABLE} = \frac{\text{AVERAGE NET ACCOUNTS RECEIVABLE}}{\text{ONE DAY'S SALES}}$$

To compute the ratio for the beginning of the year, substitute beginning net accounts receivable for average net accounts receivable. To compute the ratio for the end of the year, substitute ending net accounts receivable for average net accounts receivable.

3. **Ratios that measure ability to pay long-term debt**

The **debt ratio** measures the relationship between total liabilities and total assets.

$$\text{DEBT RATIO} = \frac{\text{TOTAL LIABILITIES}}{\text{TOTAL ASSETS}}$$

The **times-interest-earned ratio** (also called the **interest-coverage ratio**) measures the ability of a business to pay interest expense.

$$\text{TIMES-INTEREST-EARNED} = \frac{\text{INCOME FROM OPERATIONS}}{\text{INTEREST EXPENSE}}$$

Remember that income from operations does not include interest revenue, interest expense, or income tax expense.

4. **Ratios that measure profitability**

Rate of return on net sales measures the relationship between net income and sales.

$$\text{RATE OF RETURN ON NET SALES} = \frac{\text{NET INCOME}}{\text{NET SALES}}$$

Rate of return on total assets measures the success a company has in using its assets to earn a profit.

$$\text{RATE OF RETURN ON TOTAL ASSETS} = \frac{\text{NET INCOME} + \text{INTEREST EXPENSE}}{\text{AVERAGE TOTAL ASSETS}}$$

$$\text{AVERAGE TOTAL ASSETS} = \frac{\text{BEGINNING TOTAL ASSETS} + \text{ENDING TOTAL ASSETS}}{2}$$

> **Study Tip:** In reality, the rate of return on total assets (ROA) can be calculated in different ways depending on the use. Be careful when using real data to analyze companies, as the numerator may be different.

The **rate of return on common shareholders' equity** shows the relationship between net income and common shareholders' investment in the company.

$$\text{RATE OF RETURN ON COMMON SHAREHOLDERS' EQUITY} = \frac{\text{NET INCOME} - \text{PREFERRED DIVIDENDS}}{\text{AVERAGE COMMON SHAREHOLDERS' EQUITY}}$$

$$\text{AVERAGE COMMON SHAREHOLDERS' EQUITY} = \frac{\text{BEGINNING} + \text{ENDING COMMON SHAREHOLDERS' EQUITY}}{2}$$

Earnings per share (EPS) is the amount of net income per share of the company's common shares.

$$\text{EPS} = \frac{\text{NET INCOME} - \text{PREFERRED DIVIDENDS}}{\text{NUMBER OF COMMON SHARES OUTSTANDING}}$$

> **Study Tip:** Remember, if the number of common shares outstanding has changed during the year, the denominator is changed to reflect the **average** number of common shares outstanding.

5. **Ratios used to analyze shares as an investment**

The **price/earnings (P/E) ratio** is the ratio of the market price of a common share to the company's EPS.

$$\text{PRICE/ EARNINGS RATIO} = \frac{\text{MARKET PRICE PER COMMON SHARE}}{\text{EARNINGS PER SHARE}}$$

Dividend yield is the ratio of dividends per common share to the share market price.

$$\text{DIVIDEND YIELD} = \frac{\text{DIVIDENDS PER COMMON SHARE}}{\text{MARKET PRICE PER COMMON SHARE}}$$

The formula for calculating **book value per common share** is as follows:

$$\frac{\text{BOOK VALUE}}{\text{PER}} = \frac{\text{TOTAL SHAREHOLDERS' EQUITY - PREFERRED EQUITY}}{\text{NUMBER OF COMMON SHARES OUTSTANDING}}$$

Objective 6 - Use ratios in decision making

Ratios should be 1) evaluated over a period of years and 2) compared with industry standards.

When a problem is found, the items used to compute the ratio should be analyzed to determine the nature of the problem. At that time, possible solutions to the problem can be suggested.

Objective 7 - Measure the economic value added by operations

Economic value added (EVA®) is one measure many companies use to evaluate whether the company has increased shareholder wealth from operations. The formula for EVA® is

$$\text{EVA}^{®} = \textbf{Net income + interest expense – capital charge}$$

where **capital charge = (notes payable+ loans payable + long-term + shareholders') × cost of capital**
$$\qquad\qquad\qquad\qquad\qquad\qquad\qquad\qquad \text{debt} \qquad\quad \text{equity}$$

The **cost of capital** is the weighted average of the returns demanded by the company's shareholders and lenders. Newer companies, because of the added risk, have a higher cost of capital compared with older, more established companies. The underlying assumption behind EVA® is that returns to both shareholders and lenders should be greater than the company's capital charge. If the calculation results in a positive value, this indicates an increase in shareholder wealth. If the result is negative, shareholders may consider selling the shares which, if done in large enough amounts, could lower the price of the shares. Obviously, companies who use this measure strive to achieve a positive result.

There are **limitations of financial analysis.** A sudden drop in a company's ratios signal that there is something wrong, but does not tell us what is wrong. You must analyze the ratios collectively and in light of the current business situation. Is a drop in profitability due to increased expenses, or decreased sales? Has new competition come into the market, or has there been a slowdown in the economy due to higher interest rates and decreased consumer spending?

In an **efficient capital market**, share prices reflect all information that is available to the public. Financial statement analysis helps to identify and evaluate the inherent risks in potential investments.

TEST YOURSELF

All the self-testing materials in this chapter focus on information and procedures that your instructor is likely to test in quizzes and examinations.

I. Matching   *Match each numbered term with its lettered definition.*

_____ 1. accounts receivable turnover
_____ 2. working capital
_____ 3. common-size statements
_____ 4. days' sales in receivables
_____ 5. dividend yield
_____ 6. inventory turnover
_____ 7. return on total assets
_____ 8. times-interest-earned ratio
_____ 9. vertical analysis
_____ 10. acid-test ratio

_____ 11. current ratio
_____ 12. debt ratio
_____ 13. horizontal analysis
_____ 14. price/earnings ratio
_____ 15. return on net sales
_____ 16. book value per common share
_____ 17. return on common shareholders' equity
_____ 18. benchmarking
_____ 19. earnings per share
_____ 20. economic value added

A. analysis of a financial statement that reveals the relationship of each statement item to the total, which is the 100% figure
B. common shareholders' equity divided by the number of common shares outstanding
C. current assets divided by current liabilities
D. current assets minus current liabilities
E. financial statements that report only percentages (no dollar amounts)
F. measures the number of times that operating income can cover interest expense
G. measures the number of times a company sells its average level of inventory during a year
H. ratio of the market price of common shares to the company's earnings per share
I. measures the success a company has in using its assets to earn a profit
J. net income minus preferred dividends divided by average common shareholders' equity; a measure of profitability
K. ratio of average net accounts receivable to one day's sales
L. ratio of dividends per share to the stock's market price per share
M. ratio of net income to net sales; a measure of profitability
N. study of percentage changes in comparative financial statements
O. tells the proportion of a company's assets that it has financed with debt
P. tells whether an entity could pay all its current liabilities if they came due immediately
Q. the ratio of net credit sales to average net accounts receivable; it measures a company's ability to collect cash from credit customers
R. used to measure if a company has increased shareholder wealth from operations
S. the practice of comparing a company with other companies with a view toward improvement
T. the amount of a company's net income per share of its outstanding common stock

II. Multiple Choice   *Circle the best answer.*

1. In vertical analysis, the relationship between net income and net sales is shown by the

   A. income from operations percentage
   B. net sales percentage
   C. rate of return on sales
   D. gross margin percentage

2. Which of the following measures profitability?

   A. debt ratio
   B. current ratio
   C. dividend yield
   D. earnings per common share

3. Which of the following current assets is *not* used to compute the acid-test ratio?

   A. accounts receivable
   B. cash
   C. prepaid expenses
   D. short-term investments

4. Which of the following is a common measure of a firm's ability to meet short-term obligations?

   A. working capital ratio
   B. rate of return on sales
   C. net assets
   D. price/earnings ratio

5. The times-interest-earned ratio measures

   A. profitability
   B. ability to pay interest expense on debt
   C. ability to pay current liabilities
   D. ability to collect receivables

6. The proportion of a firm's assets financed by debt is measured by the

   A. current ratio
   B. debt ratio
   C. debt yield ratio
   D. times-interest-earned ratio

7. Assume that a company's current ratio is greater than one. If the company pays current liabilities with cash, the new current ratio will

   A. increase
   B. decrease
   C. remain unchanged
   D. cannot be determined

8. The dividend yield evaluates

   A. the ability to pay current debt
   B. profitability
   C. shares as an investment
   D. ability to pay long-term debt

9. The excess of current assets over current liabilities is

   A. a measure of profitability
   B. economic value added
   C. a measure of short-term liquidity
   D. a measure of long-term debt-paying ability

10. Book value measures

    A. profitability
    B. short-term liquidity
    C. long-term debt-paying ability
    D. shares as an investment

11. Which of the following measures would be used to evaluate a company's operating performance?

    A. current ratio
    B. economic value added
    C. times-interest-earned ratio
    D. working capital ratio

12. For a ratio to be useful it must

    A. have a high number; the higher the better
    B. have a low number; the lower the better
    C. be compared to something else
    D. be considered in isolation

13. The practice of benchmarking is to

    A. compare your company to other competitors
    B. compare your company to itself over time
    C. compare your company against the industry average
    D. all of the above

14. The use of the cash flow statement in financial analysis

   A. is dependent on whether the direct or indirect method is used
   B. allows you to evaluate the use of cash
   C. should be used only with the acid-test or quick ratio
   D. needs to be analyzed using vertical analysis only

15. The working capital ratio

   A. is used to determine the ability to pay long-term debt
   B. is used to determine the ability to pay current liabilities
   C. is used to determine the profitability of a company
   D. is used to determine the investment in shares of a company

III. Completion   *Complete each of the following statements.*

1. The study of percentage changes in comparative financial statements is called _____ analysis.

2. Vertical analysis percentages on the income statement are computed by dividing all amounts by _____.

3. Vertical analysis percentages on the balance sheet are computed by dividing all amounts by _____.

4. Working capital is _____.

5. _____ and _____ are the two ratios that use current assets and current liabilities.

6. Leverage _____ the risk to common shareholders.

7. The _____ ratio indicates the market price of one dollar of earnings.

8. The rate of return on total assets equals _____.

9. The most widely quoted of all financial measures is _____.

10. The _____ is the recorded accounting value of each common share outstanding.

11. The _____ statement is used to determine if a company is generating enough cash from operations to cover major capital outlays.

12. _____ measures the proportion of a company's assets that is financed with debt.

13. The rate of return on net sales is considered a _____ ratio.

14. _____, also called _____ is encountered when a company earns more income from borrowed money than the related interest expense on the borrowings.

15. _____ is used to evaluate a company's operating performance.

IV. True/False

For each of the following statements, circle T *for true or* F *for false.*

1.   T F   Trend percentages are a form of horizontal analysis.
2.   T F   Vertical analysis is one means for analyzing change over time.
3.   T F   Common-size statements contain no dollar amounts, only percentages.
4.   T F   Benchmarking involves comparing one company to itself, another company, or the industry average.
5.   T F   Rate of return on sales measures a company's profitability.
6.   T F   Working capital can be a negative value.
7.   T F   Quick assets consist of cash, short-term investments, net accounts receivable, and inventories.
8.   T F   Inventory turnover measures a company's ability to sell on credit and collect cash for those credit sales.
9.   T F   Earnings per share is calculated by dividing net income less preferred dividends by the number of shares outstanding at the end of the year.
10.   T F   The price/earnings ratio divides earnings per share into the book value per common share.
11.   T F   The acid-test ratio should always be greater than the current ratio.
12.   T F   EVA® stands for extra value added.
13.   T F   Benchmarking relates one company's results with another company's or the industry's.
14.   T F   Generally, the greater the inventory turnover, the lower the accounts receivable turnover.
15.   T F   Trading on equity occurs when the income generated from borrowings exceed the interest expense, thus benefiting the shareholders.

V. Exercises

1. Net income was $700,000 in Year 1, $1,200,000 in Year 2, $3,450,000 in Year 3, and $2,900,000 in Year 4. What were the percentage changes in net income?

2. Singh Industries had the following information for 2006:

Cost of goods sold	$1,700,000
Beginning inventory	540,000
Ending inventory	680,000
Net credit sales	2,125,000
Beginning accounts receivable	345,000
Ending accounts receivable	275,000

A. What is the inventory turnover?

B. What is the accounts receivable turnover?

C. What is the days' sales in average receivables?

3. The following information is given for Carleton Corporation for 2006:

Net sales	$825,000
Net income	60,000
Average common shareholders' equity	3,150,000
Average total assets	4,225,000
Interest expense	75,000
Preferred dividends	20,000
Common dividends	55,000
Common shares outstanding	240,000 shares

A. What is the rate of return on net sales?

B. What is the rate of return on total assets?

C. What is the rate of return on common shareholders' equity?

4. The following information is given for T-Bot.com Inc.:

Assets:	
Cash	$ 299,000
Marketable securities	85,000
Accounts receivable	175,000
Inventory	350,000
Equipment (net)	1,600,000
Total assets	$2,509,000
Liabilities and Shareholders' Equity:	
Accounts payable	$ 75,000
Salaries payable	39,000
Long-term bonds payable	660,000
Common shares	475,000
Retained earnings	1,260,000
Total liabilities and shareholders' equity	$2,509,000

A. What is the working capital?

B. What is the current ratio?

C. What is the acid-test (quick) ratio?

D. What is the debt ratio?

5. Fashion Connection Inc. has a price/earnings ratio of 12, dividends of $0.90 per share, and earnings per share of $1.28.

A. What is the market price per share?

B. What is the dividend yield?

VI. Critical Thinking

1. The operating cycle is the length of time between the purchase of merchandise and its conversion to cash following the sale and receipt of payment. Using the information in Exercise 2 above, calculate the operating cycle for Singh Industries.

2. Explain why leverage can be both positive or negative for shareholders.

DEMONSTRATION PROBLEMS

Demonstration Problem #1

Mariposa Industries, headquartered in Toronto, Ontario, is a clothing retailer. Figures from its 2006 annual report follow:

Mariposa Industries
Statement of Consolidated Earnings
For the Year Ended December 31, 2006

Net sales	$7,730,000
Cost and expenses	
Cost of products sold	4,820,000
Selling, delivery, and administration	277,500
Amortization	190,000
Discount on sales of receivables	4,500
Interest expense	175,000
Other (income) expense, net	12,000
Total costs and expenses	5,479,000
Earnings before income taxes	2,251,000
Income taxes (40%)	900,400
Net earnings	$ 1,350,600
Average number of shares outstanding	1,500,000

Mariposa Industries
Consolidated Balance Sheet
December 31, 2006

	2006	2005
Assets		
Current assets:		
Cash and short-term investments	533,800	907,300
Accounts receivable, less allowance	750,000	690,000
Inventories	1,590,000	1,235,000
Notes receivable	20,000	35,000
Prepaid expenses	45,000	33,000
Total current assets	2,938,800	2,900,300
Property, plant, and equipment—net	6,150,000	3,400,000
Brands, trademarks, patents, and other intangibles—net	2,100,000	200,000
Other assets	32,000	25,000
Total	$11,220,800	$6,525,300

Liabilities and Shareholders' Equity		
Current liabilities:		
Accounts payable	$ 1,400,000	$ 980,000
Accrued liabilities	110,500	144,000
Income taxes payable	320,000	275,000
Short-term debt	45,000	50,000
Current maturity of long-term debt	120,000	30,000
Total current liabilities	1,995,500	1,479,000
Long-term debt	5,300,000	1,300,000
Other obligations	17,700	18,600
Future income tax liability	66,300	54,500
Shareholders' equity		
Common shares—authorized, 5,000,000 shares,		
issued, 1,500,000 shares	3,000,000	3,000,000
Retained earnings	850,600	700,000
Cumulative translation adjustments	(9,300)	(26,800)
Total shareholders' equity	3,841,300	3,673,200
Total liabilities and shareholders' equity	$11,220,800	$6,525,300

Required:

Assume annual dividends of $0.80 and a market price of $11.20 per share. Compute the following for 2006:

A) working capital

B) current ratio

C) acid-test (quick) ratio

D) inventory turnover

E) accounts receivable turnover

F) days' sales in receivables

G) debt ratio

H) times-interest-earned ratio

I) rate of return on sales

J) rate of return on total assets

K) rate of return on common shareholders' equity

L) earnings per share

M) price/earnings ratio

N) dividend yield

O) book value per common share

Demonstration Problem #2

Vega Corporation's balance sheets and income statements are presented below:

Vega Corporation
Balance Sheet
Years 2006 and 2005

	2006	2005
Assets		
Current assets:		
Cash	$ 13,300	$ 20,350
Short-term investments	8,200	8,000
Receivables, net	26,000	24,000
Inventories	45,000	40,000
Prepaid expenses	2,500	4,650
Total current assets	95,000	97,000
Property, plant, and equipment—net	185,680	196,500
Land	40,000	35,000
Intangibles and other assets	2,400	2,400
Total assets	$323,080	$330,900
Liabilities and Shareholders' Equity		
Current liabilities:		
Notes payable	$ 10,000	$ 10,500
Current installments of long-term debt	3,550	3,445
Accounts payable—trade	14,447	18,500
Accrued liabilities	3,670	1,605
Total current liabilities	31,667	34,050
Long-term debt, less current installments	95,500	93,330
Capital lease obligations, less current portion	1,100	2,150
Deferred income share and future income		
tax liability	4,813	4,370
Total common shareholders' equity	190,000	197,000
Total liabilities and shareholders' equity	$323,080	$330,900

Vega Corporation
Income Statements
For the Years 2006 and 2005

	2006	2005
Net sales	$416,500	$406,316
Cost and expenses:		
Cost of goods sold	322,593	315,812
Operating expenses	41,219	43,200
	363,812	359,012
Income from operations	52,688	47,304
Interest expense	3,251	3,150
Earnings before income taxes	49,437	44,154
Income taxes	7,437	6,554
Net income	$ 42,000	$ 37,600

Required:

1. Prepare a horizontal analysis of the balance sheet for 2006, using the 2005 amounts as the base.

Vega Corporation				
Balance Sheet				
Years 2006 and 2005				
	2006	2005	Amount Increase (Decrease)	% Change
Assets				
Current assets:				
Cash	$ 13,300	$ 20,350		
Short-term investments	8,200	8,000		
Receivables, net	26,000	24,000		
Inventories	45,000	40,000		
Prepaid expenses	2,500	4,650		
Total current assets	95,000	97,000		
Property, plant, and equipment—net	185,680	196,500		
Land	40,000	35,000		
Intangibles and other assets	2,400	2,400		
Total assets	$323,080	$330,900		

Liabilities and shareholders' equity				
Current liabilities:				
Notes payable	$ 10,000	$ 10,500		
Current installments of long-term debt	3,550	3,445		
Accounts payable—trade	14,447	18,500		
Accrued liabilities	3,670	1,605		
Total current liabilities	31,667	34,050		
Long-term debt, less current installments	95,500	93,330		
Capital lease obligations, less current portion	1,100	2,150		
Deferred income and future income tax liability	4,813	4,370		
Total common shareholders' equity	190,000	197,000		
Total liabilities and shareholders' equity	$323,080	$330,900		

2. Convert the 2006 and 2005 income statements to common-size statements, using net sales as the base figures.

Vega Corporation				
Income Statements				
For the Years 2006 and 2005				
	2006		2005	
	Amount	%	Amount	%
Net sales	$416,500		$406,316	
Cost and expenses:				
Cost of goods sold	322,593		315,812	
Operating expenses	41,219		43,200	
Total costs and expenses	363,812		359,012	
Income from operations	52,688		47,304	
Interest expense	3,251		3,150	
Earnings before income taxes	49,437		44,154	
Income taxes	7,437		6,554	
Net income	$ 42,000		$ 37,600	

SOLUTIONS

A. TEST YOURSELF

I. Matching

1. Q	5. L	9. A	13. N	17. J
2. D	6. G	10. P	14. H	18. S
3. E	7. I	11. C	15. M	19. T
4. K	8. F	12. O	16. B	20. R

II. Multiple Choice

1. C   The rate of return on sales is net income / net sales.

2. D   The debt ratio measures the ability to pay long-term debts. The current ratio measures the ability to pay current liabilities. The dividend yield is used in analyzing shares as an investment.

3. C   Only the most liquid current assets are used to calculate the acid-test ratio.

4. A   Working capital is current assets less current liabilities. It measures a firm's ability to meet short-term obligations.

5. B   The times-interest-earned ratio measures how many times operating income is greater than interest expense.

6. B   The current ratio measures the ability to pay current liabilities. Debt yield ratio has no meaning. The times-interest-earned ratio measures the ability to pay interest on debt. The debt ratio is total liabilities ÷ total assets.

7. A   Let CA = current assets, CL = current liabilities, and X = the amount of cash paid on current liabilities. Then, given that CA > CL (or CL < CA), show that:

$$(CA - X) / (CL - X) > \quad CA / CL$$
$$CL(CA - X) > \quad CA(CL - X)$$
$$CL(CA) - CL(X) > \quad CA(CL) - CA(X)$$
$$-CL(X) > \quad -CA(X)$$

dividing by -X: $\quad$ CL < $\quad$ CA

> **Study Tip:** In a firm with current assets greater than current liabilities, the current ratio can be improved by using cash to pay current liabilities.

8. C   Dividend yield compares the amount of dividend per share with the current market price and therefore is one way to evaluate a share as a potential investment.

9. C   Working capital (the excess of current assets over current liabilities) measures short-term liquidity.

10. D Book value indicates the value of each common share outstanding and is one way to analyze shares as an investment.

11. B EVA® is used to measure the operating performance of a company.

12. C Ratios must be compared to something else to be useful; your own company over time, a competitor, or the industry average.

13. D Benchmarking is comparing yourself to either yourself (trend), industry average, or a competitor.

14. B Cash flows allow one to see what is happening with the cash of the business

15. B Working capital is used to determine the ability to pay current liabilities.

III. Completion

1. horizontal
2. net sales
3. total assets (or total liabilities plus shareholders' equity)
4. current assets minus current liabilities
5. Working capital, current
6. increases (Leverage is the practice of increasing the debt financing of an entity with respect to owner financing. Leverage is a two-edged sword, increasing profits (and returns to shareholders') during good times, but compounding losses during bad times.)
7. price/earnings
8. (net income + interest expense) ÷ average total assets
9. earnings per share
10. book value per common share
11. cash flow
12. Debt ratio
13. profitability
14. Trading on equity, leverage
15. Economic value added (EVA®)

IV. True/False

1. T
2. F Vertical analysis only looks at one year's activity and therefore is not a way to analyze change over time.
3. T
4. T
5. T
6. T

> **Study Tip:** When current liabilities exceed current assets, the result is negative working capital. Negative working capital always exists when the current ratio is less than 1.

7. F For most industries, inventory is excluded from quick assets.
8. F Inventory turnover tells you nothing about collecting cash owed from customers.

9.   F   The denominator is the average number of shares for the year. You would use the year-end figure only when there has been no change in outstanding shares throughout the year.

> **Study Tip:** This is one of the most frequent mistakes students make when calculating ratios. Just remember, net income reflects the entire accounting period; therefore, we should relate it to something with a similar basis.

10.   F   The price/earnings ratio is computed by dividing earnings per share by the market value per share.
11.   F   The acid-test ratio can never be greater than the current ratio.
12.   F   EVA® stands for economic value added.
13.   T
14.   F   The two are unrelated.
15.   T

V. Exercises

1. Year 2 = $500,000 / $700,000 = 71.4%
   Year 3 = $2,250,000 / $1,200,000 = 187.5%
   Year 4 = ($550,000) / $3,450,000 = (15.9%)

2. A. Cost of goods / Average inventory = $1,700,000 / [($540,000 + $680,000) / 2] = 2.79 times (rounded)
   B. Net credit sales / Average accounts receivable = $2,125,000 / [($345,000 + $275,000) / 2] = 6.86 times (rounded)
   C. Average accounts receivable / One day's sales = [($345,000 + $275,000) / 2] / ($2,125,000 / 365) = 53.25 days (rounded)

3. A. Net income / Net sales = $60,000 / $825,000 = 0.073 = 7.3%
   B. (Net income + Interest expense) / Average total assets = ($60,000 + $75,000) / $4,225,000 = 0.032 = 3.2%
   C. (Net income - Preferred dividends) / Average common shareholders' equity = ($60,000 - $20,000) / $3,150,000 = 0.013 = 1.3%

4. A. Current assets – Current liabilities = ($299,000 + $85,000 + $175,000 + $350,000) – ($75,000 + $39,000) = $795,000
   B. Current assets / Current liabilities =($299,000 + $85,000 + $175,000 + $350,000) / ($75,000 + $39,000) = 7.97 (rounded)
   C. (Cash + Short-term investments + Net current receivables) / Current liabilities = ($299,000 + $85,000 + $175,000) / ($75,000 + $39,000) = 4.90

> **Study Tip:** Remember, only the assets that will convert to cash "quickly" are called quick assets. Inventory does not do this.

   D. Total liabilities / Total assets = ($75,000 + $39,000 + $660,000) / $2,509,000 = 0.308 = 30.8%

5. A. Market price per common share / Earnings per share = P / $1.28 = 12;
   P = $15.36.

   B. Dividends per share of common share / Market price per common share = $0.90 / $15.36 = 0.059 = 5.9%

VI. Critical Thinking

1. The operating cycle for Singh Industries is 184.05 days (184 rounded). Instruction (C) in the exercise asked you to calculate the days' sales in average receivables. The correct figure was 53.25 days. Another way of characterizing this result is to say that it takes approximately 53.25 days to collect an average account receivable. Instruction (A) asked you to calculate inventory turnover. The correct amount was 2.79 times—in other words, inventory "turns" approximately 2.79 times each year. Divide this result into 365 to convert it to days, or 130.8 days. In other words, it takes 130.8 days on average for an item to sell and 53.25 days on average to collect a receivable. Therefore, the operating cycle is 184.05 days (184 rounded).

2. Leverage or trading on equity occurs whenever an organization takes on debt. The debt is invested to generate a profit. If the profit is greater than the interest charged on the debt, then the excess funds will benefit the shareholders. For example, if $1,000,000 is borrowed at 8% interest and invested to generate a return of 12%, then the profit is $120,000 ($1,000,000 × 12%). The $1,000,000 borrowed funds are returned to the lender and interest is paid of $80,000 ($1,000,000 × 8%). The difference (profit) of $40,000 ($120,000 - $80,000) goes to the shareholders and increases their wealth.

Alternatively, if the funds are invested poorly, say 6% return or $60,000 ($1,000,000 x 6%), the lender is still paid their $80,000 interest and the shareholders are $20,000 worse off ($60,000 - $80,000). Thus, borrowing (leverage) can be profitable or unprofitable, depending on whether it is invested to generate a return greater or worse than the interest to be paid.

DEMONSTRATION PROBLEMS

Demonstration Problem #1 Solved and Explained

A) Working capital = Current assets - Current liabilities = $2,938,800 - $1,995,500 = $943,300

B) Current ratio = Current assets / Current liabilities = $2,938,800 / $1,995,500 = 1.47 (rounded)

C) Acid-test (quick) = Quick assets / Current liabilities
= ($533,800 + 750,000) / $1,995,500 = 0.65 (rounded)

This means Mariposa has 65 cents of quick assets (cash and short-term investments plus net accounts receivable) for every dollar of current liability. Notes receivable is listed after inventory, indicating that it is not liquid.

D) Inventory turnover = Cost of goods sold / Average inventory
= $4,820,000 / [($1,590,000 + $1,235,000) / 2] = 3.41 times

Mariposa "turns" its inventory 3.41 times each year. Another way of stating this ratio is to convert it to days by dividing the "turn" into 365. For Mariposa, the turnover averages 107 days (rounded) (365 / 3.41).

E) Accounts receivable turnover = Net credit sales / Average accounts receivable
= $7,730,000 / [($750,000 + $690,000) / 2] = 10.74 times (rounded)

F) Days' sales in receivables   =   Average net accounts receivable / One day's sales

                                          =   \$720,000 / (\$7,730,000 / 365) = 34 days

The numerator for this ratio was the denominator for the previous ratio.

G) Debt ratio =   Total liabilities / Total assets

                   =   \$7,379,500 / \$11,220,800

                   =   0.658 or 65.8% (rounded)

This means that 65.8% of the Mariposa assets were financed with debt. Notice the numerator (total liabilities) was not presented on the balance sheet but had to be calculated by adding together total current liabilities, long-term debt, other obligations, and future income taxes.

H) Times-interest-earned   =   Income from operations / Interest expense

                               =   \$2,426,000 / \$175,000

                               =   13.86 times

Note that we used earnings before income taxes plus interest expense as the numerator because interest expense had already been deducted from the earnings before income taxes amount.

I) Rate of return on sales =   Net income / Net sales

                           =   \$1,350,600 / \$7,730,000

                           =   0.175 or 17.5%

J) Rate of return on total assets   =   (Net income + Interest expense) / Average total assets

                                            =   (\$1,350,600 + \$175,000) / [(\$11,220,800 + \$6,525,300) / 2]

                                            =   0.172 or 17.2%

This ratio measures the return on assets generated by this year's operations.

K) Rate of return on common shareholders' equity =   (Net income - Preferred dividends) / Average
                                                                       common shareholders' equity

                                               =   (\$1,350,600 - 0) / [(\$3,841,300 + \$3,673,200) / 2]

                                               =   0.360 or 36.0% (rounded)

Mariposa does not have preferred shares outstanding, so the numerator is the same as net earnings.

L) Earnings per share = (Net income - Preferred dividends) / Average number of common shares outstanding

                           = (\$1,350,600 – 0) / 1,500,000

                           = \$0.90

This should be calculated for each "net earnings" amount. Companies are required to include these per share amounts on the income statement, not in the footnotes.

M) Price/earnings ratio =   Market price per share of common shares / Earnings per share

                         =   \$11.20 / \$0.90 = 12.44 (rounded)

The earnings per share is calculated in part L.

N) Dividend yield = Dividend per common share / Market price per common share

= $0.80 / $11.20

= 0.0714 or 7.14%

O) Book value per common share = (Total shareholders' equity - Preferred equity) / Number of common shares outstanding

= 3,841,300 / 1,500,000

= $2.56 per share

As emphasized in your text, these ratios would have more meaning if you did them over consecutive years. In addition, to properly evaluate a company you would also want to compare the ratios with those of competitors and with the industry as a whole.

Demonstration Problem #2 Solved and Explained

1.

Vega Corporation
Balance Sheet
Years 2006 and 2005

	2006	2005	Amount Increase (Decrease)	% Change
Assets				
Current assets:				
Cash	$ 13,300	$ 20,350	$(7,050)	(34.6)
Short-term investments	8,200	8,000	200	2.5
Receivables, net	26,000	24,000	2,000	8.3
Inventories	45,000	40,000	5,000	12.5
Prepaid expenses	2,500	4,650	(2,150)	(46.2)
Total current assets	95,000	97,000	(2,000)	(2.1)
Property, plant, and equipment—net	185,680	196,500	(10,820)	(5.5)
Land	40,000	35,000	5,000	14.3
Intangibles and other assets	2,400	2,400	0	0
	$323,080	$330,900	$(7,820)	(2.4)
Liabilities and shareholders' equity				
Current liabilities:				
Notes payable	$ 10,000	$ 10,500	$ (500)	(4.8)
Current installments of long-term debt	3,550	3,445	105	3.0
Accounts payable—trade	14,447	18,500	(4,053)	(21.9)
Accrued liabilities	3,670	1,605	2,065	128.7
Total current liabilities	31,667	34,050	(2,383)	(7.0)
Long-term debt, less current installments	95,500	93,330	2,170	2.3
Capital lease obligations, less current portion	1,100	2,150	(1,050)	(48.9)
Deferred income and future income tax liability	4,813	4,370	443	10.1
Total common shareholders' equity	190,000	197,000	(7,000)	(3.6)
	$323,080	$330,900	$(7,820)	(2.4)

2.

Vega Corporation
Income Statements
Years 2006 and 2005

	2006		2005	
	Amount	%	Amount	%
Net sales	$416,500	100.0	$406,316	100.0
Cost and expenses:				
Cost of goods sold	322,593	77.5	315,812	77.7
Operating expenses	41,219	9.9	43,200	10.6
Total costs and expenses	363,812	87.4	359,012	88.3
Income from operations	52,688	12.7	47,304	11.6
Interest expense	3,251	0.8	3,150	0.8
Earnings before income taxes	49,437	11.9	44,154	10.8
Income taxes	7,437	1.8	6,554	1.6
Net income	$ 42,000	10.1	$ 37,600	9.2

Points to remember:

1. When presenting horizontal analysis, each year's change is divided by the base-year amount (in this case, 2005) and converted to a percentage. While the change in any single item in any single year may not be significant, applying horizontal analysis over a number of years may highlight significant changes.

2. Common-size statements for a single year are only meaningful when the results are compared to other companies or industry data. However, common-size statements covering two or more years permit analysis of the particular company being examined. In this case, we see that 2006 results improved over those of 2005 due to lower cost of goods sold and lower operating expenses.

3. Financial ratios are mathematical formulas that quantify the relationship between two or more items reported in the financial statements. Ratios are used to assess and compare a firm's liquidity, profitability, rate of return, and ability to meet debt obligations.

Study Tip: One of the most common mistakes students make is forgetting to use the average amount of inventory, accounts receivable, or shares outstanding in some of the formulas. It is important that an average be used to reduce distortions that might occur if only year-end balances were used.

APPENDIX A— SUN-RYPE PRODUCTS LTD. 2004 ANNUAL REPORT

Appendix A presents the 2004 Annual Report of Sun-Rype Products Ltd.

APPENDIX B—MULLEN TRANSPORTATION INC.
2004 ANNUAL REPORT

Appendix B presents the 2004 Annual Report of Mullen Transportation Inc .

APPENDIX C—TYPICAL CHARTS OF ACCOUNTS FOR DIFFERENT TYPES OF BUSINESSES

Appendix C presents typical charts of accounts for different types of businesses.

APPENDIX D—TIME VALUE OF MONEY: FUTURE VALUE AND PRESENT VALUE

Because you can earn interest on your money over time, the value of invested funds is greater in the future than it is today. This refers to the **time value of money**. To determine what a **future value** will be, you simply apply an interest rate to the amount of your investment and calculate the amount of interest. Add this result to your original amount and the sum becomes the future value at the end of one interest period. Repeat this process for additional interest periods, remembering to add in the interest each time. Therefore, there are three factors involved in determining a future value: 1) the amount of the original investment, 2) the length of time, and 3) the interest rate. Obviously the longer the time, the more calculations are involved. Fortunately, mathematical tables are available to ease your task. Review Exhibit D-2 carefully. This is the table used to determine the future value of a single investment, again assuming time and interest rate.

Instead of investing a single amount for a specific period, you might wish to invest multiple amounts over time. This is an example of an **annuity type investment**. In other words, you invest identical amounts for several years—what will the future value of these multiple investments be in the future? Of course, you could calculate each individually and add the results, or you could consult mathematical tables that do the multiple calculations for you. Review Exhibit D-4 carefully. This is the table used to determine a future value of multiple investments, again assuming time and interest rate. This table is used to answer questions like "If I start setting aside (investing) $500 each year for the next ten years, what will it be worth, assuming I can invest this money at 8%?" Exhibit D-4 shows the value 14.487 at the intersection of 10 and 8%. Multiply this value by your annual investment ($500) and the result is $7,243.50.

Another way to look at present and future values is to begin with the future value and work backwards. In other words, in order to have X amount sometime in the future, how much would one need to set aside today? Again assumptions need to be made about the time and the interest rate (this is always true).

As with the preceding discussions, you could calculate the result manually, but the longer the period the more calculations you would have to complete. Once again, mathematical tables are available to use. Study Exhibit D-6 carefully.

Rather than determining the present value of a single amount, you may be interested in the **present value of an annuity-type investment**. In other words, what is the present value of an investment that will give you the same fixed amount over a number of periods? As with earlier discussions, this value can be calculated manually, but it is time-consuming. Once again, tables are available to simplify the process. Study Exhibit D-7 carefully.

> **Study Tip:** BEFORE PROCEEDING, BE CERTAIN YOU UNDERSTAND IN WHICH CIRCUMSTANCES YOU USE WHICH TABLE. This is vital to understanding the topics that follow.

In Chapter 8 you learned about long-term liabilities, primarily bonds payable. What is a bond? It is a way for a company to borrow funds. When a company issues a bond, what happens? The company promises to pay the face value of the bond at maturity and, during the life of the bond, the company also promises to pay a fixed amount of interest periodically. The face value at maturity is a single value, whereas the interest payments are like an annuity. Therefore, when a company issues bonds, it needs to know what price should be asked (remember bond prices are quoted as percentages of face value) in order to attract investors. To determine this, consult the appropriate tables—in this case D-6 and D-7 in your text. Using the market rate of interest, the first table will give you the present value of a future single amount, the second will give the present value of an annuity. Sum the results and you have an estimate of the market price of the bonds. The market rate of interest is used because this is the rate potential investors will demand for the use of their funds. If the market rate is higher than the contract (or stated) rate of interest, the bonds will have to be sold at a discount to attract investors. Conversely, if the market rate is lower than the contract rate, the bonds will sell at a premium.

In Chapter 8, you learned about capital leases. When a company acquires an asset with a capital lease, the company needs to record the asset at "cost." What is the cost when the lease requires payments over the life of the lease? Using present value tables, specifically Exhibit D-7, you can value the asset because the fixed payments over the life of the lease are like annuities and you want to determine the present value (i.e. cost) of all those payments.

Appendix D Exercises

1. When you began college four years ago, your aunt, a CA, set aside $10,000 in a special savings account and promised to give you the total amount in the account when you graduate IF you major in accounting and earn a B average in all your accounting courses. Assuming the savings account earns 5% each year and you meet the terms of her offer, what amount will you receive at graduation?

2. Your uncle, a high school teacher, promised to save $600 annually on your behalf for the four years you are an undergraduate student and give you the total amount at graduation if you choose teaching as a career. The $600 will earn 6% annually. Assuming you choose teaching as a career, what amount will your uncle give you upon graduating?

3. You have just purchased a new car and estimate it will last you for 10 years. Assuming a replacement will cost $20,000 in 10 years, and your present car will have a trade-in value of $2500, what amount should you set aside now to ensure you have sufficient cash on hand in 10 years to buy a replacement car? You believe your fund will earn 7% annually.

4. A company needs to borrow $500,000 and decides to offer 10-year debentures carrying 9% interest, payable semi-annually. If the market rate of interest is 8% when the bonds are offered, at what price should the bonds be sold?

5. Assume the same facts as in Exercise 4, but the market rate of interest is 10%. At what price should the bonds be sold?

6. Levine Laboratories Ltd., has located a warehouse to lease. The company is offered a capital lease for 20 years requiring annual payments of $10,000 in addition to a $25,000 payment upon signing the lease. Present the journal entry to record the cash down payment, assuming a current 6% market rate.

Date	Account and Explanation	Debit	Credit

Appendix D Critical Thinking

Examine the situations presented in Exercises 1 and 2. What decision should you make?

_____
_____
_____
_____
_____

SOLUTIONS

Exercises

1. To answer the question, you have two options: (1) calculate the future value manually or (2) use Table D-2 in the text. Either way, the result should be the same. Calculating it manually requires the following:

   Year 1: $10,000 × 1.05 = $10,500
   Year 2: $10,500 × 1.05 = $11,025
   Year 3: $11,025 × 1.05 = $11,576.25
   Year 4: $11,576.25 × 1.05 = $12,155.06 (rounded)

   Table D-2 lists the value 1.216 at the intersection of 5% and 4 periods. $10,000 times 1.216 equals $12,160.

2. The $600 is like an annuity, so use Table D-4 to calculate the answer. 6% and 4 periods intersect at 4.375. Multiply this value by $600.

   $600 × 4.375 = $2,625

   The answer can also be calculated manually, but would require 10 separate calculations.

3. This exercise requires a present value for a future amount, so use Table D-6. 7% and 10 periods intersect at 0.508. Apply this value to $17,500 to determine the amount of cash that needs to be invested now.

   $17,500 × 0.508 = $8,890

   Note we use $17,500 and not $20,000 because the present car's trade-in value of $2,500 will reduce the amount of cash needed in 10 years time.

4. To determine the asking price of the bonds, we need to know the present value of a future amount and the present value of an annuity. The present value of the $500,000 is determined by consulting Table D-6 while the present value of the annuity (the interest payments) is determined by Table D-7.

   Present value of $500,000 = $500,000 × 0.456 = $228,000

   Use the 4% column and the 20 periods row to find the value 0.456. Because the bonds will pay interest semi-annually and the market rate is 8%, there are 20 periods at 4% each period. Apply this same logic to find the present value of the interest payments by consulting Table D-7. The semi-annual interest payments will be $22,500 ($500,000 and 4.5%) so

   $22,500 × 13.590 = $305,775

   Now add the results as follows:

   $228,000 + $305,775 = $533,775

   Because the bonds carry an interest rate higher than the current market rate, they can be offered for sale at a premium. Therefore, they will be offered for sale at 106.755% ($533,775 divided by $500,000).

Study Tip: Ignore the contract interest rate when using both tables in this exercise. The key figure is the market rate.

Study Tip: Remember bond prices are listed as percentages, not as dollar amounts.

5. Following the logic explained in Exercise 4, the calculations are

   $500,000 \times 0.377 = \$188,500$ and $\$22,500 \times 12.462 = \$280,395$
   These results add to \$468,895, so the bonds will be offered at 93.779% (\$468,895 divided by \$500,000).

6. Use Table D-7 because this is an annuity.

   $10,000 \times 11.470 = \$114,700$; in addition, the lease calls for an initial down payment of \$25,000, so the "cost" (present value) of the capital lease is \$139,700, recorded as follows:

Warehouse	139,700	
Cash		25,000
Lease Liability		114,700

Critical Thinking

The answer is obvious—become an accounting teacher!

APPENDIX E—SUMMARY OF GENERALLY ACCEPTED ACCOUNTING PRINCIPLES (GAAP)

The Canadian Institute of Chartered Accountants (CICA) has the responsibility for issuing accounting standards, which form the basis for generally accepted accounting principles (GAAP) in Canada.

The Canadian Securities Administrators, the *Canada Business Corporations Act*, and the *Ontario Securities Act* have all designated the *CICA Handbook* as GAAP. Thus both the federal and provincial governments have delegated responsibility for GAAP to the CICA, effectively giving the *CICA Handbook* the force of law. The basic objective of financial reporting is to provide information that is useful for investment and lending decisions. Information should be relevant, reliable, comparable, and consistent. Relevant information is useful. Reliable information is unbiased and free from significant error. Comparable and consistent information can be compared from period to period.

Concepts

The **entity concept** provides that the transactions of the organization be accounted for separately from the transactions of other organizations and persons, including the owner(s) of the entity.

The **going-concern concept** is an assumption that the business will continue to operate in the future. This concept enables accountants to assume that a business will continue long enough to recover the cost of its assets.

The **stable-monetary-unit concept** assumes that the value of the monetary unit never changes. Accountants ignore the effects of inflation and make no accounting adjustments related to changes in the purchasing power of the dollar.

The **time-period concept** provides that financial information be reported at regular intervals so that decision makers can compare business operations over time to assess the success or failure of the business. This concept is the basis for accruals and adjusting entries prepared at the end of an accounting period.

The **conservatism concept** requires that income and assets be reported at their lowest reasonable amounts. This does not mean that assets or income should be deliberately understated. It does mean that when different values can be assigned to a transaction, the less optimistic value should be used. The lower-of-cost-or-market method (LCM) for valuing assets is a clear example of conservatism.

The **materiality concept** requires accountants to accurately account for significant items and transactions. Information is significant (or material) if it is likely to cause a statement user to change a decision because of that information. The accounting treatment for a $3 pencil sharpener is not likely to affect any decisions; the pencil sharpener is immaterial. However, failing to record a $1 million liability would affect the decisions of many users. Thus, the $1 million is material.

Principles

The **reliability (objectivity) principle** states that accounting information should be based on the most reliable data available.

The **cost principle** states that transactions are to be recorded at cost. When assets are purchased, they are recorded at cost, and the accounting records of the asset are maintained at cost. The actual cost of an asset or service is considered to be a verifiable, objective evidence of value.

The **revenue principle** tells the accountant when to record revenue and how much revenue to record. Generally, revenue is recorded when it is earned and not before. Three conditions must be met before revenue is recorded:

1. The seller has done everything necessary to expect to collect from the buyer.
2. The amount of revenues can be objectively measured.
3. Collectibility is reasonably assured.

Generally, these conditions are met when the seller delivers the goods or renders services to the buyer.

The **matching principle**, in conjunction with the revenue principle, governs income recognition. Recall that expenses are matched against revenues.

The **consistency principle** is enhanced by using the same accounting methods from period to period.

The **disclosure principle** requires that a company's financial statements report enough information for users to make knowledgeable decisions about the company. In order to satisfy the disclosure principle, companies add to the financial statements notes that disclose significant accounting policies, probable losses, and accounting changes.

Financial Statements and Notes

The **Balance sheet** presents the accounting equation (assets = liabilities + owners' equity) at a point in time.

The **Income statement** lists revenues and gains less expenses and losses. The difference is either net income or net loss for the period.

The **Cash flow statement** lists cash receipts and cash disbursements during the period. These are grouped under operating, investing, and financing activities.

The **Statement of retained earnings** lists the changes in retained earnings during the period.

The **Statement of shareholders' equity** explains all changes in each shareholders' equity account during the period.

Financial statement notes provide information that is not included on the face of the financial statements. The notes are an integral part of the statements.

APPENDIX F—CHECK FIGURES

Appendix F presents the check figures.